Blessings for the
Fast Paced and
Cyberspaced

D0967525

"This book is an absolute joy, filled with treasures. The stories, wise insights and blessings galore will inspire you and nudge you to find deeper meaning and joy in your life.

"You will be glad that you have read this book. William Fitzgerald's poetic yet practical reflection on our daily blessings is a gifted piece of writing, in tune with our times. In a culture that keeps yanking us away from deeper meaning by keeping us so busy, Fitzgerald's approach to cyberspace life helps us sink deep roots and maintain awareness of the sacred in our midst. Don't miss this book or you will miss a significant blessing."

—Joyce Rupp, Author, *Out of the Ordinary*

"Reading Bill Fitzgerald's new work, **Blessings for the Fast Paced and Cyberspaced** reminds us that gratitude and grace are essential if we are to stay grounded in a runaway world.

"Pick up this book and you will be refreshed — it will energize your soul."

—Jim Conlon, Director of *Sophia Center* at Holy Names College in Oakland, CA. Author, *Ponderings from the Precipice* and *The Sacred Impulse*

"This is a wonderful book that knits the material and spiritual aspects of our lives in a practical way, leading one to see the divine in the mundane. It has helped me as a scientist to refocus spiritually on both the grandest, deepest truths in our universe and the daily little tests and miracles that fill our lives."

—Dr. Jack Kasher, Professor of Physics, University of Nebraska at Omaha

"A unique book of prose, poetry and blessings that transforms the pressures and stresses of modern life and allows them to be opportunities for prayer and spiritual renewal."

—Charlotte Karlen, past Arts and Marketing Director of the Minnesota Orchestra

"If you need a lift, be sure to read this book. It communicates a quiet joy and a whispered wisdom."

—Father Val J. Peter, Executive Director of Boys Town USA

BLESSINGS FOR THE FAST PACED AND CYBERSPACED

Parables, Reflections and Prayers

WILLIAM JOHN FITZGERALD

FOREST OF PEACE
Publishing

Suppliers for the Spiritual Pilgrim
Leavenworth, KS

Other Books by the Author:

One Hundred One Cranes

Seasons of the Earth and Heart
(available from Forest of Peace Publishing)

A Contemporary Celtic Prayer Book

Words of Comfort

Stories of Coming Home: Finding Spirituality in Our Messy Lives

BLESSINGS FOR THE FAST PACED AND CYBERSPACED

copyright © 2000, by William John Fitzgerald

Library of Congress Cataloging-in-Publication Data

Fitzgerald, William, 1932-
    Blessings for the fast paced and cyberspaced : parables, reflections, and prayers / William John Fitzgerald.
        p. cm.
    ISBN 0-939516-50-0
    1. Spiritual life. 2. Benediction. I. Title.

BL624.F543 2000
291.4'32—dc21

00-026462

published by
Forest of Peace Publishing, Inc.
PO Box 269
Leavenworth, KS 66048-0269   USA
1-800-659-3227
www.forestofpeace.com

printed by
Hall Commercial Printing
Topeka, KS 66608-0007

1st printing: May 2000

DEDICATED TO:

**Bill and Kitty Fitzgerald
who set me upon a blessing path**

REMEMBERING:

Colleagues and friends who have worked with me and
who have passed through the holy dark into blessed light:
Jack Gould, Marguerite Keithley, Joyce Kreikemeier,
Margaret Crull, Bill Weidner, Tom McDermott and Larry Dorsey.

REMEMBERING:

the old 32nd Avenue neighborhood — the holy ground of my childhood.
It's alleys were blessing paths of fun, play and exuberance.
Remembering the Rohmeyers and Hautzingers — my playmates —
and all the other folks who helped make our neighborhood a community.
May the old neighborhood remain a shrine of good memories,
an enchanted place to return to on pilgrimage.

Special thanks to Susan Lamb, Jeannie Beal, Charlotte Karlen,
John Bernbrock, S.J., and Dr. Jack Kasher for their help,
and to Tom Skorupa, my editor, for helping me
get to the heart of the matter.

PRAYERS AND BLESSINGS

CONTENTS

FOREWORD
BY SUSAN LAMB-BEAN

Every Tuesday and Thursday evening, I take my goddaughter and her best friend to practice Mexican folklorico dancing (my husband calls it "advanced skirt-swirling"). There I sit, the only Anglo among the local Hispanic equivalent of soccer moms, watching the girls tap and twirl to some of the happiest music in the world. Many of the mothers have had very full days, but still they faithfully bring their children to experience their traditions, their talents and their joy.

One mother, in particular, is determined to keep dance a part of her three daughters' lives. Now single through a sudden tragedy, Mercedes works full-time in a busy office, but she is also a full-time mom, dropping off and picking up her girls at school every day, buying them shoes and hairclips and groceries, cooking their dinner and doing their laundry and keeping their home in order. She even sews the elaborate costumes for their folklorico performances. Mercedes is kind and good-natured and her daughters try to help, but she's also weary and she often takes herself to task for not being patient and cheerful with her beloved children every moment of every day.

Last Tuesday, I took the manuscript of this book to dance practice with me, to read again before writing this foreword. Mercedes glanced over my shoulder and asked if she could read it too, so I gave her the first eighty pages or so. At the end of practice she handed them back to me, her eyes shining, and asked: "Can you bring this again on Thursday?"

What was it, I wanted to know, that she liked so much about the book?

It's so understanding," she explained. "It makes me feel happy to realize that my life is so full of good things just the way it is. Sometimes I read magazines for advice on how to be a better person, how to be more cheerful. But all they tell me is to say 'no' more often, to change everything around and put myself first. They give me rules for living a life that my heart can't believe in. Reading this feels so different — it's for real people, people who want to do the best they can for their families."

Mercedes is right, of course. Father Fitz reveals the blessings of what is, rather than agitating for the ever-elusive what could be. There is something very liberating about this book. Genuinely compassionate and never scolding, it gently reminds us with dozens of delightful illustrations that we do indeed lie in the palm of God's hand.

This is not to say that Fitz recommends we be mere lumps, meeting life in an utterly passive way. Rather, *Blessings for the Fast Paced and Cyberspaced* advocates making the choice to seek God everywhere, in every moment. We are reminded of a basic spiritual paradox: that being swept up in the anxieties of our time is actually the passive choice. To stop striving and simply allow the divine to reveal itself — this is a decisive act.

All the religious traditions addressed in this book have a long history, an antiquity that can lend our faith resonance, but sometimes because religion is so ancient its teachings can seem out of touch with the modern age. Father Fitz translates ancient and medieval metaphors, revealing that the old dungeons of fear and doubt are made deeper and darker in our day by a lack of time, by a prickly array of choices and by contradictory advice on health, work, relationships and food. Fearsome dragons lurk in the mall and on the internet. But he also assures us that although they have changed in appearance over the centuries, the snares and monsters that would menace our lives are still powerless when we armor our souls with gratitude, faith and prayer.

Father Fitz looks present-day trials square in the face, redefining well-worn terms such as pilgrimage to help us transcend such frustrations as hellish commutes and plagues of phone calls, as well as the fear and anger engendered by fire-breathing bosses and bureaucrats. He relates traditional religious teachings and vocabulary to contemporary models from quantum physics to biology. A highly original (one could say quirky) thinker, Fitz expertly whittles the scariest of bogeymen down to size with his unfailing wit and playfulness, with insights from a variety of spiritual traditions and with observations of the flora and fauna of the natural world.

Schoolteachers know that the more time they squander on children who are interfering with the learning of others, the more problems all of the children in the classroom will cause. Shifting attention to students who are enthusiastic about learning can change the character of a class from chaotic to comprehending. By the same token, although he identifies some things that disrupt the joy and harmony of our lives, Father Fitz is intent on recognizing the blessings that surround us every day no matter what our circumstances may be. He shows us how in naming our blessings we actually magnify them, leaving less room in our lives for evil and misery. In effect, he shows us how we can mold reality. As this new millennium unfolds, perhaps if we each celebrate the good things in our lives, collectively magnifying them, together we will shape a world less burdened by suffering.

Susan Lamb-Bean

Susan is a writer and educator in the field of natural history, culture and religion. She lives with her husband, photographer Tom Bean, in the forest outside of Flagstaff, Arizona, where she is a member of the parish of San Francisco de Asis.

Among her many published titles are: *Channel Islands National Park* (Southwest Parks & Monuments Association, due out in 2000). *Mesa Verde National Park* (Sierra Press, 1999). *Wildflowers of the Pacific Northwest* (Companion Press, 1999). *Pueblo and Mission: Cultural Roots of the Southwest* (Northland Publishing, 1997). *A Guide to Pueblo Pottery* (Southwest Parks & Monuments, 1996). *Wildflowers of the Plateau and Canyon Country* (Companion Press, 1996). *The Smithsonian Guide to Natural America: The Southern Rockies* (1995). *Grand Canyon: The Vault of Heaven* (Grand Canyon Association, 1995). *Wildflowers of California* (Companion Press, 1994). *Petroglyph National Monument* (Southwest Parks & Monuments, 1993). *A Guide to Navajo Rugs* (Southwest Parks & Monuments, 1992). *Ancient Walls: Indian Ruins of the Southwest* (Companion Press/Fulcrum, 1992).

Her works in progress include *Mesa Verde National Park* (Sierra Press, 2000). *The Bishop's Woman: A Novel of the New West. Garden Pollinators* (in collaboration with Norwegian photographer Carll Goodpasture). *Flower Companions of the Hopi* (with Eric Polingyouma).

PROLOGUE

My favorite head covering is a jaunty wool cap from Ireland. On the inner lining of the cap is stitched a blessing: "Joy and health to you who wear this!" It's signed by "T.O. Gorman the hatmaker." How wonderful that a hatmaker from far across the sea would work a blessing for me right into the fabric of my cap. So, everywhere I go, I walk with a blessing overhead!

That is what this book is all about—holding in mind an awareness that everywhere you go, whether on the information highway or a busy freeway, you can carry a blessing with you! Even more, you can put a blessing to work!

Our ancient ancestors knew how to put blessings into their work. Many ancient peoples walked a blessing path and marked their trails with petroglyphs or wayside shrines. When the buffalo appeared or the crops ripened, these peoples had a sense of being blessed. They took time in the midst of their real life — their hunting life or their farming life — to recognize what the Celts called "the long hand of God at work."

We cultivate an awareness of blessings only by pondering. Yet our very lifestyles usually war against opportunities to ponder. Today, we live within a time-warped paradox. We pride ourselves on timesaving technology, and yet the time we "save" is quickly filled up with more to do. And there is never enough time to do what we "have to do." Our paths are marked across the sky by the quickly fading contrails of jets hurtling us at 500 miles an hour through different time zones or by the wound-up messages on our answering machines — each message making a new demand upon us.

A world without blessings is a sterile world, an egocentric world, an ungrateful world. A blessing is a "yes" to goodness, to grace, to an ultimately friendly universe. Blessings connect us to the wellspring of our very being. To be blessed is to taste and savor being favored. This book is intended not only to enhance our awareness of the blessings in our lives, it has built-in opportunities to reflect on and savor those varied blessings. This volume is meant to help you carve out moments to ponder in the midst of the busyness and to pray on the way to deadlines.

As a conveyer of words, I offer you this blessing:

A BLESSING FOR THE READER OF THIS BOOK

May the words of this book give you pause to ponder,
and may each of its chapters unfold for you a blessing path!

May it help you recognize the blessings that saturate your world,
those already in your home and church and quiet corners of your life.

May it lead you on a road of reverence and right relationship toward earth
and open you to awe at God's grandeur and grace.

May it assist you in using modern technologies in our cyberculture
as instruments of blessing rather than turning them into a curse:

May your information highway wind through delightful glens
and pass over all dead-end alleys.

May your cell phone enlarge your freedom
but not infringe on the rights or safety of others.

May your E-mail bring your friends closer
and readily send your blessings afar.

And may the long hand of God
draw up joy from the well of creativity within you
and guide you to spread it throughout your world.

— from the bookmaker,

William John Fitzgerald

BLESSING PATHS

Like the crew of the Starship Enterprise…we are approaching
a velocity called "warp speed," a velocity that can warp our
behavior and our most basic values…a velocity sanctioned by
a society committed to speed.

—Stephen Bertman, "Hyper," *The Futurist*

A PRIMER PARABLE

Once upon a time, a simpler time, a slower time, there were two playmates
— Dick and Jane (and a dog named Spot). Dick lived on the shady side of
the street, and Jane lived on the sunny side. Dick and Jane grew up in a
neighborhood with quiet streets and even alleys where children could
safely play. After they grew up, they married different partners and had
children of their own. Dick's son, Richard, was raised on the shady side
of their street and Jane's baby, Jan, was raised on the sunny side of their
street.

They too grew up, got jobs and became very busy adults. And, lo and behold, Richard moved into a condo on the shady side of the street, while Jan moved into a condo across the street — on the sunny side.

Now this is the way a typical day in Richard's life unfolds: When his radio alarm goes off in the morning, he pulls his pillow over his head to muffle the incessant blare of rock music. After napping ten more minutes in a semi-coma state, Richard finally emerges from his bed like a lumbering bear coming out of his cave. He staggers over to the window, pulls back the drapes and is face-to-face with a blinding light. Blinking and muttering, he shuffles into the bathroom, reaches in the shower and turns the first knob he touches. Pajamas go off in a heap. In he goes, only to be blasted with a surge of ice-cold water. "Damn that infernal water heater!"

Running behind time, his rushed shaving results in a prickly nick on his left chin. Quick, first aid! Now, what to wear? Decisions! Decisions! The black charcoal suit looks good. Grab the yellow tie, the white shirt, and dress quickly.

At breakfast, the morning paper brings him up to date on the latest rape, pillage and mayhem. Belching after a rushed breakfast, Richard grabs his briefcase, emerges into the hall and waits and waits for the elevator. Up, up it goes — floor, 12, 14, 15 — where it stops, nobody knows! Richard nervously pushes the down button again even though he knows this infernal machine will follow its own wisdom.

Finally its doors slide open, and Richard squeezes into a herd of other dour-faced commuters. The elevator grinds to a halt on the ground floor, and he bursts into the lobby like a racehorse bounding from the starting gate. He has to go top speed; he's almost 10 minutes late.

Rushing out from under the condo awning, he looks furtively up toward the window ledge where two pigeons are eyeing him with great interest. "Damn Nazi birds! You're like the Luftwaffe, dropping your poop bombs! But you won't get me today — I'm moving too fast for that."

He rushes into the garage, jumps into his car and is off for the forty-minute commute. As he waits for the red light to turn green and let him drive up the expressway ramp, he drums his hand on the gearshift. At the first verdant cast from the signal, up he roars...only to be merged into bumper-to-bumper traffic — slow, meandering, a constipated "free"way.

Richard utters a bathroom term that seems to sum up the beginning of this hectic day very well. Starting and stopping, talking on the cell phone, a gap emerges, and a car on the left cuts right in front of Richard, causing him to shake his fist and draw even deeper from his bathroom vocabulary.

After a tortuous journey, Richard rushes into the office fourteen minutes late and plunks down at his computer terminal, only to be greeted by Roger at the next cubicle, "How's it going, Richard?"

He breathlessly replies, "It ain't…I don't think I'm long for this world!" Then he boots up and taps nervously as the computer, which also has its own mind and is sometimes beyond his control as it hisses, beeps and goes through its own morning calisthenics. Richard waits nervously, already yearning for the smoke break that is two hours away.

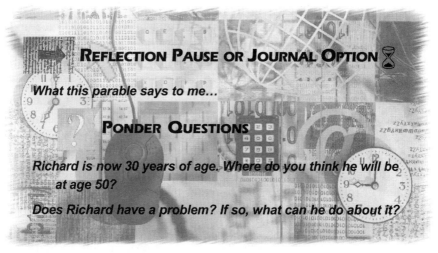

REFLECTION PAUSE OR JOURNAL OPTION

What this parable says to me…

PONDER QUESTIONS

Richard is now 30 years of age. Where do you think he will be at age 50?

Does Richard have a problem? If so, what can he do about it?

The very same morning, Jan's alarm buzzes. She is groggy but, after a few moments, gets out of bed. She moves toward the window, pulls open the drapes and greets the sun with a smile, saying, "Thanks, blessed light, for faithfully returning." As she turns to make her bed, she stubs her toe on a little wooden bed support. "Damn! Gotta slow down!"

In her bathroom, Jan lights a candle, which gives a pleasant aroma, takes her time turning on the shower and going in. The fresh water soothes every pore of her skin and her soul, and she exclaims, "Ah! This is wonderful!"

Afterwards, as Jan dresses, she puts on a pleasant perfume and savors its scent as she goes downstairs for breakfast. She turns on some music, makes a sign of the cross, says her table blessing, then relishes her first cup of coffee. The aroma drifts into her nostrils, and sip by sip the energizing nectar opens her still sleepy eyes to the new day. "Mmm, good!" she exclaims.

When she gets up to put the butter back in the refrigerator, she smiles as she takes a second to glance at one of the family snapshots pasted to the refrigerator door. Breakfast finished, she looks into the eyes of her cat, Celine, and pats her furry head. Celine licks her chops; Jan laughs and reaches for the cat food. Celine now purrs contentedly. Jan grabs her briefcase and heads out into the hall on her way to the office. She passes the elevator and goes to the stairwell instead, choosing a little exercise in the form of five flights of stairs. When she emerges from the building, she feels the cool morning breeze on her face and notices the graceful birds flying between the high-rises. The sidewalk is crowded with scurrying people, and she picks up her pace to go with the flow.

Jan reaches her car and pulls out onto the street. The light at the entrance of the freeway is red; she checks her watch — no problem, she has extra time. When she merges into the freeway traffic, her first reaction is "Here we go again." When traffic grinds to a halt and settles into gridlock, she does some deep breathing and tries to relax. In a moment of relative quiet in a space that is hardly ever quiet, she decides to make this a prayer moment. Looking at the car ahead, she wonders what the passenger's story might be: their griefs, their triumphs. And she prays! "I ask your blessing, O God, on the occupants of that car. May your love surround them today, these people I don't know and will probably never meet. Bless too my circle of loved ones and friends." Even when the stop-and-go traffic resumes, it's hectic, but Jan muses about how it's just one little blip on life's radar screen.

When she finally walks into the office, she has a smile for fellow workers. She goes to her cubicle, which in a sense is a little shrine — for several pictures of loved ones grace the walls. When she boots up her computer, a little hourglass comes up on the screen and lingers, and Jan prays her usual morning offering: "O God, thank you for the gift of time. Bless this time, and bless my work."

REFLECTION PAUSE OR JOURNAL OPTION

What this parable says to me...

PONDER QUESTIONS

Is Jan a Pollyanna?
Is Jan's morning experience similar to or very different from mine?
Do I find myself in some ways in the parables of both Richard and Jan?

WALKING A BLESSING PATH — THE NATIVE AMERICANS

Is Jan a Pollyanna? Can anyone really develop an approach to life like hers? Is greeting the sun "far out"? The Native Americans would not think so. The ancient Apaches always situated their wickiups so that the entrance flap faced the east. Upon rising, they would open the flap and greet the sun with a blessing prayer of thanks that the sun had returned once more. Then they would pray "for all our relatives." That included all creatures, from pigeons to buffalo!

This attitude was not unique to the Apaches. Listen to an ode to the dawn as prayed by the Guami:

From the great rock I see it, the Daybreak Star, the sign of the dawning;
    above the mountain it rises and my heart dances.
Now the light comes,
    the light that makes me one with all life.
Like the tinamou I am,
    who sings in the dawn, who is humble with love,
Who walks in the circle of the greater love and the greater power.
               — "A Song Heard in the Dawn"

There is much that can be learned about walking a blessing path from the Native Americans. They see much more than just the glare of the morning sun. Their light joins them to all creation. And in the great, blazing power of the sun they become humble with love. I once experienced a seminar with Buck Ghost Horse. At one point, he had us on hands and knees upon the grass to "experience the earth as the little creatures close to the earth do." He did not explain the exercise. He left it to us to realize that we too are close to the earth — to the *humus*. For the Native Americans, "becoming *humble* with love" meant being close to the earth and all our earth relatives.

How different from our "masters of the universe" modern day view. Despite our pretensions, we are not really giants traipsing over the earth. We all share the same sunlight and the same dark with other creatures, large and small. We share the blessings of our earthen planet. From the earth we come and to the earth we return.

Ashes

I recently took part in the Ash Wednesday blessing at a U.S. Naval Air Training Station. It was a moving experience as the assembly came up one-by-one to be signed with the ashes and reminded: "Remember man — remember woman — that you are dust, and unto dust you shall return!" This was a blessing, not a curse, to be reminded that we are of earth. But it is also humbling, for it calls our attention to how we have only a limited time on earth to walk a blessing path. Every size, shape, color, nationality and rank came up to receive the ashes. A tall and stately admiral approached, covered with braids and decorations. Right behind him was a diminutive non-commissioned woman sailor. At that moment, neither rank nor height mattered. "Remember" applied to all.

Walking — Not Running upon the Earth

In their daily walking, Native Americans enter the "circle of a greater power." And the Navaho sing and speak of walking a "blessing path." But in our modern fast-paced, cyberspace culture, we disdain "going around in circles." We move straight forward — racing ahead frantically, never really arriving because once we think we have arrived, we realize we are behind someone, somewhere or something else and must race faster and faster, on and on over the ever-increasing obstacles that stand in our way.

Native Americans of different tribes are renowned for their running. Many can run endless miles without stopping. But they don't run all the time! Although they possess the grace and endurance of great runners, they're not always "on the run." Rather, Native American spirituality is intent on walking a "blessing path," being connected to the rhythms of the earth, moon and sun. They haven't written books about blessings, but they know intuitively what blessings are. They take time to notice. Perhaps in our ever-accelerating lives, we too need to discover the meaning of blessings. We need to take time to notice them and cultivate the ability to walk a blessing path.

So, What Are Blessings?

It's fine, you might say, to consider Native American pieties, but we live in busy, fast-paced communities — not out on the plains hunting buffalo. So, what are blessings for us and our time? A fair enough question! It's difficult to be aware of blessings unless they break through our busy schedules. Sometimes on TV we see the Pope blessing people from his balcony. When the Pope makes the sign of the cross, we know it is a blessing. But we may be puzzled when we see him alight from a plane, stoop down and kiss the ground. Is that also a blessing?

If we reflect on blessings, many questions can come to mind. A priest praying over a religious medal is imparting a blessing. An evangelist laying on hands is definitely imparting a blessing. But what about a priest praying over a beer? What about the "Aha!" of discovery, the "Wow!" of exuberance or the orgasmic moan — can these also be blessings?

A basketball player seems to be performing a blessing when making the sign of the cross before an important free throw. If the shooter misses, does it still count as a blessing? Are high fives blessings?

On rare occasions, a bishop anoints an altar table with oil, setting it aside for sacred use. We know that's a blessing, but what about being rubbed with oil during a refreshing massage? Is that a blessing too? A baby is a "blessed event." What about a honeymoon? Isn't it true that the more sensual or erotic an activity, the less we might be inclined to use the word "blessing" or "holy?" But why isn't that a blessing too?

How about affirmations? Is "I love you!" a blessing? Surely it is, and one of the most powerful of blessings! Do we adequately identify simple but significant words and gestures as blessings?

Besides invoking a blessing on someone, something, some place or some activity, we also experience *being* blessed. Think about the blessing of a hug from your child, a kiss from your spouse, a cool drink on a hot day or a hot bath at the end of a long day. We can be blessed by a kind word, a friendly smile, a hug or a pat on the back.

And what about beauty? When we glimpse a beautiful sunset or share the peacefulness of a tranquil lake, we might exclaim, "What a blessing!" Yet, how often are we that conscious? Are we attentive to the blessings all around, or is our path through life so hectic that too many of the blessings all around are lost in a blur?

Perhaps we all need a graduate course in blessings. Perhaps we simply need to pay more attention to blessings close at hand. If we do, we might well develop a deeper consciousness about blessing and being blessed. This could help us develop a blessing-centered spirituality that might further empower us both to give and receive blessings. When we learn to do that, we walk a blessing path.

But we are on the run, and if we are to reap a harvest of blessings, we need sometimes to cease our frantic pace, to stop, look and listen! When we do stop, the first logical question might be, "Well, just what are blessings really?

THE MEANING OF BLESSING

The dictionary gives several definitions for the verb "to bless": to consecrate or sanctify, to request divine favor, to bestow good of any kind, to protect or guard from evil. And to *be* blessed is to be divinely or supremely favored, according to Webster.

Perhaps that is the place to start when considering a spirituality of blessing. The primal blessing is God's love overflowing, bestowing divine favor on the blessed. As Genesis assures us, in the very beginning God looked at what was created and said it was "very good!" This was the origin of each and every blessing.

BLESSING IN A COFFEE SHOP

One day as I was on a rushed journey, I took time to stop at a small coffee shop on the East Bay in California. There I discovered a smiling Buddha. His pleasant face looked out from a small shrine behind the counter. A small food offering had been placed in front of his statue. Something about that sight changed my consciousness. All of a sudden, there was something special about the coffee in the Styrofoam cup being served by a smiling Chinese woman. As I turned around, something else in the little shop caught my heart. A beaming, toothless Chinese elder stood gazing proudly into a stroller. The faces of two women, who were probably aunties, glowed as they focused full attention on the infant that the grandpa was babysitting. I don't know Chinese, but the way their faces lit up and the wonder in their chatter proclaimed, "Ah! This is very good!" and I felt a multiple blessing — the beautiful infant, the happy relatives, the smiling Buddha and the steaming coffee! What a holy coffee break! What a wonderful pause in the midst of a swift journey! We can discover blessings all around — if we take the time to pay attention.

MY OWN BLESSING JOURNEY

My own awareness of the power of blessing and the depth of its meaning has changed through the widening and deepening of my consciousness as the years have passed. "When I was a child, I spoke as a child, I reasoned like a child..." (1 Corinthians 13: 11). At one time I thought that a blessing turned something worldly into something spiritual. There was an element of magic in this kind of thinking. And, of course, only priests had the power to bless. Blessings took place on clerical turf. The blessing arena was very small and narrow.

In college, at a Benedictine abbey, I learned that there were more church blessing prayers than I had ever imagined — even a blessing for beer! That bemused me even though the monks have had their hand in "spirit making" from time immemorial, evidenced in Benedictine Liqueur and Christian Brothers Wines. My ministry in the 50s and 60s spanned the shifting of consciousness in my denomination from a Vatican I to a Vatican II spirituality. Priests were still the "official blessers," but there was a growing awareness of the baptismal priesthood of the laity. It would not be long before parents were urged to place their hands upon the heads of their children and bless them.

THE PRIMAL BLESSING

In the second half of my life I began to reflect on the new creation story. For the first time in human history, a new picture of an evolving universe was beginning to capture the imagination of mainstream thinking. Pioneers and prophets like Thomas Berry were reminding us that creation had been unfolding for some fifteen billion years, that the whole universe is a multiform energy event. Moreover, it's an event that's an unfolding cornucopia of blessings!

Where stories start is extremely important — as important as where they lead. Up to this time, my own starting point for the spiritual journey was the story of Adam and Eve after their fall — a story that emphasized a curse from sin. It makes a big difference whether one's consciousness of beginnings focuses on a curse as opposed to centering on blessings.

The shift from a curse fixation to a blessing outlook in my own consciousness came from the insight that creation was "very good" before humans ever arrived on earth. It was all an evolving gift from the Creator. It remained an enduring blessing even after sin and the curse entered the picture — which is very late in the story indeed. God took lots of time to unfold the creation story. Unlike people in contemporary culture, God was never in a rush.

I now live near the Grand Canyon. To stand at its edge and look down, one can trace each epoch of its development by examining the lines in the rock. These lines, in some sense, the are fingerprints of the Creator revealing a gradual development over millions of years. To pause, to look and to reflect on this monumental unfolding is truly awe-inspiring.

In one of the Chevy Chase *Vacation* movies, he and his family are on a frenetic, stop-and-go vacation. They drive up to the rim of the Grand Canyon; they clamber out; they peer over the edge for perhaps twenty seconds, and then Chevy says, "Well, we've seen this now; let's get back in the car and get going!" His remarks are barely a caricature of the hurried times in which we live.

GOD'S TIME — NOT OUR TIME

After the eons of pre-development that followed the great fireball 550 million years ago, the clams and snails evolved, and the God of Genesis looked out over it — and it was very good. Then 510 million years ago vertebrate animals appeared, and God looked out — and it was very good. And 150 million years ago the birds took to the sky, and this was a blessed event. Cats and dogs came along 35 million years ago — long before any human arrived. What an ancient wisdom they possess, and what a blessing they have come to be to so many humans!

No wonder that Meister Eckhart, the medieval mystic, could

proclaim that every creature is a book about God. A wonderful thought! But if this is so, then the unique library from which humans can learn so much about God is shrinking with the depletion and destruction of so many species. If multitudes of species continue to be destroyed, the earth will become quite bleak, and mankind, in turn, will be deprived of many blessings.

ANCIENT ANIMAL BLESSINGS

When I wrote my book *One Hundred Cranes: Praying with the Chorus of Creation*, my awareness exploded into the realization that other creatures have the power to bless us. (Some have the power to eat us alive which would not seem to be much of a blessing. Yet we have been given the unique gift as humans to protect ourselves from such a fate, while at the same time receiving blessings from our cousins in creation.) The creatures with whom we share planet Earth are much more blessings for us than they are curses, and so I wrote:

Blessed be! Blessed be! Blessed be!	
Dolphins leaping	Lame leaping
Whales breaching	Blind seeing
Horses racing	Brides blushing
Falcons diving	Grooms glowing
Bears rumbling	Parades strutting
Rams butting	Dancers strutting
Seahawks flocking	Birthday candles blazing
Cardinals singing	Soldiers returning
Colts frolicking	Spirits lifting
Lions roaring	Clowns laughing
Broncos bucking	Hearts beating
Children skipping	Tides rolling
Lovers kissing	Fortunes shifting!
Blessed be! Blessed be! Blessed be!	

Creation dances all around us on Mother Earth and in the surging seas, continually blessing us! As humans, we are divinely and supremely favored just to be a part of the great dance and the chorus of creation.

MERRY-GO-ROUNDS

Do you remember when you were a child and you were lifted up and placed upon a "bucking horse," and the merry-go-round went round and round. There was no destination, no need to rush — just a joyful ride, up and down, round and round. The music played, and you and the horsy dipped and rose, turned and turned. The journey was not product-oriented. In some intuitive way you were in touch, even as a little child, with the turning of the spheres, the chorus of creation, the rhythm of life.

However, in our plastic and spastic culture we charge full-speed ahead, always trying to get ahead. Our motion must always get us somewhere. We always must be on the climb — higher status, bigger houses, more prestigious vehicles. Yet, while we are always climbing, all too often we are not satisfied. And rarely do we move in the blessed circle of what really counts — sharing life among graying elders, a circle of friends, laughing and skipping children. Have we not been told, "Unless you become as children, you cannot enter the kingdom" (Matthew 18: 3)? We need to get off our high horses and join the children in the blessed merry-go-round of life.

If we are on a racehorse, all we see is a blur. To walk a blessing path, we must stop the "rat race" for awhile in order to pay attention, gain perspective and reflect a little. These are the conduits that allow the life-giving waters of the natural world to flood our parched spirits.

ATTENTION TO THE NATURAL WORLD

The natural world that encircles us wants to bless us. Even in our paved-over cities we can catch glimpses of the natural world and of other creatures worthy of our attention. In some cities, the almost extinct peregrine falcon is being reestablished in friendly business towers. I know of one skyscraper where a TV camera focuses on an falcon's nest, and workers on their lunch break marvel at this high-flyer love nest!

From the dawn of human history peoples who live close to the earth have believed that creatures of nature have messages and blessings for us. The Native Americans and ancient Celts believed that those creatures who were here before humankind have something to teach the later-arriving humans. Ancient shamans valued animal guides. And in the Scriptures, Jesus is a lamb, the Spirit is a dove and the evangelists a lion, ox and eagle!

We certainly don't eclipse the significance and the symbolic power of animals and birds when we name our sports teams Tigers, Broncos, Marlins and Seahawks.

Recently, I rode down a busy avenue with two lovely friends, both in their eighties. Joe's a retired airline pilot, so Fran and he have flown all over the world. Fran has slowed down now, and her knees will not take her everyplace she would like to go. However she is in love with life and is attentive to small happenings. In heavy traffic, we came to a stop at a traffic signal. The light was attached to an extended white pole that reached out over the center of the road. "Oh, look!" said Fran. "The tiniest bird just flew into a hole in that steel pole! Amazing!" Yes, indeed, for someone who has eyes to see and a heart to enjoy, an unexpected blessing from the natural world can come even in the midst of heavy traffic.

Yesterday, the very day I wrote about the peregrine falcon, I had a conversation with a lady who lives along a dry Arizona wash. She was very moved at observing a rare falcon across the wash. That sighting led us into a further conversation about the powerful symbolism that such creatures can bring into our human lives. She remembered the tragic death of her son a year before by suicide. She said that shortly after his death she was looking out of her picture window in her home, and a beautiful crane was framed for a moment in time as it lifted skyward. Her son had worked in Alaska, and his ashes were to be sprinkled on a high Alaska lake. As the family was making the trek up the mountain, a spot where they would have least expected it, two cranes floated by in front of them. (In Japanese lore, the crane's role was to bear up slain warriors to a better place.) She did not explain what the sighting of those cranes meant to her; she did not have to. In some sense, they spoke to her grieving heart, and that by itself was a marvelous blessing.

For the most part, our cities provide limited opportunities to encounter animals or birds, and yet there is hardly anyplace where interesting creatures do not dwell. Even sports stadiums in the hearts of great cities provide havens for an amazing variety of swallows and other birds. More and more waiting rooms are incorporating tropical fish tanks or even aviaries. They do so because we are starved for the blessings that nature wishes to bestow.

If we pay attention, our perceptions sharpen; we see much more of what we previously missed. And when we see deeper and wider, we reflect on the mystery and wonder of life — and our soul, which searches for treasure, finds gold at its very doorway.

PERCEPTIONS

The Missouri River is the second longest river in the United States. It makes an epic trek from the mountains of Montana down to the lowlands of Missouri. I am especially familiar with its meanderings between Nebraska and Iowa. It separates the cities of Omaha, Nebraska, and Council Bluffs, Iowa. Stand on its Omaha bank and look across, and its wooded eastern bank is pretty much as it was when Lewis and Clark made their adventurous journey almost two hundred years ago. One change particularly stands out now. A riverboat gambling casino is moored on the other shore. If you were to take a variety of people to that Nebraska shore and ask them what they see, their answers might be:

What do you see, gambler? "A casino and the possibility of big bucks!"
What do you see, pessimist? "A dirty brown river."
What do you see, fisherman? "Some big catfish lurking under the surface."
What do you see, historian? "The path that Lewis and Clark trod."

These would all be correct, but very limited perceptions.

And what do you see, spiritual seeker? "I see a mighty river, always flowing yet never the same. I see a river that speaks of the flow of life. I see a river that is a fountain of life, blessing humans with life-giving waters purified for drinking. I see the eyes of deer peeking out from the forested banks, survivors between two cities, knowing when to bound and when to stand still. I see a river that keeps moving, that floods in springtime and freezes in winter, reminding me that there is a time to flow out and a time to slow down. I see all of this and much more!"

ATTENTION

To walk a blessing path demands attention — really looking about with a spiritual perception. It's an attitude of reverence that is always open and alert to blessings all around. Thomas Aquinas, thirteenth century philosopher and theologian, wrote that everything is perceived through the mode (attitude) of the perceiver. His insight is still true.

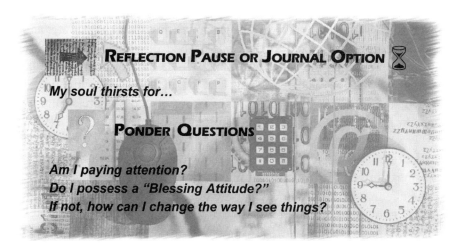

REFLECTION PAUSE OR JOURNAL OPTION

My soul thirsts for...

PONDER QUESTIONS

Am I paying attention?
Do I possess a "Blessing Attitude?"
If not, how can I change the way I see things?

THE HEBREW SCRIPTURES' BLESSING PATH

One of the oldest historical and spiritual journeys, and a significant chapter in Judeo-Christian history and spirituality, is the journey of the Exodus. In this story we can glimpse a people's struggle to walk a blessing path. There is attention and lack of attention. There are both correct and misguided perceptions. There is impatience with the slowness of the journey. And there is a spiritual sense of God very close in crossing the sea and plodding through the desert.

We might see the Hebrew people as unseeing and untrusting. God saw them that way sometimes. But we can also see them as Sprit-driven and God-seeking. They did not see their desert journey in ordinary terms. God was with them, and God spoke to them through gushing water from the rock and in quail cast upon the desert. When they did reach the Promised Land, they marveled at its blessings — a land flowing with milk and honey. Their journey through the sea, over the desert and beyond the mountain passed on a tradition of a blessing path — a path that Jesus would later walk.

JESUS AND THE BLESSING PATH

At the end of each chapter in this book there will be Scripture references that look at how Jesus was on the blessing path, as well as references from the Hebrew Scriptures that reflect on a people grounded in blessing. In my own experience and awareness of creation's ability to bestow the blessings of vitality, fertility, energy and healing, the Gospels have taken on new vibrancy. Jesus was in touch with air, sea, water and earth, and he recognized their goodness and power. Jesus walked a blessing path upon the earth. He walked — he did not rush — and he was attentive to the earth beneath his feet. In fact, if you took a highlighter and marked the passages where Jesus is out-of-doors, there would be very little of the text left unmarked. He knew and experienced the fertility of water — filling a net to sinking — as well as the sea's tempest. At the pool of Bethsaida and Siloam he knew that water was already holy, and he allowed the waters of the Jordan to bless him. (There is no evidence that he found it necessary to make a sign of the cross over it before being immersed.) He made frequent use of images of earth and seed and plants to describe the kingdom.

His most famous sermon (which will be considered in the last chapter of this book) was his litany of blessings on the mount of Beatitudes: Blessed be…Blessed be…Blessed be…. This litany came so naturally to Jesus because the pious Jew of his day often prayed a hundred blessings every day!

What is Holy?

Blessings are identified with the "sacred." If Jesus did not invoke ritual blessings over the water and mud he used to heal, what is holy water and what is holy earth? When the Pope descends from an airplane and kisses the ground, he first receives the earth's blessed welcome and in turn blesses the earth with a kiss. Thus, before any water receives a special blessing for church use, it too is already holy! For water is as rare in the universe as a diamond in the desert. On earth we could not sustain our lives without its blessed presence. So, blessed be rare and precious life-giving water!

Curses

There is only one recorded instance of Jesus cursing. Jesus cursed a fig tree. The reason he did so was because of its refusal to bestow its blessings. Because it was turned in upon itself, it would shrivel up — as will our sprits if we fail to bless and be blessed. Jesus' cursing the ungiving fig tree only highlights the fact that he walked a blessing, healing path of affirmation. To affirm is to recognize goodness, even when it is poorly wrapped. Jesus even blessed outcasts and notorious sinners.

The paradox about blessings, of course, is that we can appreciate them more because there are also curses. The nightly news reminds us of that. Perhaps one of the greatest discernment challenges of our days is to know the difference between blessings and curses. Yellow poppies that ripple across a field and are harvested for medicine are blessings. The dope that is extracted from them for addicts is a curse. Too often we don't know the difference. And too often, humans use their ingenuity to turn blessings into curses. Moreover, in our daily experiences, we too often receive curses from others in the form of words, gestures or put-downs.

AFFIRMATIONS

It has never been recorded that anyone ever died from an overdose of affirmation! But some have died without it! At the turn of the twentieth century, it was discovered that babies who had been placed in orphanages and who were not held and cuddled often died. They shriveled up and faded away without the affirmation of hugs and affection. Affirmations are recognitions of goodness. Young or old, we all need them. Affirmations reveal an awareness of the goodness that permeates all reality.

One of the most joyful affirmations and ardent hugs in the New Testament took place in the garden when Mary Magdalene thought she was talking to the gardener, and Jesus turned and said, "Mary!" Her eyes widened in wonder and surprise, and she exclaimed, "Rabboni!" She immediately threw her arms around Jesus and hugged him with all her heart. Finally, Jesus smiled and said that she should not continue to cling to him for she had a blessing to deliver to his men friends, most of whom had abandoned him on the cross (See John 20: 11-18). I wonder if even Jesus needed a hug after the agony of the cross? It would seem so. And what an affirmation the scene was for Mary — she was to be the witness and apostle of his resurrection.

STRUCTURED AFFIRMATIONS

When I was a pastor, our pastoral team did semi-annual evaluations. We would go around the group, and each member would verbally give five affirmations to each member with only one opportunity to offer a possible area for growth. At the end of the morning, each member of the team glowed after receiving fifty affirmations. We felt this practice needed to be structured into our format because too often we forget to affirm.

Joyce Brothers claims that each married partner needs at least five affirmations to make up for one negative comment or put-down that might occur. She claims such a ratio is vital for a healthy relationship. Such a practice of affirmation is part of walking a blessing path.

REFLECTION PAUSE OR JOURNAL OPTION

When I think of _____, who is dear to me, I would affirm these five blessings that his/her presence brings to me:

PONDER QUESTIONS

When was the last time I blessed my closest loved ones with five affirmations?

Am I receiving enough affirmations? Giving enough? (Perhaps these two answers are related)

Were I to give myself five affirmations, would they would be?

BEGIN THE DAY WITH BLESSINGS

When we walk a blessing path, we take nothing for granted. Gratitude is at the heart of blessings. I have developed my own little morning prayer ritual. When I get up, I go to the east window in my bedroom and pull open the drapes. Arizona is home for me, and so most mornings I greet the *sun* with gratitude. If it is a cloudy day, I praise God for the variety and change in the weather. Next to the window is a collage picture of friends and loved ones. I look at them and thank God that they are such gifts in my life. Next to that hangs a calendar. As I look at it, I thank God for giving me this day. This little ritual starts me walking a blessing path each day.

IRISH BLESSINGS

Alan, an affable Irishman from Galway who lives in our rectory, makes a daily commute on the freeway to the adjoining city of Phoenix. One evening when he arrived home, we sat down to a meal and discussed daily blessings. He told me how much blessings are woven into the fabric of daily life in Ireland. "If you meet someone in the field or perhaps digging turf or feeding livestock, the common parting words are, "God bless the work!" The customary response is, "And bless you too!"

The Irish greeting *Céad Míle Fáilte!* means "100,000 Welcomes!" What a blessed greeting! *Sláinte!* — "Health!" is the blessing that echoes through Irish pubs. "May the road rise to meet you, the wind be always at your back, the rain fall soft upon your fields," and "May you be in heaven a half hour before the devil knows you're dead!" are well-known Irish blessings. No wonder Ireland is famed for its hospitality. Besides the beauty of its countryside, it is a land filled with blessings.

Perhaps another hidden blessing is that its roads are often winding lanes, which precludes driving through the countryside at breakneck speed.

THE CURSES OF ROAD RAGE

If there is anything symptomatic of the hyperpaced culture in which we live, one need look no farther than road rage. After talking about the blessing culture of Ireland, Alan went on to describe an incident that happened on his commute home from downtown Phoenix. "A lady arrived in the turn lane just as the arrow switched to yellow. She stopped. The driver behind her (maybe Richard?), a young businessman in a suit and French cuffs, screeched to a stop, jumped out of his car, ran up to the woman's car window and berated her with curses and obscene gestures — all for not running the light!

In a society that is almost manic in its acceleration and stress, there seems to be more and more cursing and fewer and fewer blessings. Consider a 1996 study by the AAA Foundation for Traffic Safety, which reported that road rage incidents in the United States had increased 51% in the six preceding years. In the study's final year, 12,828 people were killed or injured as a result of aggressive driving. The *Scottsdale Tribune* reported the experience of one city truck driver:

> Doug Eden, a driver for Performance Delivery Systems of Tempe has had a gun pointed at him while driving. "I'm not special," he says. "Ask the truck drivers who work this town — at least half of them have had a gun pointed at them at one time or another."

This is a worst-case scenario. But aren't all us often rushed to the point of inner consternation? There are a lot of grim and angry people out on the freeway. They dress well, drive nice cars or utility vehicles and have nice homes, yet they are sour, grumpy and even resort to violence behind the wheel. It's so easy for all of us to be caught up in this mad frenzy. We need pauses in the whirlwind. We need prayer. We need blessings. One natural pause that could provide a prayer opportunity for us is the red light. Instead of gritting my teeth about waiting at a red light, I have begun to use it a couple times a day as an opportunity for prayer. When I am waiting at a red light, I sometimes use the moment as an opportunity for quiet reflection or I say a little blessing prayer for the person ahead of me. Yes, even the crowded roadway can be turned into a blessing path.

In our rushed and busy lives it is quite difficult for many people to find extended times for prayer, although if we really prioritized our lives most of us could find more fruitful time than we realize. I once bought a guitar with the intent of learning to play. But it sat in corner for months. One of my friends asked, "Have you started to play?" I responded, "I would like to but I haven't had time." She responded, "Oh? Do you only have a twenty three-hour day, or are you like the rest of us who have twenty-four hours? I'd guess you can find the time to do what you really value."

There certainly is one way for almost everyone to find time for prayer — a time to bless, a time to reflect, a time to speak to the Spirit of God who is all around, no matter where we are. This newfound prayer time can come in the intervals where circumstances force us to wait: at a traffic light, the doctor's office, the checkout line…. These short pauses are like cracks in a sidewalk, from which amazingly a flower may sometimes take root and bloom. These cracks in the concrete of life can become pauses in the whirlwind — providing us opportunities to bless and be blessed.

ROAD SIGNS ON THE BLESSING PATH

If there were road signs on the Blessing Path, they might be posted at consecutive intervals to remind us to:

Pay Attention — Notice!
Stop! Look! Listen!
Deer Crossing! We Were Here First!
Perceive!

Reflect!
Have Open Eyes and Hearts!
Have a Gratitude Attitude!
Have a Reverential Spirit!
Notice Other Creatures!
Find Rest Stops on the Fast Track!
Make Pit Stops into Prayer Stops!
Affirm! Affirm! Affirm!
Slow Down to Live!

SCRIPTURE IMAGES AND PASSAGES FOR REFLECTION

Hebrew Scriptures

Psalm 103: 8-22 — *Bless our God*

...Bless our God, you heavenly host,
    you faithful ones who enforce God's will!
Bless our God, all creation,
    to the far reaches of God's reign!
Bless, Adonai, my soul!

Christian Scriptures

Matthew 6: 28-29 — *Jesus' words regarding the Blessing Path:*

Look at the lilies of the field,
    not even Solomon in all his glory
    was arrayed like one of these!

 ## PAUSES IN THE WHIRLWIND

Prayer Starters for Busy People:

At the sighting of the first flying bird of the day:

Holy Spirit, graceful dove, soar above me this day.
Let me fly beyond what might drag me down.

At the stoplight:

O God, send your angel to guide this person in front of me.
Ease his/her burdens, and grant him/her peace and joy this day.

At the checkout line:

How fortunate I am, O God, that I have found what I needed.
Help each of us in this line to find even more:
your love and your life.

In the Post Office line:

How much we want to communicate, O God!
I pray for the recipients of the messages being sent.
May they be blessed and respond with love.

In the doctor's office:

O God, let me be one, in compassion,
with everyone waiting here.
Bless the doctor.
Bless the nurses.
May we all find healing.

BLESSINGS FROM THE HOLY DARK

PARABLES OF TWO QUESTING KNIGHTS

I will give you the treasures of darkness
and riches hidden in secret places
—Isaiah 45: 3

THE KNIGHT IN SHINING ARMOR

Once upon a time, a certain knight, a prince of the realm, wanted to be a perfect knight. He knelt before his lady and pledged to her that his escutcheon would never be sullied. His armor always shone so gloriously that he was dubbed the "Knight of the Shining Armor." He rode forth on his sacred quest, his pennant brilliant in the noonday sun. He rode along roads well traveled. His proud stallion was sure of foot and capable of galloping swiftly. The shining knight avoided muddy byways and crooked detours. He searched far and wide for dragons and monsters to slay, but he only rode during the daytime and in brightly lit places. There were road signs along the way pointing this way and that. But whenever the road forked, he would always chose the road that looked most traveled.

One day he came to a junction where the two branching roads both appeared rocky. Carefully deliberating, he chose what seemed the less rough of the two. After a while, at the side of a mountain, he came upon a dark and fearsome cave. His squire announced to him, "Sire, it is said that a fierce dragon lives within this cave, and the one who vanquishes this creature will be the noblest knight in the realm!"

"Very well," said the Knight of the Shining Armor, "I shall challenge the beast!" So he stood at the entrance, sword in hand. He prayed a blessing and then dared the monster to come out of the dark cavern and engage him in a battle. But from the cave, only darkness and silence greeted him.

Thus it ever went. He only journeyed forth and prayed in the noonday sun. He only traveled the smoothest roads. He disdained venturing forth on an unknown or unexplored path, and he only threw down his gauntlet in the light of day. He prayed often, asking blessings for his quest, and shouted out many challenges, but no monsters ever emerged from any of the caves he approached in his sunlit quest. On his long journey, he was so much in the light that his sight began to fail. Finally, the day came when he could not see at all.

The knight, therefore, returned to the castle, his eyes blinded by the noonday sun, his head down, his heart deeply depressed. He had journeyed far. He had blessed the light, but never had he prayed in the dark or encountered monsters in the black recesses of unexplored caves. In the end, he had experienced so much light that he was forced into his own dark. For the rest of his life, he would remain in the castle. His old shiny armor rusted in a corner, and he could be heard to mumble from time to time, "If only…if only I had taken another path and found the dragon."

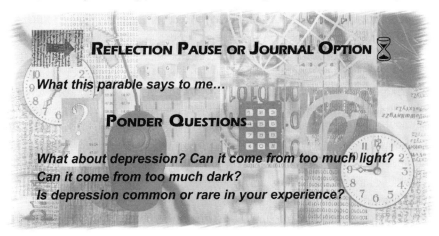

REFLECTION PAUSE OR JOURNAL OPTION

What this parable says to me…

PONDER QUESTIONS

What about depression? Can it come from too much light?
Can it come from too much dark?
Is depression common or rare in your experience?

THE PRINCE WITH MUDDY FEET

Once upon a time, another prince, son of a powerful and mighty king was sent forth by his father on a vision quest into wild places to seek his destiny. His father told him to search for a messenger in a forbidding place, a messenger who would direct him to a less traveled road. After many miles, the road wound around to a junction. At the crossroads there were two options: One sign said, *First Class Oasis — Twenty Miles. AAAA* (Ancient AAA) *Recommended Hotels*. The other said, *Winding Path to the River: 50 Miles*. His instincts told him to take the path toward the river even though there was no indication of moisture anywhere. In fact, the narrow path apparently only wound through barren desert.

As he made this difficult journey, he learned to rise early before the dawn and walk in the cool of night, guided by the stars. At noontime, in the fiery desert sun, he would pull up his hood and nap in what little shade he could find. He would resume his journey in the late afternoon and into the dark of nightfall.

After several days, some green shrubbery could be seen on the horizon. It was a thin green line that indicated water was near. Sure enough, as he reached the green foliage, he could hear running water just beyond.

Finally, he reached the riverbank. The stream was peaceful, and it flowed some fifty feet below him through carved-out muddy banks. There were people camped nearby. Standing there was a tall, rough-looking man, a real "desert rat," tanned, well muscled. He came over to the prince and introduced himself: "I'm a wilderness guide — do you need one?"

"Yes, I think so," said the prince. "I would welcome a guide to point the way on my search for my destiny, but first I must bathe in the flowing river and wash away the grit and grime of a long journey." And so he did. When he finally emerged, he was energized, strengthened, his body cleansed, his spirit lifted. However, there was no way to climb the bank without his feet getting muddy.

So it happened that the Prince with Muddy Feet would stay in the wild man's camp for several days. Finally, the day came for the prince to journey forth and continue his search for his destiny. As he was about to leave, the wild man looked at him and said, "I now believe that I am the messenger the king said you should meet in this wild place. Your very destiny has brought you here — not to a palace but to a place of muddy feet. I also believe that you are a beloved son, affirmed and blest by your father even though you have not been given an easy path.

"You are to enlarge and extend your father's kingdom at great cost to yourself. You shall be a valiant prince striving against great odds. Now you must continue your vision quest. But from here the journey is more difficult. It is a trackless waste between this place and the great city of your destiny. The foxes have holes is this wild country, but you shall have no place to lay your head." The wild man pointed to the prince — and called out to his followers, "Look! This royal visitor is special indeed!" Then, motioning toward the horizon, he said to the prince, "Follow that way. It shall be a blessing path. Befriend the night by following the stars. Take this water and journey on. I sense that there will be other messengers and a great joust on your heroic journey."

So the prince set out. The journey was just as the wild man had prophesied. Again, the prince befriended the night and followed the stars. He was now the prince with dusty and aching feet. In the intense heat of noonday he rested as best he could. He journeyed many days through the searing heat.

Then, just before dawn, out of the dark came a vision. A handsome figure appeared and declared to the prince: "I am a prince of the darkness, but I am also called 'Light Bearer.' I am strong and wise, and I can help you reach your full stature and obtain the glory to which you are entitled. Let me show you! But first, are you hungry?"

"Yes, indeed!" replied the prince.

"Well then, since you are the son of a powerful king, and I am even more powerful than he is, it is my will that you turn these stones into bread and that we shall both feast."

The Prince with Muddy Feet responded, "I answer only to my father's command."

The Prince of Darkness replied, "Very well, but let me show you now how you can create a great spectacle." And at that moment, the dark prince used his great power and swept the vision-questing prince high up on a precipice. "Test your father's power of kingship. Throw yourself down and test his power!" Again, the prince refused.

Finally, the Prince of Darkness swirled his cape and took the young prince to noonday, showing him all the kingdoms of the earth glistening in the noonday sun — temples, palaces and all the high-rises of ages to come. "Look at their glory! Sense their splendor! Behold these houses of gold, resplendent and glittering in the yellow sunlight. Kneel and worship me; seek my blessing and it all shall be yours!"

The young prince looked at his tempter and noticed that the persuasive huckster cast no shadow in the noonday sun! So he replied, "I know who you are! You are not just a prince from the darkness — you are the noonday devil! Away with you!" At that moment, the vision evaporated. Now, out of the holy dark powerful knights led by their captain Michael came to the young prince from his father's realm — just as they had descended some thirty years before on a midnight clear. They ministered to the prince, this stage of his vision quest now complete. As he lay down to rest, dreams of a better vision came to dwell in the dark and holy cave of his imagination. He awoke with the dawn and now saw more clearly — but not yet fully — the direction in which he must go.

Now strengthened, his journey continued. The prince blessed the night and welcomed the day. He journeyed on to his own coronation, toward his destiny as a king who would pass the test, who would suffer grievously, but in the end would triumph.

And that is the story of the Prince, the Knight with the Muddy Feet. Like all noble knights, his destiny took him through the night to a better dawning.

Have you ever noticed that the words "knight" and "night" are so alike?

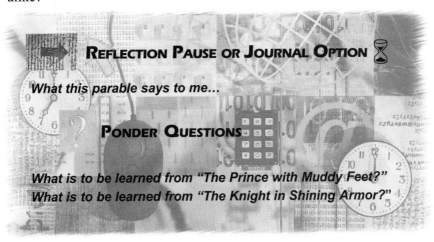

REFLECTION PAUSE OR JOURNAL OPTION

What this parable says to me...

PONDER QUESTIONS

What is to be learned from "The Prince with Muddy Feet?"
What is to be learned from "The Knight in Shining Armor?"

Light and Darkness

In our cyber-culture we can easily become confused about light and darkness. We need to find a blessing path through both light and dark. Yet in our age we live mostly in the light, with bright TV and computer screens in well-lit offices and cities illuminated with incandescent and neon. We can live twenty-four hours every day without ever walking in the pitch dark. Yet stories and myths throughout the ages assure us that to walk a blessing path we must sometimes make our way through darkness. There are blessings in the dark as well as in the light.

Perpetual Light

Like the Knight in Shining Armor, our "enlightened" culture beguiles us into trying to live our lives and seek our quests in perpetual light. In the ancient Roman liturgy, "Let perpetual light shine upon them" was a prayer for the dead, pointing to their place in heaven, not a prayer for those living on earth! In our time we are led to believe that *light* is good and *dark* is bad. This is a dangerous and simplistic illusion. We can have too much dark, but we can also have too much light.

Too Much Light

Our journeys are from light to light. From our morning rising to our going to bed, we are enveloped in light. The only total darkness we experience is that small window of time between lights out and night's dreams. We hardly ever really experience the night's exterior darkness. In order to know with our hearts the splendor of a black and star-sprinkled sky, we must journey out of our cities and take time to look up. Yet how seldom most of us take the time for such inner essentials. Rarely are we ever enmeshed in the great darkness of the holy night. Even in the darkness of wintertime, our journey from Thanksgiving to Christmas is ablaze with holiday lights.

Our pursuits seldom take us to mysterious caves, shady glens or sacred wells. More and more for many of the affluent and even the non-affluent, gaudily lit casinos offer our primary modern heroic quests and jousts. There, against great odds, modern knights and ladies do battle with one-armed bandits. America's great modern pilgrimage shrines may well be the casinos of Atlantic City or Vegas where the sun shines year-round and night is always as bright as day.

Our Cyber-Image-World

Yes, we live and work in perpetual light. Whether at work or at play, so many of us spend more and more time gazing into a bright word-processing screen or television screen. And it is here that we can be beguiled into believing that the "holy grail" is some consumer item that we must have in order to be fulfilled. Like the Knight in Shining Armor, we can be blinded by too much glitter. In the bright lights of advertising everything looks good and attractive, and we are conned into believing we can buy perfection. Indeed, not everything that emanates from our light-dominated culture is good. What first appears as a blessing can turn into a curse.

In his insightful book *The Age of Manipulation*, Wilson Bryan Key calls attention to the seduction that reaches out from our bright screens:

> (In the United States) People have been conditioned to accept mindlessly word or picture symbols as realities — even when they lack any conceivable relationship to perceivable reality. Ads supply the model for language.... Human populations can be unconsciously (subliminally) conditioned to any desired design.

He is writing about the subliminal perceptions that pervade our experience because of the manipulative advertising that constantly bombards us from our bright and alluring screens. Even the movie screen has become a billboard. In a 1999 movie called *Edtv,* the plot centers around an ordinary guy named Ed who has been chosen to be filmed every waking hour and broadcast live over the course of many days. On one level, the film is a satire of an invasive and prying culture and the resulting loss of privacy. Yet, while this film professes to decry the manipulation of Ed, it simultaneously manipulates the viewer! Inserted at the bottom bar-lines of each of the TV shots is a continuous series of commercial ads. We can't help but be subtly yet strongly influenced in simply watching the action on the screen!

Writing about our "postmodern" culture in the *Arizona Republic*, Richard Nilsen says that postmodern "reality" blurs the distinction between TV and real life. Our lives in some way blend in and merge with TV images. Consumers become extensions of TV's marketing!

We wear billboards on our ball caps and T-shirts. We look

for the swooshes on our jogging shoes. It doesn't strike anyone under the age of 40 as odd that we should name a stadium after a snack food or a long distance telephone company.

Never before in human history has the human psyche been flooded with so many images designed to allure, captivate, motivate and program us to the designer's desire. And all of this is presented brightly, smartly and convincingly.

HOLY CARDS

When I was a child, it was a great treat to receive "holy cards," colorful pictures of Jesus, Mary or a saint. There was wisdom in giving out such cards: They were treats for the imagination, and long after catechism questions and answers might be forgotten the images of Jesus and the saints would linger. Granted, this was before color TV and invasive billboards. Now, of course, there are different "colored pictures" that linger in the minds of the children and adults. Nike, for example, runs a sixteen-page spread of near-naked athletes in *Sports Illustrated*, knowing that we will eventually be lured by their logo on the sixteenth page. Some colorful images are funny, like the Bud frogs; some are harmless, like Charlie the Tuna or the Pillsbury Doughboy. But some, like Joe Camel and the Marlboro Man are extremely harmful. Wayne McClaren, one of the models for the Marlboro Man, died of lung cancer at age fifty-one. Riding on the wide-open range, he projected the image of freedom in the sunshiny West, riding carefree with no fences in the way. Yet he died gasping for breath — a lung-locked victim of the product he promoted.

Despite stories like this, teenagers today are still buying the image. More than a third of high school kids now smoke regularly, with Marlboro preferred by more than 60%. The power of images! Marshall McCluhan termed advertising "the cave art of the twentieth century." Indeed, its seductive images do often cater to primitive needs and emotions.

Josh Anshell, CEO for a Phoenix ad agency, commenting on the allure of the Marlboro Man, reinforces the immense power of such images that flood into our consciousness with these words, "For many people, your image of yourself or what others think of you becomes more important than anything, even death."

SPIRITUAL SEEKERS IN CYBERSPACE

In the midst of a glut of images, is it not increasingly difficult for spiritual seekers to walk a blessing path that quests for the good, the true and the beautiful? Is it not difficult to travel a path that leads toward real treasure rather than toward death masquerading in bright tinsel and glaring billboards?

In our age, that challenge has gone to another level because we have the Internet. Turn on the blank computer, and it floods with light and images. Emerging from its dark, mysterious inner microchips, the whole world is at our fingertips. It can be a cornucopia overflowing with beauty and knowledge or a sewer pipe spewing forth poison and garbage. We need a spiritual approach to integrating this new force for good or evil into our lives. I find more and more good-willed people seeking counseling after being hooked by Internet porn. To walk a blessing path through the Internet, could we not use frequent "blessing prayer breaks," asking God directly to bless our search when we log on to the net? There is much more throughout this book, particularly in Chapter 7, on the need for discernment as we travel along the bright ways of the Internet and utilize other "marvels" of modern technology. But we need to begin the process here to help keep us on the path as we explore the blessing way.

Indeed, there are both buried treasure and hidden demons along the information highway. So we need to be careful neither to demonize the technology itself nor to give over too much power to the trash dragons that hang out there. To raise too much fuss with the dragons is to give them too much power. However, there is an ancient folk wisdom that might be applied to the Internet: "Curiosity killed the cat!" Aren't we all tempted sometimes to prowl and sniff out the dankest corridors of this alluring maze? Maybe praying gentle blessings as we log on can keep our consciousness focused on a search for treasures that can ennoble us.

In their day, many of our grandparents found it very important to teach our parents table blessings. It is still important. In our day, we might also teach our children blessing prayers to use with computer tables. This practice could begin as early as children go on-line.

DUNGEONS

As with the light, not all darkness is holy or even beneficial. Morbid curiosity can lead us into some of the dungeons and unhealthy webs that lurk in the darker recesses of the net. Eric Harris, one of the two "Trenchcoat Mafia" assassins at Columbine High in Littleton, Colorado, had a Web site code named "Darkness." Marc Fisher of the *Washington Post* said that their fascination with the morbid and the macabre was symptomatic of a Gothic subculture among some teens. In the article entitled "Eager Descent into Darkness," he described Harris and Klebold as immersing themselves in "a pseudomedieval world of dark images." He went on to underline how the tragedy was preceded by these two youths using the Internet as a resource for anger and hatred:

> They were confused, angry kids drowning in a sea of lurid imagery and frightening violence. Like many in a generation that has grown up on-line, they sprinkled bits of make-believe and reality all over the Internet — a line drawing of a gun-toting attacker here, a self-portrait as a marauding avenger there…. And amid it all a page on Harris' Web site appears with plans for constructing bombs.

OUR PASSAGE

If we are pilgrims on the blessing path trod by the Prince with Muddy Feet, we must make our way neither blinded by the light nor overwhelmed by the dark. And we must discern the difference between garbage and soul food. To do so in our age we need blessings for our paths through cyberspace.

DISCERNMENT

Do we need discernment regarding images? How many images of mayhem, sadism and war are enough? How many are too much? The ancient Native Americans had petroglyphs. The medieval peasants had stained glass windows. But that was the extent of the images in their lives. Their waking days were filled with actual interactions with the reality surrounding them. For large numbers of people in our lifetime, a large portion of each day is filled with virtual reality — a flood of images flowing across our screens. How much of an effect do they have on us? Can the distinction between reality and projected reality become blurred? We really do not know. One thing is certain: Never in the history of mankind have the human senses been deluged with such a variety and volume of daily transmitted images.

Every week, the average American child between the ages of 2 and 11 watches 1117 minutes of TV and spends 39 minutes talking with his or her parents. Fifty-two percent of kids between 5 and 17 have a TV in their bedroom. Every year, the average teenager spends 900 hours in school and 500 hours watching television. In any given period during prime time viewing hours, there are at least 50 people killed, shot or raped across the spectrum of broadcast and cable television.

Those "Trenchcoat" youth in the Columbine High tragedy were obsessed with a "world of dark images." None of us can avoid disturbing images entirely, but we can be aided by some sort of "image discernment" about how much is too much. We need dark images from time to time through art, cinema and drama in order to face into the dark side of life and experience a catharsis. Yet how many young people today watch contemporary professional wrestling, which stresses dark impulses and sadism, go to hockey games regularly and cheer the often-approved mayhem, have a steady diet of "Terminator" violence, regularly play shoot-and-kill video games or search the Web for the sordid and foul. Especially for youth who do *all* of this, isn't it quite likely they will cross over the line of too many dark images, jeopardizing their psychological and spiritual health? Because of the glut of images and the fact that all of these options are readily available to so many children, don't we need to discern what is too much? The old spiritual discipline of fasting needs to apply to more than food.

How much is too much? Morbidity, negativity, the shadowy and dark are all givens in contemporary arts and entertainment. In the midst of this barrage some teenagers affect dark poses just to be different or to stand out. One lesson that seemed to come out of Littleton was the need for parents to audit images and to dialog with teens about any morbid attitudes they may be acting out.

In the Jewish tradition of the kabbala, even well meaning spiritual seekers were discouraged by the rabbis from delving into the deeper, darker and hidden spiritual mysteries prior to the age of forty. Before probing the shadowy depths of mysticism, the seeker was advised to master the Talmud. The message was: Before exploring the dark deeply, one ought to be clothed with the armor of light and spiritual maturity.

MASKING DARKNESS

The darkness can also wear a mask. What we see is not always what we get. Hitler danced a jig and burst into smiles after conquering France. For that moment, he looked like a very happy innocent little boy. Milosovec, "the Butcher of the Balkans," was in many ways charming. Too many dark images can corrupt. Too many dark images can addict. Too many dark images can desensitize. Too many dark images can deceive.

We are flooded with so many images that even in our personal relationships we can be tricked into believing fully the "image-persona" — the smile, the wink, the wide-eyed innocence — that is projected as the "real thing." It is said of the great saints that they shone with a certain radiance. It emanated from deep within. But we must also be aware that sometimes people who wear masks can fool us with false and shiny personas that reveal nothing of what lies deeper.

The Shadow

Beware of knights in shining armor, people who acknowledge no darkness in themselves but rather project it out onto someone "less spiritual" or "less radiant" or "less principled." Such knights and ladies often seem "perfect" in all that they do and demand perfection in those around them. Then a day comes when they do something completely out of character. Monsters that they could not acknowledge in their own darkness burst forth upon the scene. Better to befriend our shadow — that raw, unexplored and perhaps frightening realm of our psyche. When we are gentle with our own darkness, compassion grows for the foibles and shadows of others, lessening our tendency toward self-righteous condemnation.

Might racism have its origin in the dualistic worldview that sees light as all good and dark as all evil? The paradox is that darkness, like the night itself, covers over both bad and good.

Black Can Be Beautiful

O God, black can be beautiful!
Let us be aware of black blessings:
   Blessed be the black night that nurtures dreams.
   Blessed be the black hole out of which creation sprang.
   Blessed be the black cave of imagination that births creativity.
   Blessed be dark wombs that cradle us.
   Blessed be black loam that produces nourishing food for our bodies.
   Blessed be black jazz that nourishes our souls
   Blessed be black energy that swirls into gracefulness.
   Blessed be black coal that heats us.
   Blessed be black boiling clouds
      hurling down lightning and cleansing rain.
   Blessed be even our own darkness,
      our raw, undeveloped cave of shadows.
   O God, help us to befriend black and not deny its power.
   Help us to not cover over the dark with fear
      but to open to it with your grace

and to be open to your life within the dark.
May we discover the blessings that lie
    deep within our holy dark
    so that we may freely affirm that
Black is beautiful indeed!

SCRIPTURAL IMAGERY

Imagery from the Sacred Scriptures often emphasizes the goodness of light and the evil in the dark. Light is the first gift God gave when creating, and darkness is the place where evildoers seek to hide their deeds. John's Gospel reveals Jesus as the true light that has come into the world, a light that was not overcome by the darkness. Because of the consistent contrasts between light and dark in the Bible, it may take Christians some effort to give the darkness its own due.

Yet even if at first it seems hidden, there is a balance that points to another dimension of darkness. It was out of the dark void that God brought forth creation (See Genesis 1: 2). It was in the dark earth that the great treasure of the kingdom is buried (See Matthew 13: 44). It was in the dark depths of the sea that the pearl of great price was to be found (See Matthew 13: 45). It was the dark depths of the tomb that became the womb of Jesus' resurrection (See Luke 23: 50 - 24: 9). And John Marsh in the *New Testament Commentaries on John's Gospel*, makes a similar salient and paradoxical point. In referring to Jesus' betrayal by Judas in the dark garden of Gesthemane, he writes:

> The moment of greatest tension and apparent darkness is at
> the same time that of the greatest release from tension and from
> light.

THE HOLY DARK

Darkness can hide evil and has been portrayed in this way not only in Scripture but throughout literature. However, as the above Scriptural references suggest, the darkness holds much more than evil. All potency dwells there. Darkness has the potential for birthing good. Darkness is the realm where fertility broods. All life — human, animal and plant — is fertilized in the dark. We begin our human journey with a nine-month sojourn in the dark. And it is the holy night that cools our fevered brow and covers us over with a quilt of dreams.

Matriarchal cultures with a feminine perspective have always placed a strong value in the dark depths of Mother Earth. Patriarchal cultures, on the other hand, tend to value mountain peaks and illumination. Yet, instead of having to choose either one or the other as most highly valued, it would seem wise to view light and dark as both/and rather than either/or. Perhaps because of strong patriarchal roots in our Western world we need to stress the holiness of the dark to put things in balance and attain a proper perspective.

The mystics and poets can teach us a great deal about the paradoxical beauty and latent potency of the dark. For example, three spiritual classics, *The Interior Castle* by Teresa of Avila, *Dark Night of the Soul* by John of the Cross and *The Cloud of Unknowing* all contain "illuminating" images of darkness. John of the Cross tells us it is precisely in the dark that the soul is closest to God!

> Well hidden, then, and well protected is the soul, in these dark waters, where it is close to God.
>
> —John of the Cross, *Dark Night of the Soul*

T.S. Eliot echoes John of the Cross:

> I said to my soul, be still, and let
> the dark come upon you
> Which shall be the darkness of God.
>
> —T.S. Eliot, "The Four Quartets"

The Depths

Jesus knew that the fish were down in the murky deep even when his apostles doubted. When they cast their nets into the depths, they brought up a treasure hoard of fish; so much that the boat began to sink.

Jesus understood that a dark fertile hidden place covers over the swarming fish. He knew well that the dark earth must cover over the seed in order for new life to sprout forth, for unless the seed falls into the dark soil beneath the surface it remains just a seed. Seeds of all kinds take life and flourish when covered with rich, black loam.

It is worth noting that the most blessed events in Christ's life emerged out of the sacred dark: his birth upon a midnight clear, his death under a glowering sky and his resurrection from the pitch-black tomb. The dark is not just a hiding place for evil, it is also filled with divine potential!

THE NATIVE AMERICAN EXPERIENCE

The Native Americans realized this and cultivated underground spaces called kivas where they descended for discernment and prayer. They also entered the dark of the sweat lodge for purification and for gaining insight. In these dark spaces, the Native Americans listened for the voices of the spirits. When our focus is always on the exterior brightness and working in the light, we may ignore important inner voices and lose touch with the feel of our inner spiritual terrain. My personal experience of the sweat lodge has proved to be a deeply moving and cleansing spiritual encounter. Enwrapped in darkness and enveloped in steam, sitting close to the earth — not in control, not doing anything — not only are the pores opened, so is the soul.

SENSORY DEPRIVATION TANK

The most similar experience I've had to a sweat lodge was being immersed in a sensory deprivation tank. Entering into this pitch-black enclosure was almost like being buried alive. Contained within the tank is a liquid that allows the occupant to float in the dark. I lost all sense of direction and movement and of being in a particular time or place. It felt like simply floating in the void. This kind of immersion in darkness requires a letting go and a trust that all will be well, even without doing anything to ensure that all will be well. There is nothing to do and nowhere to go. In a sense, it mirrors the human predicament when we must let go of what is familiar and sink into some new unknown depth. It demands an attitude of letting it happen rather than setting a goal or plotting a course. There's no way to be in control in this tank. There's no place to go.

This sinking feeling of letting go demands great trust. When I had just began to write my first book, I was the pastor of a large suburban parish. My start there had been rocky, but in my seventh year things had come together. I had assembled a terrific pastoral team and seeds that we had been planting were blooming all around. It was a good space to be in. I went to the Archbishop and asked him if he would give me some time off to finish my book. I was hoping for a few months. I explained to him what I was trying to write, and he agreed that the project was worthwhile. Then he stunned me. He said, "I will give you a leave to write as much as you want. Afterward, come back and I will have a challenging job for you. But of course, you must resign as pastor of your present parish."

I left confused; I had certainly got more than I had bargained for. I remember talking to my spiritual director and doing some discernment, and most of the conversation was in tears. When I finally made my decision and told my staff I was going to resign as pastor, I went home and wept uncontrollably. I was pulled in opposite directions. I did not want to leave, but I felt a need to write, so I had to leave. In the wake there was darkness. But the Spirit of God is precisely present in the depths and darkness of our consciousness, not forcing us, not telling us precisely what to do, but directing us gently toward a blessing path. It feels like launching out into the deep and dark, only vaguely aware of where the journey finally leads. To follow the Spirit's seemingly imprecise movement always demands some kind of discernment and letting go. In hindsight, I know the decision to write was Spirit-initiated and Spirit-led, but there was little sense of security in the process.

More and more in our cyberspace world, there is less and less job security. An era of phased-out workers and downsized jobs creates an atmosphere of insecurity. When we are between jobs, there can be a pervasive inner sense of being suspended. At such times, cultivating a trust in the darkness, an attitude that something will surface, can be of great help. We might call this all-too-common predicament a journey into a "Job-Security Deprivation Tank." This journey of insecurity may well lead us to something new, to a different life direction. Imagination can flourish in the dark, if we let go and let it simmer up from our own depths. For it's in those creative depths that the Spirit dwells. Joseph Campbell suggests that we "follow our bliss." From a faith perspective that means following our deepest heart's desire nourished by the Spirit of God. Yet at first that desire often seems obscure, for what is deepest is often enveloped in the holy dark.

IMAGINATION

Imagination brews in the dark! A man described how he volunteered to be a subject in an advertising survey:

> We would receive $50 for bringing forth from our memories good images of Jeeps and then coming up with ideas for advertising their attractiveness. Do you know what they had us

do? We lay on the floor; they dimmed the lights, put on soft music and had us muse in the dark. When the lights came back on, it was amazing the ideas that surfaced out of the dark!

HOUSES OF MEMORY

In ancient Ireland, the Celts had "Houses of Memory," which Caitlin Matthews describes as quiet, dark huts with only a few flickering candles. In these abodes of imagination an aspiring poet would sometimes be assigned a subject to ponder. The student would be in the dark, undisturbed for many hours. Sometimes a stone would be placed on the poet's chest to ensure lack of movement. Within this incubation chamber, imagination would flourish.

BLESSING FROM THE DARK

We live in an electric age. Light is everywhere. But this is a very recent human phenomenon. (As recently as the 1940s many homes lacked electricity.) In a very short span of years, we have moved into an electric age. Now we have too much light. We need the dark. We need the blessings of the dark. We need to pray in the dark. We need to explore dark caves. There are not only monsters there; there are also treasures to be seized. The cave of darkness can be a blessing cave.

The ancient shamans knew that the holy dark is our seedbed for something new. And Jesus never tired of images of growth and fertility — of the boundless possibilities — from the holy depths of dark ground:

> Sower Jesus, you go out to sow.
> Oh, not all of the seed takes root in me,
> for you, Alpha and Omega, are too much!
> But some seed burrows into my depths and germinates.
>
> Holy Sower, bless the dark places of my psyche,
> the shadowy places where doubts lurk,
> where I may fear being submerged in chaos,
> smothered by cares.
> Day by day, little by little,
> watered by hope and tended by love,
> may your word grow within my holy dark.

PONDER QUESTIONS

When has the imagination been most active in your life?
Can you recall experiences of creativity that have followed
*   times of solitude and silence?*
What is your clearest sense of your deepest heart's desire?
What do you need to do in order to access this seat of your
*   "bliss," of your truest possibilities?*
Do you have any fears in coming near these depths of your
*   heart's desire?*

In the parable of the Prince with Muddy Feet, it was Lucifer, the light bearer, the noonday devil, who cast no shadow. To walk a blessing path we need to walk both in the light and the dark, just as the prince did on his spiritual quest. In a marvelous book *Make Friends With Your Shadow*, William Miller cautions good people who are on a spiritual quest seeking to be enlightened never to forget that there is within them a dark side. It is filled with great potential like fertile black soil, but it can also be a cave with its own dragons. We are to walk gently with the dragons and come to know them, lest they overcome us from behind. This is the path that will bless us. Miller writes:

> To the extent that I have to be right and good, he, she, they or it will become the carrier of all the evil, real, and potential, which I do not acknowledge within myself. If I do not face my inner enemy, it is inevitable that I will be driven to create an enemy outside.

As the centuries turn, echoes of the holocaust have returned in "ethnic cleansing." This misnomer created by propaganda once more reveals the lie of the noonday devil. There is nothing clean about it. It gives us "exhibit one" of people not acknowledging their own shadow side and inevitably being "driven to create an enemy outside."

Too Much Dark

We are confused about light and dark. Just as our culture tends to bask too much in the light, at the same time, paradoxically it can produce too much dark. In our time perhaps the most common journey into the dangerous side of darkness is the experience of depression. Some who study the growing incidence of this illness say that despite all our advances in technology and medicine, we are living in an age of melancholy. Myrna Weissman, a Columbia University epidemiologist, states that depression has almost doubled since World War II:

> ...due to factors such as more stress, fewer family and community ties, even nutritional deficiencies. Depression is on pace to be one of the world's second-most disabling disease....
> In the United States, depression afflicts 18 million people at any given time.

This situation exists despite the fact that the U.S. is the most advanced, affluent and health-conscious nation on earth. In this cyber-age, we have the world at our fingertips, but lurking behind our busy fingers and bright screens is the threatening specter of depression. The very technology that supposedly should free us up and lighten our burdens can enslave and possess us. The degree of this possession is humorously exhibited in a letter to the editor of the computer page of the *Phoenix Republic.* The headline reads, "Exorcise Password Demon!" — an interesting choice of religious imagery! The question for the editor was: "Whenever I start Windows 98 it requests my password, *which drives me nuts.* Can I start Windows 98 without typing the password?" And the editor replied, "To exorcise your system of the password demon, do the following...."

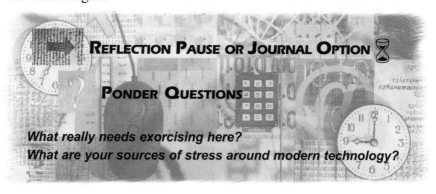

REFLECTION PAUSE OR JOURNAL OPTION

PONDER QUESTIONS

What really needs exorcising here?
What are your sources of stress around modern technology?

Relentless Darkness

When I was a child, we would visit relatives on a farm in the Platte Valley of Nebraska. Their farmhouse was located about one hundred yards from the main line of the Union Pacific railroad. I have vivid memories of being awakened in the middle of the night by the great black steam engines hurtling through the dark. They shook, rattled and roared. As they did, the house itself would tremble and the earth quake.

In our turn-of-the-century, fast-paced, demanding world, stress can be like some roaring, runaway steam engine that rattles our consciousness and propels us into a tunnel with no seeming exit — a passage leading only into deepening darkness.

But stress is only one engine pulling us into the no-man's-land of depression. There are many other tracks into its dark tunnel, and its causes are extremely complicated and varied. We need to operate at many levels — psychologically, medicinally, socially and spiritually — to assist the eighteen million people suffering from depression on their journey through its dark. There *is* a path through depression, but the catch-22 is that the depressed person seems stuck with no place to go.

Heroic Quests

No longer do we go out on knightly quests, riding horses with pennants flying. Perhaps the great search for the grail today includes passing through and finding a way out of the dark tunnel of melancholy. It used to be that the stories of heroic journeys through this passageway could never be told. It was as though we could share, without any shame, a terrible toothache or a broken leg, but the realm of depression's pain was taboo. When Edmund Muskie, a highly talented man who had held many high government posts, dared to cry in the snows of New Hampshire, he was canceled out as a presidential candidate. Would that more of our leaders would own some of the darkness and cry over it.

In our day, George Stephanopolis, a presidential assistant under Bill Clinton, wrote a best-seller, in which he admitted being beset by bouts of depression. The fact that his journey into the dark could be fully accepted is progress. More people need to tell of their heroic quests through depression to give hope to those who are in the stage at which depression is an all-enveloping darkness. For those who have passed through, hindsight can often reveal how something new was brooding in the dark of depression and how that gestating reality proved to be a blessing. In his book *Quest for Beauty*, prominent psychologist Rollo May shared that in his youth he experienced a breakdown. He said that it eventually woke him up to life. In the end, the experience proved to be a blessing. It was precisely as a result of this woundedness that new possibilities emerged. Yes, a passage through depression can be a blessing path. Jesus, the Prince with the Muddy Feet, felt the full force of the depths of depression and anxiety in the garden. Yet when he was ready to embrace the cross, he was also very close to resurrection!

Midway Through Life's Journey

When I was in college we studied Dante's classic work *The Divine Comedy*. Later in my life its opening verses would echo in my soul:

> Midway in our life's journey, I went astray
> > from the straight road and I woke to find myself
> alone in a dark wood. How shall I say
> > what wood that was! I never saw so drear,
> so rank, so arduous a wilderness!

This path of darkness, midway through the woods, would be a prophecy for my own experience of deep clinical depression in the midyears of my life. When I received what I experienced as a rejection by significant people in a parish to which I was newly assigned, I began a downhill slide that eventually ended in the tunnel of clinical depression.

There are two images that have remained with me from that experience. In the midst of my melancholy, one of my friends gave me a carving of an ox. Upon its back was a prostrated figure literally hanging on for dear life. I realize now what that image was saying to me: "Hang on! Have courage! It's a slow ride, but hanging on will get you beyond this stuck place." In fact, my friend said, "The day will come when you will get beyond this. Hang on." The day did come, but it took a lot of hanging on. When it did come, I passed the oxen on to another friend who was experiencing his own bout with depression. It then occurred to me that it was the slow-plodding but always-moving-forward oxen that pulled the pioneers in their prairie schooners across the Midwest and into their promised land. They were plodding creatures, but they kept moving.

I was fortunate to get the multifaceted help I needed. After listening to my anger, another friend suggested a woman psychiatrist. I was offended. My friend gently responded, "Think about it; I think it could help." I realize now that the truest and most valuable friends are those who love us enough not to try to rescue us but who are wise enough to gently point out a possible direction for a blessing path.

In my work with this superb psychiatrist I came to learn that there were certain thinking patterns that needed changing. Always very imaginative as a little boy, I had chosen for my grade-school heroes dark figures who were valiant but met tragic ends. The script I tended to follow was, "No matter how hard you push the rock up the mountain, it will probably roll back on you!" Not a happy ending!

Perhaps some of this came from my Celtic heritage, for, after all, the Irish had been oppressed for 800 years, and until their rising in 1916 the rock did keep rolling back on them. Indeed, there does seem to be a melancholic strain in the Irish. As C.K. Chesterton once wrote, "...for the great Gaels of Ireland are the men that God made mad — for all their wars are merry and their songs sad."

My wonderful psychiatrist friend had me work on changing my script by revisiting my favorite childhood story, "The Little Engine That Could." That's the one to follow she encouraged, not the tragic heroes who lost in the end. She also indicated that I suffered from SAD — a deficiency of light during the long Midwest winters. Not enough light — too much dark! I would eventually heed her advice and move to Arizona, with wonderful results.

Of course, she prescribed medication. At the same time, I was receiving wonderful spiritual direction from someone who lived in the dark but did so with much verve and good humor. My spiritual director was blind! He encouraged me to seek spiritual friends who could know me as I truly was. They proved to be spiritual companions on a wonderful blessing path of friendship.

During this period of struggling to move out of depression, another image came to me that illustrated a heroic blessing path through the dark. I took a short vacation to Colorado in September when all the aspen leaves were turning golden amber and dancing in the fall breeze. Despite all that beauty, I felt the heavy weight of depression. Then one day, I went out for a drive. When I was returning, I noticed a strange sight. As I approached a railroad crossing, walking ahead of me on the road was a man with a white cane and a dog. I slowed down, wondering what on earth this blind man was doing walking this mountain road. I pulled up beside him and asked, "Can I help you? There is a railroad crossing just ahead." He smiled and replied, "Thanks a lot, but we know where we're going."

That evening, I told the clerk in the grocery store about the blind man on the road and asked, "Do you know what he would be doing up here in the mountains?"

"Oh sure I do," the clerk replied, "he's getting ready for the ski season."

"The ski season!" I exclaimed. "What does he have to do with the ski season?"

"Oh, he's a ski instructor," the clerk returned. "He teaches other blind people how to ski."

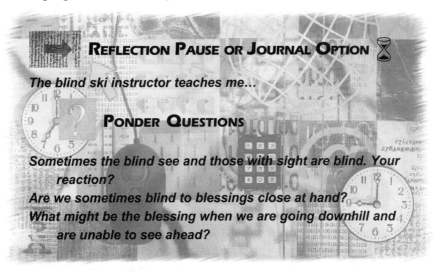

REFLECTION PAUSE OR JOURNAL OPTION

The blind ski instructor teaches me...

PONDER QUESTIONS

Sometimes the blind see and those with sight are blind. Your reaction?
Are we sometimes blind to blessings close at hand?
What might be the blessing when we are going downhill and are unable to see ahead?

In the midst of my own darkness, that image of the blind ski instructor touched something very deep within me. It remains for me today a reminder of courage and fortitude in the midst of darkness.

GLEANING BLESSINGS FROM THE PATH OF SORROW

Not everyone experiences the darkness of depression, but sooner or later everywoman/everyman walks the shadowy path of suffering, sorrow and loss. It is a given in the human condition.

What are the blessings to be gained from this walk? There are several, and any or all of them may appear when we are enrolled in the school of suffering. One of the first blessings gained is humility, which happens when one is finally forced to the realization that none of us is in complete control.

In his novels *Bonfire of the Vanities* and *Man in Full*, Tom Wolfe masterfully depicts the passage of the high-and-mighty into humpty-dumptys who have a great fall. However, one does not have to be haughty to be deflated. Any experience of losing ego control is humbling. Think of the fine actor, Christopher Reeves, who played Superman. Now paralyzed from head to toe, "Superman" has been humbled — grounded. Yet he has shown so much poise, grace and resilience in his accepting this humbling that his fall lifts us up! His willingness to turn it to positive energy is an inspiration to many.

Conversion is another blessing that can be gleaned from suffering or loss. Many of the great saints underwent serious illnesses, great challenges or severe wounds that opened the door to a change of life. Saint Paul, for example, had to be blinded before he could see things in a new way.

Compassion, the ability to suffer with those who are suffering is another blessing that can accompany suffering. Many who have been wounded have become wounded healers. In *Insearch: Psychology and Religion* James Hillman describes this kind of experience as a coming home:

> So it is often little wonder that it takes a breakdown, an actual illness, for someone to report the most extraordinary experiences of, for instance, a new sense of time, of patience and waiting, in the language of religious experience, of coming to the center, coming to oneself, letting go and coming home.

So in our fast-paced cyber-culture, after we have raced under the noonday sun of our accelerating communications and our frantic comings and goings, and after we have explored the dark caves where both angels and dragons may dwell, there will always be a need to let go and to come home again. And, indeed, home is where the path of blessing always leads.

Scripture Images and Passages for Reflection

Hebrew Scriptures

Exodus 32: 1-35 — *The Golden Calf*

When the people became aware of Moses' delay in coming down from the mountain, they gathered around Aaron and said to him, "Come, make us a god for a leader...."

Christian Scriptures

Matthew 15: 10-20 — *What comes from within*

Jesus summoned the crowd and said to them, "Hear and understand. It is not what enters one's mouth that defiles that person; but what comes out of the mouth is what defiles one...."

John 8: 1-11 — *Jesus writing on the ground*

The scribes and the Pharisees brought a woman who had been caught in adultery and made her stand in the middle....

Blessing Prayers

Blessing Prayer for Going On-line

Out of the depths we cry to you O God,
Out of the depths of microchips,
Out of the depths of surging power,
Out of the depths of files and storage,
Help us to bring forth
> what is useful,
> what is helpful,
> what aids the work,
> what enlivens our spirits.

BLESSING OF A CHILD GOING ON-LINE

Angels of God,
> swift messengers of heaven,
> guide my flight through cyberspace.
May this screen before me
> light up my mind,
> and bless my journey.

DISCERNMENT PRAYER

In my imagination,
my holy dark,
what do I love to entertain:
> Newspaper images?
> TV News images?
> Internet images?
> Movie images?
Which are most immediately memorable?
Which do I want to fill my soul?
Images of violence, destruction, speed, revenge —
> Holy Spirit, lead me out!
Images of love, romance, mystery, comedy, compassion —
> Holy Spirit, lead me in!

THE BLESSINGS OF CREATIVITY

See, I am setting before you today a blessing and a curse.
—Deuteronomy 11: 26

THE PARABLE OF THE LAST WORD

Once upon a time in Ireland, there lived a bachelor named Patrick Kelly and a thirty-year-old spinster named Brigid O'Rourke. Pat lived on the family farm with his widowed mother, and, being the eldest son, he had the care of the farm and his mother. To be sure, this was not unusual, for that's the way it was with many bachelors in Ireland. (Someone once said that Jesus must have been Irish, for at the age of thirty he was still single and living with his mother!) Pat's mother, Peg, was a dear old lady in Patrick's eyes, but she was also a crotchety perfectionist. When Pat came in from the fields, he would always hose and scour his Wellington boots even though they were never to enter the house. They had to look spotless even sitting outside the door. That's the way it was living with Peg. She noticed every detail of daily life and would never let Pat rest easy until things were just the way she wanted them. After years of accommodation, he adjusted and eventually became just as persnickety as his dear old mother.

Brigid lived down the road from the Kelly's. Her mother had died a few years before, and she now managed the small cottage by herself. When visitors would meet her and sometimes inquire about her husband, she would put her hands on her hips and respond, "Well, there is none! I've never been taken!" In all of this there was more than a wee hint that she would not mind "being taken" if the right broth of a lad came along. After all, she was right at thirty, and the clock was running.

When Patrick had passed his fortieth birthday, his dear mother was called home to God. After a year by himself, Patrick began to think that he might be approaching the marrying age — but still, there was no need to rush.

One Sunday, after Mass, Pat was visiting with the pastor, when the priest nodded at Pat and looked toward Brigid who had just past by: "Would you look at that, Pat, a fine broth of a woman; any man should be proud to hang his underwear on the clothesline next to her petticoat!" This was the pastor's picturesque and somewhat crude way of giving Patrick a hint that here was a lovely woman who had "never been taken."

Pat was missing his mother something terrible, so after awhile he called upon Brigid O'Rourke. Lo and behold, after a year of courting, Brigid agreed to be his wife. After the wedding Brigid moved out of her cottage and into the Kelly homestead. But she had a mind of her own, and she insisted that her mother's cottage remain in her name. At the same time, she might have gotten a clue early on as to whose ghost still reigned in the new manor, for when Patrick nailed up their wedding picture on the wall, it went just below that of his dear mother. Had he added a caption, it might have read, "Mama's watching you! Do it right!" Well, Brigid did a lot of things well, but not always to Peg's expectations, which lived on in her son, Patrick.

They lived in a well-swept, whitewashed cottage with a sturdy thatched roof. Brigid was a wonderful cook and had lots of creative recipes. She also had a green thumb and placed flower boxes in all the windows. Moreover, she could knit beautiful sweaters, which were the envy of the village. In her housekeeping she was neat but not obsessive. Brigid would light a good peat fire in their hearth, but once in awhile an ash or two would light on the floor, and for Pat that would not do at all. Sometimes he followed Brigid around like a watchdog. But Brigid was not to be cowed. She could care less about what Pat's dear old mam would think, and she often told him so. This would usually spark a conflict, and once the honeymoon was over fierce spats peppered their relationship. Pat had a varied vocabulary and often would end a quarrel with, "Well, mark my words, Brigid, someday I'll have the last word! On that day, I'll dance on your grave! Do you hear me? I'll dance on your grave!"

The funny part of it was, Patrick didn't practice what he preached! He was something of an inventor and even took top prizes at the fair for some clever farm tools he'd designed. His little workshop in the shed was sacred to him, yet did he keep it as spotless as the main house? Not at all! It was always in some kind of a mess because it was the one place his mother never entered. He left junk behind the shed that went to rust and old leaky cans of oil that seeped into the soil. Patrick's perfectionism only extended to the house where his dear old mother set the standards.

Eventually, two fine girls and a boy were born to Brigid and Patrick, and as they grew up they knew Pat's chant by heart: "I'll have the last word, you know; some day, I'll dance on your grave!"

Well, life went on, and the children grew up and moved out. Pat, now in his eighties, would hobble around, sputtering about things not being as perfect as he would like them to be. Brigid would roll her eyes and make a face at the picture of Patrick's mother, which she had long since removed to a hallway wall. Like her namesake, St. Brigid, she was no namby-pamby. Through the years, she maintained the title to her mother's homestead, collecting the rent and using it as she saw fit.

It is said sometimes that the "good die young and the ornery just get ornerier." While she was not quite young any more, Brigid died suddenly at the age of seventy. When the children gathered, they reminded eighty-one-year-old Patrick that their mam had made her own will to dispose of the cottage to which Patrick had never had title. So they called the lawyer and had a meeting the night she died. Perhaps she might also have left some last requests about her burial.

The lawyer brought out the will to the house, put on his glasses and solemnly read Brigid's last testament. Much to Patrick's pleasure, Brigid had bequeathed the extra cottage to Patrick to do with as he pleased. She also allotted various keepsakes to the three children. As the lawyer paused, Pat spoke, "Well, that's it now; it's all done."

"Just a moment," said the lawyer. "Brigid has one last request of you, Patrick."

"Well, then, let's hear it." said Patrick. "I'm not one to deny a dying woman her last request."

"Very well, here's what she says on the last few lines: 'And Patrick, do you remember all the times you muttered at me, "Mark my words, Brigid, the day will come when I'll dance on your grave?" Well, the day has come, Patrick, and my last request of you is this: Please bury me at sea!'"

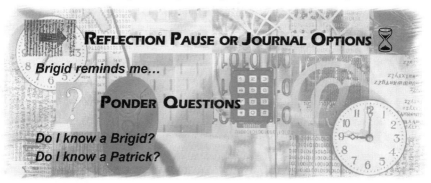

REFLECTION PAUSE OR JOURNAL OPTIONS

Brigid reminds me...

PONDER QUESTIONS

Do I know a Brigid?
Do I know a Patrick?

SUBLIME BLESSINGS

Imagination and the creativity that flows from it are wonderful and sublime blessings bestowed on humankind. They allow us to share in the divine process of creation. Brigid was so imaginative and creative that she could in some sense come back from the dead to win her duel with Patrick. She ultimately had the last laugh. Was her last word a blessing or a curse? Probably a blessing if Patrick had the good sense and good humor to let go of his controlling persona and have a good laugh — the last laugh being on him.

RESURRECTION

From the beginning of the ages, the feminine and creativity have been linked. The "wisdom" that "played" with creation in the beginning is identified as feminine in the Scriptures. Is it not also historically true that women have been more interested in bringing something new out of the holy darkness and more intent on building up creation rather than tearing it down? Perhaps we are entering a time when we need to do more than simply ignore feminine wisdom; we need to integrate it into our culture. After the recent tragic shootings at a Jonesborough, Arkansas, school, the governor of Arkansas remarked, "Our children are living in a culture unlike anything before in history." True enough. In the wake of last century's two world wars, the holocaust, the atomic and hydrogen bombs, the advent of terrorism and now school shootings, we need more than ever to heed women's wisdom in creating and building up. In the past century technology has for the most part been the domain of male inventors and has brought us wonderful creations — from microwaves — to computers. But it has also perfected weapons of mass destruction and threatens to poison the earth — the source of life itself.

In New Testament times, it was Roman male ingenuity that thought up driving nails into condemned hands and feet and exposing suffering fellow human beings to die an agonizing death, tying them to poles and using them as torches to light up a Roman bacchanalia.

We also find that quite often in the Gospels the men disciples were debating over who would be first — who would have the power and the glory. Usually, it was the holy women who displayed insight and care as they related to Jesus in creative and sustaining ways. Mary Magdalene went beyond the customary rules of hospitality and found a better way. She washed the feet of Jesus and dried them with her hair! After the death of Jesus, while the men huddled in seclusion, it was Mary and other holy women who did not fear the dark and who went with spices to anoint the body of Jesus. There they discovered an empty tomb. And when the risen Jesus revealed his restored life to Mary, her imagination was not so stilted that she would refuse the good news. She threw her arms around Jesus and gave him such a long and ardent hug of joy that he told her she could not cling forever. Then he gave her the mission of helping the slow-believing male disciples imagine what for them was unimaginable — his resurrection. Women have always known that new life can emerge from dark places. It's no wonder that the holy women were the first witnesses of the resurrection from a dark and empty tomb. Unlike Thomas, who had to put his fingers into the nail prints, the women could imagine resurrection.

> Holy women,
>> life bearers and givers,
>> you are candle bearers in the night.
> First to the tomb and Easter glory,
>> minds and hearts open,
>> enter into the caverns of our imaginations.

Stir up life in the holy dark.
Be midwives to better dreams and hopes.

The resurrection of Jesus from the dead was the greatest imaginative and creative action our world has ever seen — an unsurpassable blessing. Likewise, bringing new creation out of the darkness of the womb has ever been women's prerogative and is always characterized as the "blessed event."

The apostles had visions on a mountain. The one called "Son of Thunder" wanted to call fire down from the sky. The New Testament women often were more grounded, more down to earth: the woman at the well, the valiant women at the cross, Mary at Nazareth. This groundedness may be precisely the wisdom needed for the new millennium when what men have wrought in industrial think tanks threatens to spill a toxic waste and spoilage over the holy ground of our earth, the mother of all life.

In a May, 1999 *Phoenix Tribune* column, "Businesswomen Upbeat," Donna Hogan pointed out that more and more women are utilizing new technology: According to a 1999 survey of women in business, 98% use computers. At the same time, a majority of 69% still stay connected to their communities through donation of time; 71% donate money to better their communities. Over half also mentor other businesswomen.

Such community involvement by so many women in the workforce is remarkable. More women are working out of their homes as well. A common sight on the bike path where I often walk is young mothers whirling along on rollerblades pushing contented babies enjoying the ride of their life. Babysitting has a new creative twist: no more baby strolling — now its babies rolling! Some of these same moms will return home to conduct business on the Internet.

CREATIVITY AND MESSINESS

In "The Parable of the Last Word," Patrick was an erstwhile inventor searching for new technology, but despite his perfectionism he only left a bigger mess. In some sense, all human creativity has within it an element of messiness and chaos. Notice the artist's palette, the cook's mixing bowl, the potter's muddy wheel. And the great Sistine Chapel ceiling was birthed from the chaotic energies that crackled between Michaelangelo and his patron, Pope Julius!

In *Quest for Beauty,* Rollo May writes:

The capacity to create — which we all have, though in varying degrees — is essentially the ability to find form in chaos, to create form where there is only formlessness...we form and reform the world in the very act of perceiving it. The imagination to do this is one of the elements that makes us human beings.

Indeed, a certain amount of messiness can help engender a creative environment and get the creative juices going — after all, in the beginning, creation happened out of chaos! Yet in another sense, each time we create — and, as Rollo May says, we all do — we leave behind either a curse or a blessing. In using the tremendous creative energy with which we have been blessed, we can create further and far-reaching blessings. Or we can create a real mess that may result in long-term destructive chaos. We can create a meal carelessly and leave E Coli. We can pursue short-term technological goals and quick profits, leaving a trail of devastation in our wake. So we need to stop and ask ourselves if our creativity will bless or curse our new millennium.

THE BLESSING OF CREATIVITY

In my personal travels, several examples of the blessings of creativity stand out. One is Michaelangelo's painting on the ceiling of the Sistine Chapel. It shows God reaching down and touching an extended human hand, transmitting to it a Godly power. If, as Webster says, a blessing is a "favor or gift bestowed by God," then God's creative power transmitted to humankind is a spectacular blessing. For God is bringing us into being, and it did not have to be so! As Rabbi Abraham Heschel wrote, "Just to be is a blessing, just to live is holy!"

But God is doing even more than that. God is giving us the potency to continue the act of imagining and creating new possibilities. In doing so, God shares a Godlike power that carries enormous responsibilities. Henri Bergson, the Jewish-French philosopher, described the evolution of the human potential as God's "undertaking to create creators, that he may have besides himself, beings worthy of His love."

Indeed, creativity is a blessing that allows us to be Godlike!

Michaelangelo's face of God fixed upon the human, and the divine arm and hand reaching down artistically suggests a transmission of enormous energy from God to creature. As Adam (humankind) looks up at the face of God, the image is suffused with meaning. It is *meaning-full*. Humankind presents an open hand reaching toward God, forgetful of self. It is an image open and receptive to God's energy and God's desire. Viktor Frankl, writing of the human search for meaning, suggested that it is precisely this giving of oneself to a greater cause or being that makes earth people human. Creation is the primary blessing, and co-creating becomes our human vision quest. So the act of creation is fully divine and fully human. God is the first artist. The human is the living, breathing artifact — but not a finished product — we are capable of expanding and recreating the divine potential and imagining what is not yet thought of.

We must realize that the divine artist touches every human hand, yours and mine. Even when we experience chaos or messiness in our lives — especially then — our human challenge is to be creative.

Yes, we are all called to be artists, and our cyber-world offers us many new opportunities. But artistry will always requires quality time. Only mass production produces at breakneck speed. Watch a child build a castle at the beach. Look at a kindergartner's first art. These children are lost in creation — absorbed in timeliness. It is only a lack of creativity that produces haste or boredom.

Look into the face of a mother with her newborn; it still takes nine months and labor. Watch a football runningback do the unexpected and weave through the line with innovative darts and turns, running the full 100 yards against all odds. Savor an exquisite meal from the hands of a superb cook. Plan the details of a new home. To really create, to act artfully — to stand back and admire what flows forth from the holy dark of our imaginations — can bring into the human heart a tremendous sense of blessedness, a Godlikeness.

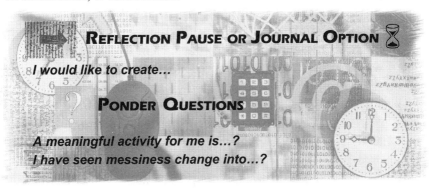

REFLECTION PAUSE OR JOURNAL OPTION

I would like to create...

PONDER QUESTIONS

A meaningful activity for me is...?
I have seen messiness change into...?

Life Assignments

When I was a college student, I had a history professor who spent a whole week describing the significance and beauty of the twelfth century Cathedral of Chartres, which is located in a small town some thirty miles from Paris. He ended the week by saying, "If you care for history, for creativity and for beauty at all — then sometime in your life, do two things. First, make a pilgrimage to Chartres and gaze at the great rose window. Second, read the Sigrid Undset's *Kristin Lavransdatter*, a trilogy about a heroic, medieval woman." It took me years to accomplish both of those assignments, but after having done so, I can respond, "Yes, Professor Nolan, you were right!"

I first read *Kristin Lavransdatter*. Sigrid Undset received a literary prize for her three-volume classic. What she gives us is an epic tale of a Scandinavian woman's life journey. Because until recently most history books have been written by men — and mostly feature their wars — we have too scant a knowledge of heroic women of the past. They were there in abundance, but most remain unsung.

Chartres

My "history assignment" eventually led me to Chartres. Like Michaelangelo's Adam reaching upward, the cathedral's tallest spire raises its Gothic index finger to the edge of the horizon and points toward the God up there and beyond.

When I first arrived at Chartres, I entered the cathedral guarded by stone-hewn saints. This entryway is not only a transit forward but also a way backward into another time. Its stone paving blocks are worn down by 800 years of footsteps. The interior is dark — a holy cavern. Out of those depths my eyes were drawn upward. A holy circle of light burst down through the dark. Sun-illumined colors splashed their brilliance through stained glass onto the ancient floor.

The great rose window is a cornucopia of disparate, vivid colors and various geometric designs. Stepping back from it, one gets "the whole picture" — the many separate elements and yet the one — a work of art that takes a chaotic mix of shapes and reforms them into breathtaking beauty. It is a vivid image of connectedness. It also mirrors the ancient holy circle — the circle of life, the circle of the womb. Joseph Campbell called Chartres "my parish church!" He described its rose window with words like "radiance," "synergetic participation" and "rapture" — each a blessing word.

MANDALAS

The rose window at Chartres is a cosmic image — like a creative womb. On the other hand, the Sistine panel depicting God and Adam, when looked at closely, has a certain loneliness about it — it points to two lone male images. (Michaelangelo himself was a lonely man driven by the importunings and impatience of Pope Julius to have the work completed.) As magnificent as it is, this most famous Sistine panel pictures God's creative blessing as entirely human centered. It gives no hint of the dynamic energies of evolution, nor does it suggest God's creative energy at work in the whole cosmos.

The Chartres rose window hints at a wider story. It's a multicolored, multifaceted circular mandala depicting wholeness and a sense of belonging. Ecological prophet Thomas Berry suggests in *Dream of the Earth* that such an image is needed for our time. Berry goes on to image the earth as the Great Mother, reminding us that the earth itself is an essential and active "actress" in the ongoing drama of creation. Relatedness is not limited to God touching Adam. The earth herself is our relative, and a vibrant, interactive, energetic relatedness pulses everywhere. Not only is the earth alive, a blessed interconnectedness is at the heart of matter. Theology has long proclaimed that the Holy Trinity, the source of creativity, is a community. Quantum physics is now revealing how creation itself is also an interdependent, energetic community. Like the great mandala of Chartres' rose window, all earth's parts come together as one community.

A COMMUNITY'S DREAM

It feels as if the great cathedral at Chartres rises up organically out of the earth. It rests on beautiful ancient farmland that has been refashioned and reformed into a new beauty. Indeed, its foundations rest on a pre-Christian, pagan fertility shrine! It rises up out of a community's fertile dream, from the imaginations of small town medieval craftpersons. It is an amazing mystery how so long ago such a small community could dream, will and create this masterpiece!

The people who erected this marvelous work of art had their own trials and tragedies. They were so much poorer than we who bask in a consumer society. But they suffered no poverty of spirit. From time to time, they experienced the chaotic discord of skirmishes and even plagues. But for the most part, their lives were filled with fruitfulness and creativity. I imagine the town of Chartres as a beehive of busy creators with little lapse into boredom because of basking in the ever-present beauty that rose up before them. In the shadow of this spiritual and architectural masterpiece, what they fashioned daily would bestow upon them the blessing of a beautiful accomplishment, a reflection of how creativity is surely one of the most rewarding of all blessings. It's no wonder that Joseph Campbell, who spent a lifetime studying the richness of the symbols, myths and images of this earth would say that one of the most meaningful activities and blessings of his life was to go and simply sit before the rose window at Chartres.

The ancient words of the psalmist still hold, reminding us that "the heavens declare the glory" of a transcendent God (Psalm 19: 1). The Gothic spire of Chartres points up and out towards transcendence. At the same time, its rose window mandala suggests an expanding circle with the immanent God, who is all around and very close. Its luminous images dancing on the cathedral floor might even inspire us to search for God deep down! Truly, the ancient dream of the Chartres community meets *The Dream of the Earth* of Thomas Berry. Like Campbell in his "parish church," Berry and other spiritual writers leading us into the new millennium suggest that the earth itself and our deep connectedness with the earth and all its creatures should be our most immediate domain for experiencing the divine. This ancient round window of Chartres calls our attention to God's mysterious immanent presence. The reality of a vibrant creative spirit is beneath our feet and all around. God's activity is deep down and all around! There is no dead matter. We are immersed in the great ebb and flow of energies — the creative dance of molecules, atoms, protons and quarks.

No Dead Matter

As I write these words, I ask myself, "What does any of this have to do with the way I lead my life?" One insight that comes to me is to consider my "environment" as having a certain soulfulness of its own rather than thinking of the things around me as simply inert matter. My most immediate environment would be the clothes I wear, the home I live in, the bed I sleep in, an immediate contact with my living flesh. To develop a consciousness that they have a history of their own and a certain soulfulness might well effect how I treat them. I am a bachelor. In many ways this bachelor is like some of the teenagers you know. For example, many bachelors' motto might be, "If a tree falls in the forest with no one to hear it, does it make a sound?" Translated: "If I mess up my room and no one sees it, is it really messed up?"

I go through streaks when I don't make my bed. When I'm in those streaks, I'm actually missing an opportunity for creating something new. Is not the simple making of a bed an expression of transforming chaos into a pleasing form? When I'm tired, I sometimes drop kick my shoes and loft them into a corner. Sometimes it is so much easier to throw clothes over a chair rather than to hang them up. What this amounts to is a basic indifference to my immediate environment.

As I look down at my shoes today, I realize that some calf gave its skin for the benefit of my feet. That skin has been remolded, reformed, tanned and cut for my feet. The jeans I wear came to me courtesy of a cotton field. I'd never seen a cotton field until a few years ago. It's a marvelous sight. In the desert sun it looks like a shimmering snow blanket. Both calves and cotton have entered into an intense process of being recreated and taking new form. They were beautiful in the old form, and they are now beautiful in a new way. They deserve respect. They are worthy of care. I begin to wonder, "Can I be a genuine environmentalist — concerned about the rain forests and the pollution of the rivers — and at the same time show little care for the clothes upon my back or the shoes upon my feet?

Perhaps to walk reverently on the earth — which is parallel to walking a blessing path — demands a certain reverence for the simple materials that touch my skin. Saint Thomas Aquinas in the thirteenth century demonstrated an intuitive insight about the hidden lives of all things when he distinguished different levels of soulfulness in all created things.

It strikes me as a good idea when I get a new pair of shoes or new jeans to say a blessing over them — asking them to serve me well and promising to show them care. Some sense of relatedness to the material things that serve us is well worthwhile. After all, don't we get attached to certain objects? We have a favorite chair, or we experience a certain feeling of being "at home" when we slip into our jeans after a time of formal work attire. Some objects in our lives take on the aura of old friends, a favorite sweater or perhaps a special old golf club that has served us through the years. Many people are driving their cars longer. Do we ever pat the hood and say, "Thanks, old friend, for getting me safely home." It may sound strange to do that anywhere, but in the privacy of our own garage is it so far-fetched? Such blessings would certainly increase our sense of relatedness to everything around us.

Conversely, my recognition that a calf gave its skin for my shoes also makes me more aware that too many calves are cursed from birth, confined to excessively close quarters and shot full of antibiotics. As a result, I refuse to order veal from any menu that utilizes calves that have been treated as though they were inanimate objects. The Latin root meaning of the word *animate* is *soul*. When we subtract soulfulness from any living creature, we degrade that creature and ourselves.

FRIENDS MADE OF STEEL

Interestingly, in the military — until recently a male preserve — we used to find airplanes with girl's names emblazoned on their noses. And salty old sailors have always referred to the collection of nuts, bolts and steel that gets them through the waters with the affectionate term "she." In some sense these planes and ships take on a personality of their own. And, lo and behold, when a ship is launched, it is always "christened" by a woman! The Irish airline, *Aer Lingus*, actually has its planes blessed, and many of them bear the names of saints. When we relate to our environment in reverent and friendly ways, it always seems that blessings follow!

REFLECTION PAUSE OR JOURNAL OPTION

I reverence...

PONDER QUESTIONS

How does the thought of God present in all things effect my spirituality?

"God is in all things and God is more than anything." Can this thought about the presence of God be reconciled with traditional Christian teaching?

My reaction to Thomas Berry's statement: "Our environment ought to be the primary mode for our experience of God"?

THE CREATION STORY

We now know more about the unfolding, evolutionary creation story than ever before. Physicist-mystic, Brian Swimme, tells us that a "divine allurement" fills the universe! Gravity itself is a form of allurement. In his book *The Cosmic Code*, Heinz Pagels claims that not only the earth but the entire universe has within it a message written in code and that this message is in a very real sense revelatory.

For more and more people, an eco-spirituality is very appealing. These are a few principles that call attention to the creative process as a source of blessings upon blessings:

1) The Big Bang Theory. Creighton University professor, Dr. Eugene Selk, writing in *Window Magazine*, warns against appealing to this theory as some sure "proof" of the existence of God but goes on to say that "Big Bang" has a wonderful consonance with the notion of God as creator. It says that all matter and potency was present in some form in the Big Bang. My body and yours as well as the stuff of the stars flew out into space as creation unfurled. It was an unfolding of blessing upon blessing. Go to the Grand Canyon and look at the lines on its towering walls. Each line traces epochs that involve millions of years of development.

To think we were one with the stars! What a blessed beginning!

The stars scatter across the sky — seemingly apart,
    isolated like broken pieces of light,
      yet they are really one.
The divine energy that hurled them into galaxies
    surges within and beneath their molecules
    and mine!
Their luster seems to flicker, dim and then brighten again.

Yet passing clouds shall not put out their light,
    nor mine!
All who suffer have a place in this universe,
    on this earth, under the stars,
      in the palm of God's hand.

2) In the original fireball there was a chaos and messiness that ever since has been the raw material for creativity. As we've already seen, whether one makes a bed or a cake, the beginnings are usually messy!

Arnold Mindell applies this principle to our life stories and points out that it is precisely from the raw material of life that we must refine our gold. Does this not apply to every human growth experience? Remember your teenage years — were they always a smooth ride? All of the recovery groups contain people who admit that their lives were messy or even chaotic. Now, these people are moving through a creative process of changing those chaotic energies into something new.

For so many of the saints, conversion came in the midst of chaos. Saint Ignatius had his leg shattered by a cannon ball. The twenty-four-year-old Saint Therese's passionate love for God flamed up in the midst of tuberculosis. The great disciple of nonviolence, Mahatma Ghandi, was sensitized as a young man through an experience of being severely beaten.

One of my spiritual friends, Carl Hammerslag, writing in *The Theft of the Spirit* about the disappointments and failures of our lives, says that too often we shovel the garbage in our lives from pile to pile rather than transforming it. Instead, he says, our life challenge is to make something out of the garbage we all pile up:

> Our task in life is not to lament, rationalize, and obsess. It is to get on with it. If you discard your garbage, then a tree can grow through it.

BLESSINGS FROM CHAOS AND MESSINESS

Blessed be wounded heroines and limping heroes!
Blessed be chaotic storms that move us.
Blessed be life's wounds that stir us.

Blessed be Ghandi, for peace out of violence.
Blessed be Franklin Roosevelt, for leading from a wheelchair.
Blessed be Ann Frank, for a spacious heart shared from confinement.
Blessed be Ruth, for loyalty out of exile.
Blessed be Joan of Arc, whose spirit rose from the flames.
Blessed be Therese, a youth consumed by TB and by love.
Blessed be Christopher Reeves, Superman while confined in a wheelchair.
Blessed be Mohammed Ali, punched but never counted out.

Blessed be the grit in our lives that reveals the gold.
Blessed be the garbage in our lives that's recycled.
Blessed be our human storms that clear the air.

3) The universe is made up of spheres not spires. The encircled Celtic cross seems an appropriate symbol for our times. We are born into a family circle. We subsist on an earth circle. We live beneath a blazing circle, sleep beneath a moody, changing circle. Our very lifeblood circulates on its journey through us. Our life journey circles around. For the Christian, Jesus is at the very center of the holy circle.

Interestingly, the Brookhaven National Lab on Long Island, searching into the mysterious heart of matter, has constructed a powerful two-and-one-half mile collider to duplicate conditions akin to those that existed one ten-millionth of a second after the Big Bang. It is, of course, a great circle.

MANY ARE ONE

Atoms do a circle-dance as they spin around the coillider. But that dance takes place all around us and within us. New science, ancient wisdom and our faith-search may all be converging to offer us a picture of reality as interconnected fields of energy. Among all these fields, prayer is one of the great energies that "can move mountains!" Research done by Doctor Larry Dossey, published in 1994 by *Natural Health*, indicates that a growing number of physicists think that non-locality may even apply to the mind. Doctor Dossey opines that the energy of prayer may be everywhere, "enveloping sender, object, and the Almighty, all at once!" In a controlled study done by Doctor Randolph Byrd, M.D. of the California Medical School in San Francisco, sick people who were prayed for, even though they were unaware of being prayed for, needed 80% less antibiotics and had fewer complications than similar sick people in the same study who were not prayed for. In this light, prayer can be seen as a circular energy that goes out and around and blesses everyone involved.

There is a growing interest in early Celtic spirituality, which connects the circle with the cross and prayer all around. As they have done for almost two millennia, the Irish today often walk around in a circle as they say their prayers in field shrines!

THE THEOLOGICAL IMPLICATIONS OF THE NEW SCIENCE

In the spring of 1997, the Episcopal Church hosted a teleconference entitled, "Exploring Chaos: the New Science and Its Theological Implications," aimed at a faith dialogue with the new science, which has made the seventeenth century static view of a mechanistic universe out-of-date. At this conference Herbert Driscoll spoke about the ancient Celts having an intuitive awareness of what quantum physicists are telling us about the dynamic interconnectedness of energies. These ancestors saw the dynamic energy of blessings all around.

Archbishop Carey of Canterbury gave a hope-filled address stressing that faith-filled people should not be afraid of dialoging with the new science. He stressed that we are made for "prayer and joy" and we need not fear encountering the dynamism or even the ambiguity of the unfolding of creation — and of our faith journeys within this unfolding.

If we are to see God's mysterious presence in the unfolding of the creation story, we must pay some heed to history in it grandest sweep. The millennial consciousness raised by our entry into the twenty-first century could be a great help in our looking back through the ages to find God's Spirit at work in so many marvelous and evolutionary ways — the unfolding of blessings upon blessings — despite all of the human error, arrogance, violence and foolishness. To appreciate this demands reflection. Part of the problem of postmodern creativity is that everything moves so fast that we have little time to assess long-term implications or to look at how past developments have unfolded into the way things are now.

Robert Reilly, a former college professor and a dean of journalism, notes the effects of fast-paced, cyberspaced culture on current generations:

> There is a disinterest in history. From reporting to reflecting, everything is happening NOW. And everything is meant to entertain. How does one find the time to step back, to meditate, to reflect on consequences?

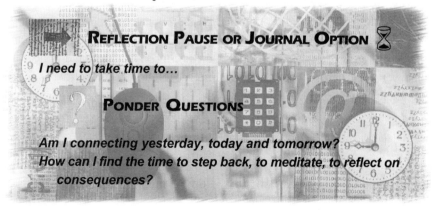

REFLECTION PAUSE OR JOURNAL OPTION

I need to take time to...

PONDER QUESTIONS

Am I connecting yesterday, today and tomorrow?
How can I find the time to step back, to meditate, to reflect on consequences?

Computerized Images — Windows to the Divine?

If we look deep down into the matter of Mother Earth, do we not discover a code for the unfolding of creative blessings from its source? The discovery of DNA moves us in that direction. In addition, the Mandelbrot Set uncovered by Benoit Mandelbrot at the IBM Research Lab in New York in 1980 gives rich food for thought and amazing images both for scientists and spiritual seekers. It comes to us as an unexpected computerized blessing. The images brought forth by Mandelbrot are termed by another scientist as the "thumbprints of God!" Through these images, we may draw closer to God, deep down, "the ground of being."

What is the "Mandelbrot Set"? By using a computer, Mandelbrot was able to display certain mathematical equations in a non-linear way. These three-dimensional images revealed the world of fractals, patterns of wholeness, that allow us to understand nature in new ways. His set is a computerized peek into the unfolding of patterns deep down below the human eye. These mathematical equations, expressed on a computer screen through a color wheel, reveal fantastic patterns merging and emerging. They appear as a pulsing kaleidoscope of patterns forming and reforming, branching out, ever expanding. If you look at the tiniest speck within this image, in some sense the whole is contained, and yet the whole keeps unraveling with slight variations.

The images of the Mandelbrot Set invalidate Newton's notion of a "clockwork" universe. Chaos and patterns dance together, forming and reforming. So many of its pulsing patterns resemble in some ways the rose window mandala at Chartres as well as other art forms and natural formations throughout the world! Disney's kaleidoscopic movie *Fantasia* would only give a slight hint at the grandeur and complexity of the striking Mandelbrot Set images.

Not only has this discovery opened a new scientific field, fractal geometry, it also inspires religious awe and wonder. The glory and beauty of the dynamic and continuing creation story is not just to be glimpsed by studying the heavens. It is revealed to us in the tiniest speck of matter that elicits marvel and awe. "Holy! Holy! Holy! Heaven *and earth* are filled with your Glory!" And I've had to wonder whether it's chance or part of a fitting pattern that the discoverer of this new vision has a name that is so similar to "mandala."

Computer Community

By revealing such mysteries as the Mandelbrot Set, the computer offers a window into mystery and the interconnectedness of matter's community. That mystery has implications for our everyday reality, opening up for many of us new opportunities to strengthen human relationships and to build community in new creative ways.

What is your experience with E-mail? If it's part of your work, it may be a mixed blessing — more communication, perhaps, than is needed. In many ways, however, it is proving to be a community builder. *US News* reported in 1999 that a three-year study underway in Sweden, Great Britain and Ireland is showing E-mail to be especially beneficial for seniors. Health questions can be answered on line by nurses. For people who are confined by age or illness, E-mail can open a window to the larger world. Isolation is often a harbinger of depression. For so many seniors E-mail allays lonliness, bringing new neighbors right into their homes.

I've had a personal experience with E-mail that has created a closer family bond. Some years ago I learned, rather belatedly, that I was not always the sweet little boy that I liked to think I was. There was a definite shadow side. Apparently, on one occasion when visiting a female cousin, I gave her a poke, which I conveniently forgot but which she clearly remembered. Years later, when I finally realized that this incident still remained somewhat a bone of contention, I simply went to her and apologized. It was a healing moment.

Since then, we have been great friends — but separated most of the time by many miles. So, over the past year or so, we have been communicating by E-mail. She often sends me jokes. There have been three particular benefits for me in this: A communication opened that was closed before, an insight into her great sense of humor, and the laughter and joy that comes from the jokes. I would count all of these as E-mail blessings.

E-mail Creativity

Since E-mail is such a new and different way of communicating, perhaps we will have to develop our own finesse and style to make it more personal and satisfying. It would be impossible to duplicate the intimacy of a scented, carefully handwritten love letter or a handwritten note of sympathy. But perhaps we might develop creative ways to make E-mail more of an art form.

I've noticed in E-mail I've received or sent that the greetings almost always are less formal, like "Hi!" or "Hello!" In its present state of development, E-mail is the computer equivalent of the ubiquitous postcard — usually just the basics.

The very way it appears on the screen invites brevity. And our hyper-culture sometimes demands limiting ourselves to a few words that can be disseminated in a few moments. That's OK as far as it goes. The challenge, however, is to creatively invest more of ourselves into these messages. Just as picture postcards often had some sort of greeting on one side and personal message on the other, we might explore the possibility of our personal E-mail becoming a unique opportunity to bless — perhaps a blessing on "one side" and an easily digestible message on the other. Some sample E-mail blessings are contained at the end of this chapter.

Some of the most famous blessing greetings are found at the beginning of the New Testament epistles. By putting a blessing at either the beginning or end of an E-mail message, we deliver not only information but also prayer! In some sense, E-mail becomes our angel, a messenger of grace. In a rapid-fire, hyper-paced world too often filled with angry curses, E-mail offers a wonderful and creative opportunity to deliver something better, something more graceful.

When I began to write books some ten years ago, I always wrote out my manuscripts by hand, feeling there was somehow more of a human dimension involved in such a hands-on approach. However, I have since changed that practice. After all, the keyboard is also a hands-on instrument that simply takes the place of a pen. The one dimension missing, of course, is that in handwriting the very personality of the writer appears in the script.

The downside of E-mail is the possibility of addiction. David Greenfield has even written a book entitled *Virtual Addiction: Help for Netheads, Cyberfreaks and Those Who Love Them!* Obsession with the keyboard can take time away from real face-to-face encounters and from the energy necessary to cultivate enriching relationships. And no machine can replace the precious value of direct contact with people.

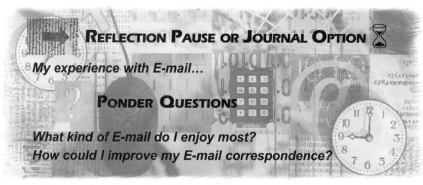

REFLECTION PAUSE OR JOURNAL OPTION

My experience with E-mail...

PONDER QUESTIONS

What kind of E-mail do I enjoy most?
How could I improve my E-mail correspondence?

FORMATTING

Of course, formatting our own greeting cards is a giant leap forward from E-mail and a wonderful way to exercise our creative potential. When I wrote my recent book *Words of Comfort,* along with prayers and reflections, I included various images that could be used as comfort greeting cards, giving permission for the user to format the words and images on cards of their own. Again, besides being opportunities for creativity, such cards offer marvelous occasions to express blessings.

MADE FOR PRAYER AND JOY

If our hearts are made for prayer and joy, then prayer and joy need to be woven into the fabric of our daily lives. There is a deep joy in mining our gifts for their gold and then sharing our gold with others. It is one of life's greatest blessings. Some psychologists tell us that we use barely 10% of our creative human potential. When we dig deeper, we can begin to mine some of our untapped resources. My friends Ron and Joanne married young in life. After leaving military service, Ron worked hard all his life at a factory, and he and Joanne raised five wonderful children. When the children were grown, Joanne went to work. They have been retired now for three years. They continue with their previous pastimes — golfing, playing cards, going to movies. Since retirement, however, Ron has taken up woodcarving and Joanne has taken a painting course. Each year, they have become more and more skilled. Recently, a shop owner invited Ron to place some of his carvings in her store. He may do that, but first he has a whole list of carvings to make for each of his grandchildren. Joanne's paintings have also developed beautifully. Most recently she presented a painting of Nancy Drew to one of her grandchildren for her first communion.

Even though their children are out of the nest, Ron and Joanne continue to send their creative blessings into the homes of their loved ones. The artistic efforts in the second half of their life together have strengthened their identity as playing and praying folks who bless the earth. And long after they have left this earth, their children's children will continue to be blessed by their creativity.

They are now talking about getting a computer and doing E-mail. Part of their reluctance to do so prior to this time is an apprehension that it may curtail their time for creativity. However, knowing Ron and Joanne, my guess is they will balance it all and apply their creativity to the word processor just as they have done to wood and paints.

We are all given a challenge to pass on to the world either a blessing or a curse. The call to provide blessings may require us to move through messiness and even chaos to create something new and worthwhile.

Despite all of the turmoil we see around us — as Archbishop Carey reminds us — we are made for prayer and for joy. In the midst of messiness — and sometimes even in chaos and crisis — prayer and joy can be present. Think of Michaelangelo lying on his back painting the great ceiling. His back must have ached and his ears must have rang from the harangues of Pope Julius, but his creativity must have flooded him with joy. Moreover, every childbirth is messy and painful, but each birth is a supremely "blessed event."

LEAVING BLESSINGS OR CURSES?

Hitler had imaginative creativity — but it brought forth gas ovens and finally his own self-destruction in a bombarded bunker beneath Berlin. The challenge for the new millennium is not simply to use our creative and imaginative energies — as essential as that is. The fundamental question is: Shall our creativity leave behind a trail of perpetuating chaos for future generations, or shall we tap into our creativity to bless ourselves and our children to come?

MEDITATION PATH

I recently returned from my morning prayer at my favorite duck pond. There, ducks and swans swam around and between each other in seemingly random patterns — the swans honking like impatient Chicago cabdrivers.

The waters swirled as they "created" thousands of unique "Mandelbrot" patterns. I chuckled as both ducks and swans did bottoms up and heads down — submerging their heads to uncover unseen treasures from the muddy lake bottom. As they did so, their bottoms wagged like disco dancers. Soon, a little three-year-old boy came by with his mother. He held a toy truck in his right hand. He stopped and gazed at the waterfowl, totally mesmerized by the scene. After awhile, he and his mother moved on.

Then another person came and scattered breadcrumbs onto the pond. The waterfowl landed and pigeons joined them for the feast. It was a delightful sight — birds of different feathers eating peacefully together. A while later, the feeder left, and another little boy came hand-in-hand with his mother. He held a stick in his hand. He let go of his mother's hand and ran into the midst of the birds trying to hit them with the stick. They fluttered, scattered and ran away. He returned to his mother, very satisfied, and said, "I did good, Mom, didn't I?" As I walked away, it seemed to me that in those short scenes I had witnessed both patterns of blessing and curse.

SCRIPTURE IMAGES AND PASSAGES FOR REFLECTION

Hebrew Scriptures

Genesis 1: 27-28 — *God's creativity and call for humans to be fruitful*
So God created humankind in
      the divine image,
        in the image of God they were created;
        male and female God created them.
God blessed them, and God said to them, "Be fruitful...."

Song of Solomon 4: 1 — *The beauty of the beloved*
      How beautiful you are, my love,
        how very beautiful!
      Your eyes are like doves
        behind your veil.

Isaiah 40: 1 — *God comforting us*
>   Comfort, O comfort my people,
>   says your God.

Isaiah 52: 7 — *The beauty of the messenger*
>   How beautiful upon the mountains
>   are the feet of the messenger
>   who announces peace,
>   who brings good news.

Christian Scriptures

John 15: 16 — *Jesus' call for us to be fruitful*

You did not choose me; I chose you. And I appointed you to go and bear fruit, fruit that will last.

E-MAIL BLESSINGS

Please know that the very thought of you is always a blessing
    for me!
May my blessings come to you on angel wings!
With the speed of light may my words brighten your day!
Peace from my house to yours!
Grace to you and peace (1 Thessalonians 1: 1).

The blessings of my love to you… "For if I were to write to
    you without love, I would only be a noisy gong or a clanging
    symbol" (1 Corinthians 13: 1).
May grace and peace be yours in abundance (1 Peter 1: 2)
May mercy, peace, and love be yours in abundance (Jude 1: 2).
Beloved, I pray that all may go well with you (3 John 1: 1).

BLESSINGS OF SPACE AND PLACE

"Home is a container for soul. The roof and walls shelter and nurture the spark of life that animates our modes of dwelling."
—Anthony Lawlor, *A Home for the Soul*

THE PARABLE OF THE HEAVENLY POLL

Once upon a time, God asked Saint Peter and Archangel Raphael to clean up the front office. As Peter entered the empty office, Raphael flew in through the window. They looked around the room, and the angel motioned toward three stacks of paper on God's desk. Peter sighed as he looked at the three piles of messages and said to Raphael, "These earthlings certainly keep God busy with all their requests. Running the rest of the universe is small potatoes compared to handling all the communications from earth." Pointing to a two-foot tall stack of papers on his desk, he added, "You know, Raphael, this whole stack of requests goes into the 'damn' file."

"The 'damn' file?" replied Raphael.

"Yes, they're all requests for God to damn someone or something. A lot of them come from the freeways, like 'Damn that Chevy!' or 'Damn that slowpoke!' or 'Damn that guy who just cut in!' Heaven gets piles and piles of these requests for damning."

"Why are they in such a hurry, Peter? God gave them each twenty-four hours in a day, and for many of them it's not enough."

"Some of them are in such a hurry," Peter added, "that they arrive at my gate — or at the other place — before their time. I often wonder what the rush is. And look at this second pile. Only half as big as the 'damn' pile, it asks for all kinds of blessings. 'Give me this. Give me that. Give me everything under the sun.'"

Gesturing toward the pile on the far side of the desk, Raphael asked, "And what about the smallest pile over there?"

"Oh, those are 'thank yous.' Only about one in ten go in that pile."

Then, after a moment of pensive reflection, Peter continued, "Raphael, I have a job for you. I'd like you to find out what these earthlings really want. Better yet, find out what they consider to be their fundamental need. Maybe you can get to the bottom of it. Interview. Ask questions. Take notes. Take a poll."

"Well, your holiness, any sense of how I should go about this? Where should I go? Whom should I talk to?"

"Oh, there are no restrictions, Raphael. You know we operate on eternal time here. You can take your poll anywhere and at any time. Poll those currently living on earth, but you can also contact people from the past, or even the future."

"I think I've got the idea," said Raphael. "I'm on my way."

"Godspeed!" replied Peter.

"Well," thought Raphael as he flew out the office window, "why not start by going way back to the first century to the Roman Empire. So he called up the emperor himself, Caesar Augustus, and asked about humankind's most fundamental need.

"That's easy," said Caesar. "It's the need for Rome's civilizing function. And most fundamental to this is our system of law, roads and military might." Raphael took out his journal and wrote down the emperor's response, as he would do for everyone he interviewed.

At the end of a day of interviewing, he read through the rest of his journal. Here is a sampling of his findings:

Humankind's Most Fundamental Need?
Raphael's Journal

Cleopatra: "The most fundamental need? Barge traffic. Just kidding. It's really to prepare our bodies for the afterlife. Look at my father's mummy. First class wrapping and first class burial. Who's ever going to beat the pyramids for chutzpah? Well, maybe Moses. But thank God he's out of here!"

Saint Paul: "Love, for without it, I am a clashing cymbal."

King Henry VIII: "Good food and a good wife — and I can never get enough of either. With your connections, can't you do something about that?"

Thomas Aquinas: "Faith seeking understanding."

Augustine of Hippo: "Our hearts are made for God and are restless until they rest in him."

Frederick Nietzsche: "The most fundamental need of humankind is "the will to power."

A twentieth century football coach: "Winning! What else is there? It's the name of the game. And if anybody thinks differently — look at my salary. It's bigger than the college president's. In fact, it's twice as much as the salary of the president of the United States. Our whole American way of life is based on winning. What's more fundamental?"

Viktor Frankl (logotherapist who went through the Holocaust): "What I learned in the horrors of the concentration camps is that the human's most fundamental need is the search for meaning."

Confucius: "The need is for the family and ethical leaders to bring about harmony."

Socrates: "Knowing one's own psyche, for the unexamined life is not worth living."

Nelson Mandela: "Freedom from oppression."

Playboy Bunny: "Sex."

Pope John Paul II: "To recognize the dignity of the human person in the eyes of God."

TV Evangelist: "To be born again."

Charles Darwin: "The survival of the species."

William Shakespeare: "I'll answer your question with another question, 'To be or not to be' — is not that the fundamental question?"

*Note to myself: So far I've asked persons from the past as well as some twentieth century folks. Do I need to ask Jesus? No, the Father can ask him himself. What about those from the future? Yes, I ought to ask a least one person.

OK, here's a woman from the mid twenty-first century.

Mary Doe, 2050: "Well, there are a lot of needs. Maybe the biggest one we are feeling right now is to get rid of all the poison and pollution that our self-indulgent ancestors bequeathed to us. It's everywhere!"

*Note to myself: I thought I ought to ask another woman from recent history, so I found a woman walking down on the road with her scraggly child. When I asked her what road she was on, she responded, "The road back to Kosovo." When I asked her about the fundamental need, she replied: "A place to be."

When I asked her what she meant, she simply answered, "Home."

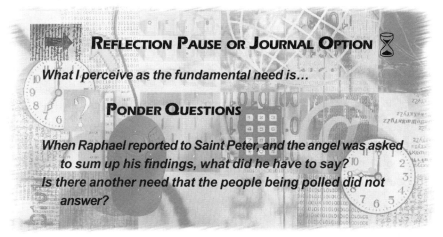

REFLECTION PAUSE OR JOURNAL OPTION

What I perceive as the fundamental need is...

PONDER QUESTIONS

When Raphael reported to Saint Peter, and the angel was asked to sum up his findings, what did he have to say? Is there another need that the people being polled did not answer?

Raphael may have been puzzled by the woman on the road who answered "home," for, after all, angels do not have to be concerned by space or place as humans do. For us humans in our present physical form, to have no space to occupy means non-existence. Perhaps as a mother she realized that in a way an angel never could. For our first home is the womb, and an infant either finds a home there or dies. "To be or not to be" may well be the fundamental question. It is also true that if the human continues his/her journey out of the womb each of the various spaces that the human occupies will turn out to be either a blessing space or a depressing space for many different kinds of reasons. One reason may have a lot to do with colors.

COLORED SPACE

One of the great revelations God made to the ancient Hebrew people was the rainbow, God's color wheel, as a holy sign of their covenant. Color is indeed one of our primal blessings, one we take so much for granted. I am old enough to remember when all TV was black, white and gray. When color first appeared on our living room screens, it was remarkable and memorable. Now we take it for granted. Advertisers, psychologists and designers do not. They have long known the influences of space and color upon our senses and our psyche. Color is one of the most pervasive yet subtle spacial influences on our daily living. Our personal experience makes us aware of how our environment influences us and how we react, consciously or unconsciously, to the colors around us. Like our place and our space, color can either curse or bless us. Our multicolored environment even influences our motivation and our health.

A few years back, a college football coach painted the walls of his team's dressing room a bold red. He knew how a bull at a bullfight reacts to the red cape — Charge! And that is exactly what he wanted his players to do, to charge out onto the field, energized and eager for battle. He painted the visiting team's locker room "sissy pink," knowing that its effects would be relaxing and subduing. "Let them relax while we charge!" was the strategy. "Get 'em before they get going." He understood well the potential power of color on our emotions. While we are all somewhat aware of the following facts about color, modern advertising and designers use this knowledge to great advantage:

Yellow is the most noticeable of all colors. For that reason, modern fire trucks often are no longer red but are yellow instead. They need to be seen. To that end, a TV network recently reworked all its own promotional commercials into yellow. At the same time, yellow, like the sun, cannot be looked at for long. **Green** is the most soothing, recreating color. It puts us in touch with nature, being one of the most basic expressions of the natural world. **Blue**, like a summer lake, is a relaxing color. It cools the mind, the senses and even the appetites. **Red** is the color of action and passion, and also of danger. Stop signs and red flags signal caution. The bridal color in China is red and from ancient times — red light districts have signaled passion for sale throughout much of the world.

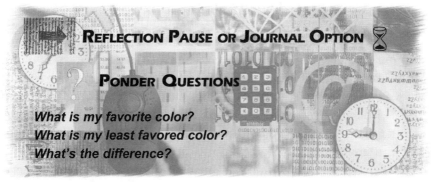

REFLECTION PAUSE OR JOURNAL OPTION

PONDER QUESTIONS

What is my favorite color?
What is my least favored color?
What's the difference?

Therapists now suggest that color can even affect our health. The swank Biltmore Hotel in Phoenix has added color therapy to its spa services because colors have various frequencies that can have definite effects on a person's body. When I spoke to Lydia, who had undergone color therapy, she described it this way:

At first I was somewhat skeptical of this new idea, but the more I thought about it, I realized it was not so new. Didn't God in the first place give us the gift of colors to brighten our lives? When I had my face painted in different colors, I noticed subtle changes in my attitude. I'd also experienced color therapy by sitting in a room where various colors flooded the senses. Added to that was a variety of scents. These different colors elicited a whole range of reactions in my bodily feelings. It's helped me be aware that perhaps at various times I may need to be more in touch with one color or another. The whole experience also raised my awareness of how color is often used to motivate us. I now understand why fast food restaurants use colors like red or yellow in their decor. They are *fast food* enterprises, and they want us to eat fast and get moving so others can take our places. On the other hand, my favorite restaurant has soft relaxing colors and a candle-lit atmosphere that makes me want to linger and relax. I need that because the rest of my busy hours are all rush and hurry. I am more sensitive now to my need for restful colors like green and brown.

Indeed, color is capable of producing blessings — the right colors can be therapeutic, delivering various relaxing messages to the body. Yet, at the other end of town from the elegant Biltmore, someone who has been called the "the toughest sheriff in the USA" has mandated that the convicts under his care wear black and white striped outerwear but also pink underwear. While this may have a calming effect, it is quite likely also experienced as demeaning. Moreover, the convicts are forced to live in "Tent City" — old khaki army tents set up in the sometimes 100-115-degree Arizona summer sun. Despite the pink underwear, every so often riots break out in these sweltering homes. So color is only one factor in environment.

There will always be a debate about the relative determining effects of heredity and environment. The more we know about how we are influenced by what surrounds us, the more we realize there are interacting energies being exchanged all the time within the field of our experience. Modern physics reveal that we swim in these energies. Just as a fish can not avoid getting wet in the ocean, so too we are all affected one way or another by the colors of our space.

THE BLESSING OF SPACE

Blessings for space and place have a long history in religious tradition, from church blessings to house blessings. Some theologians tell us that prayer itself is a unique spiritual energy. Prayers were offered at sacred sites, and a house would be consecrated with holy water — blessed and thus sanctified. It was previously thought to be a one-way communication, a person blessing an inert object. However, we are now becoming more aware of how blessed space returns the blessing to us.

Quantum physicists have been telling us that energies are constantly flowing both ways. No matter how controlled an experiment might be, the mere presence of an observer always influences an outcome. The observer, in some sense, is being observed by the object. The object, it seems, is a field of energy — in some sense, "a live thing" acting upon the observer. We not only act upon the walls or windows, but they act upon us. Perhaps we all realize this intuitively, but now we know it scientifically. We are enveloped in energy fields, and we ourselves are a bundle of energies constantly exchanging dynamic interactions with the larger fields in which we live. There is no such thing as an inert room or place! This raises the question, "If we bless space, how does space bless us?"

Church Homes

One place we expect to be blessed is in our church. For those of us who are churchgoers, our "spiritual home" is often the space where we worship with other believers — the church where we assemble on Sundays or the synagogue on the Sabbath. In fact, there are many different types of such sacred space. Traditionally, small chapels have been created as quiet, contemplative spaces, ideal for silent meditation and prayer. Other public prayer spaces might involve much more — like a church conducive to singing, learning or collective prayers, or a plaza in Europe where thousands gather to be blessed. Indeed, one of the great challenges of church life in many places is the clash among those who have different perceptions of the proper use of space. In many new churches, a compromise has been reached by building a chapel for quiet, undisturbed prayer and a larger sanctuary area for interaction and welcoming.

That is precisely what my good friend Father Larry Dorsey and I hoped to accomplish in 1998 when we served on the design committee for the new Saint Gerald's church in Omaha, Nebraska. The large vestibule gathering space with its icon of the Holy Family — Jesus, Mary and Joseph in their home at Nazareth — helped to create a welcoming and open gathering space — conducive to visiting upon entering or departing. The adjoining chapel, by contrast, possesses a quieting warmth, conducive to silent prayer and meditation. Images on the wall from the Stations of the Cross are interspersed with flickering vigil candles. Soft light from a skylight pours down over a golden, freestanding tabernacle. The light from a stained glass window splashes onto the floor and creates colored patterns there. This space speaks, but in hushed tones. "Quiet. Rest awhile. Settle down. Be in God's presence. Be blessed. Just be. Receive the blessings this place holds for you."

Serving on a design committee is a great apprenticeship for developing a deeper realization of the way the make-up of a space influences how it is used. Architect Frank Lloyd Wright is well known for his dictum, "Form follows function." That is what our design committee strived to do, to make the space best serve its purpose but also ensure that it would be a beautiful space. When this succeeds, the space itself confers blessings of welcoming, uplifting spirits and moving the humans within it toward prayer.

One of the items we struggled with was color. We all seemed to have our own favorite colors. My co-pastor, Father Larry, lobbied for blue. When we discussed this, it was agreed that blue was a cooling color, and enough cold would surround this church during the long Nebraska winters. In the end, a lighter-colored brick and light wood created a neutral ambiance that allowed the seasonal liturgical colors to stand out. Rich burgundy sanctuary carpet and upholstered pews contrasted the light wood and produced a feeling of warmth and "at-homeness" as well as a feeling that this was special and sacred space.

That is exactly what resulted — a warm and inviting spiritual home for all of the parishioners. But it didn't happen by accident. It was designed to happen. Moreover, prayer was an integral part of many of the planning sessions that led to the design of the church. In some sense, the spirituality of the parishioners was breathed into the new structure. Spirit, in fact, means breath. I asked the architect David Beringer, who worked with us for three years designing the church, how the "spirit of a people" is coalesced and breathed into a building. He responded:

> Each community that plans a building has its own unique chemistry or energy. This would be equally true for a church family or a family planning a new home. No two "families" are the same. As an architect, I feel that listening to the people who will eventually use the space is a crucial ingredient for a good design. I also find it helpful when designing a church to visit their present worship site and experience how the community is currently worshiping. After participating with them on Sunday, I try to talk to a cross section of parishioners in one-on-one input sessions.

From the listening process we used at Saint Gerald's, it became clear that the parish family was a blending of young families and older people, many with somewhat traditional ethnic backgrounds coming from a part of town that was pioneered by immigrants from several countries in central Europe. As a result of listening to where the people came from, where they were at that moment and where they wanted to go with the new church space, the church design evolved as a blending of contemporary and traditional forms. It was intended to make everyone in the diverse family that makes up St. Gerald's feel welcome and at home. When the church was completed and blessed, I think it is safe to say that the spirit of this unique parish family was "breathed" into bricks and mortar. The people dreamt a dream and blessed the space through their input in the creative process. Now their space blesses them as they use it.

OUR HOMES

Next to our churches, would not our homes be the places where we would expect most to be blessed with peace, contentment and even the presence of God. A home blessing is a wonderful ritual not only because it is an effort to connect God with the space in which we live, but it also can remind us that our home is sacred space that can bestow its own blessing on us. What are some of the blessings we might expect from our home?

God bless this house. Make it:
a safe place,
a place of warmth,
a place of ease,
a place of comfort,
a place of rest,
a place of pleasing colors,
a place of stability,
a place of memories,
a place of dreaming,
a place to talk,
a place of table hospitality,
a place of acceptance,
a place of welcome,
a place of laughter,
a place of healing,
a place of beauty,
a place of romance and lovemaking,
a place of pleasing aromas,
a place of strength and security,
a place of unconditional love,
a place where we can most truly be ourselves,

a place of refuge from hyperactivity.
In such a holy space, angels hover near.

No Space Like It

"There's no place like home" is not just a cliché. Among other things, home is the place for the most formative events of our young lives, the nest for lovers and young families, the place we turn to find comfort at old age and a solace from the storms we encounter at each stage of life.

Perhaps the most significant space in any of our houses is the front door. After all, it is the one space we pass in and out of every single day. It is the first part of our house that welcomes visitors. It is an element that is profoundly symbolic. Jesus used the door of the sheepfold as an image for himself. We use the term "open door policy." The ancient psalmist sang of "lifting high, you ancient doors." At Saint Peter's Basilica a "holy door" is sealed and only opened every fifty years.

The front door is the first message a guest receives. We know there are so many kinds of doors. Jail doors are grim and locked. Dublin is famous for its Georgian doors — brightly painted in a wide variety of colors, sometimes with the doorknob in the middle and a glass arch overhead. Sometimes they possess ornate doorknockers. One of the most beautiful is the Claddagh emblem, a heart held by two hands — standing for friendship, loyalty and love. Such a doorknocker can signal blessings within: "Come in! If you find me beautiful, you will also find beauty within."

There was another door in Ireland that preceded the Georgian doors — the half door. Often the villagers would stand in their doorways, leaning out over the half door to visit with passersby. One foreign visitor reflected, "With the end of the half doors, hospitality was halved." However, even modern day visitors to Ireland might question that sentiment, for hospitality to strangers passing through Irish doors still remains a very high priority.

The Blessings of Jewish Hospitality

Hospitality is also a strong Jewish tradition. And it begins at the doorpost. There the *mezuzah* is attached as a reminder to all who pass through the door that God loves us abundantly — the same love we should have for God and each other. This wonderful Jewish home blessing from *Renew Our Days: A Book of Jewish Prayer and Meditation* is for the occupants and the visitor:

> We ask God's blessing on this home and all who live in it.
> May its doors be open to those in need
> and its rooms be filled with kindness.
> May love dwell within its walls,
> and joy shine from its windows.
> May God's peace protect it
> and God's presence never leave it.

There is also a rabbinical saying, "Now that the temple has been destroyed, a person's table replaces the altar and every Jewish home is a temple in miniature." It is also a common theme in the Hebrew Scriptures that whenever generous hospitality is given to an unexpected stranger who has done nothing to "earn it" a blessing always rebounds to the generous host or hostess. For example, the blessing promise of Elisha the prophet to the woman who offered him generous hospitality was later fulfilled by the birth of a son she so much desired (2 Kings 4: 14-17).

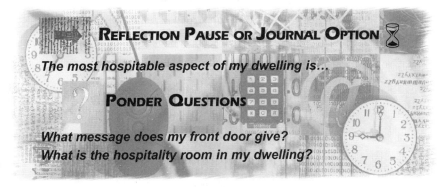

REFLECTION PAUSE OR JOURNAL OPTION

The most hospitable aspect of my dwelling is...

PONDER QUESTIONS

What message does my front door give?
What is the hospitality room in my dwelling?

DOORS

As you lie on the hillside, or lie prone under the trees of the forest, or spread wet-legged on the shingly beach of a mountain stream, the great door, that does not look like a door, opens.
—Stephen Graham, *The Gentle Art of Tramping*

> O gates, lift high your heads;
> Grow higher, ancient doors,
> Let him enter, the king of glory (Psalm 24: 7).

...the doors being shut...Jesus came and stood among them"
(John 20: 19).

Some doors are famous, like Ghiberti's baptistry doors in Florence. Each door is engraved with twenty-eight scenes from the Bible.

There are sealed holy doors at the entrance of Saint Peter's Basilica in Rome. They are opened every fifty years during the Year of the Jubilee.

Dublin boasts of its Georgian doors. Each has a bright color with a brass doorknob in the middle.

In New York, the rusting doors of Ellis Island creak in the breeze. They once welcomed "the refuse of your teaming shores."

AN ODE TO DOORS

We are either indoors or out of doors. So goes our journey:
Some are tight and trim, others hinged, squeaky talking doors,
Dutch doors, French doors, Romanesque doors,
swinging, sagging, veneered, lacquered, varnished.

Bright with a Christmas wreath,
Sad with a blackened crepe.

Secure doors, safe doors, fortress doors,
fastened, latched, bolted, chained, locked, barred —
bank doors, business doors, condo doors,
glassed, etched, numbered, posted, sealed.

Magic sliding train doors you push,
and they go "whoosh!"

Revolving, twirling doors that circle,
and bring you in and out again.

There are doors that open into welcome and life:
nursery doors, red barn doors, school doors,
church doors, theater doors, airplane doors,
kitchen doors, friends' doors, home's doors.

The risen Jesus cast aside the stone door
and passed through the locked door,
there being no closed doors from those he loved.

THE SOUL OF THE HOME

If eyes are the windows of the soul, then doors are the entrance to the soul of the home. Do houses have personalities, a certain soulfulness of their own? If churches do, then why not houses? What is the difference between a "spooky house" and a "lovely home?" What happens within? When O.J.'s home was put up for sale after the infamous trial, it was bought and then quickly torn down. The new owner in some sense saw it as cursed with bad memories, not blest. And he wanted no part of what went on in that house.

Homes, from the front door to the farthest interior corner, reflect the personality and values of the inhabitants. The walls do speak. They echo back what is important to the inhabitants. In her novel *Tara Road*, Maeve Binchy revolves her whole plot around two borrowed homes and all the memories they hold — and also, in this case, all their secrets. In my own experience as a pastor, I always try to visit the home of the deceased after a death, not only to console the bereaved but also to learn the secrets the home itself wants to tell me. I am able to use the information I glean to help make the funeral homily personal and meaningful.

The front door itself gives the first clue. If it has a feeling of welcome about it (sometimes there is an actual welcome mat), I know that this is a house of hospitality. When I sit and visit with the bereaved, the room we sit in tells a story. Often it is in the kitchen over a cup of coffee. And often in the kitchen there is a refrigerator shrine with all kinds of pictures and sometimes sayings and poems. Such shrines are surrounded by a feeling of reverence for deeply held values and cherished family members and friends. The room where the bereaved choose to sit in is more than likely the room of hospitality, the room for visiting closed off from the intrusive TV screen.

QUIET SPACE — UNUSUAL PRAYER PLACES IN THE HOME

But what of quiet space in our homes — spaces where blessings can be savored, spaces conducive to prayer? Most rooms are for interacting — or, in the case of entertainment rooms — for passive viewing.

Perhaps in some homes the only room for total private use is the bathroom! Should that be a prayer space? Perhaps so! Many people find it the only quiet place where they can read in peace and reflect in silence!

We could start our day recognizing the blessed gift of water by singing joyfully in the shower. This is a blessing prayer of joy. If water is not sacred and precious then what is? It is a primal gift and a rare one. As far as we now know, it only exists in flowing form on planet earth. Its freshening qualities affect more than the exterior of the body; its vitalizing power touches the mind and spirit as well. Just as we would pray a meal blessing, why not sometimes pray a short exclamation in the shower? Something like, "Praise God for Holy Water!"

How about our bath? I know of an English woman who once said, "I know of very few problems that can't be solved by a good hot bath!" The bathroom can definitely be a space for rejuvenation and blessings.

Or why not say a prayer on the toilet seat? Does this sound too bizarre? It is always a moment when we are humbled. We experience our earthiness. It is a moment of letting go! For people in our society it is a rare and unavoidable experience of not being in control. One such prayer in this position might be:

O God, I am of the earth and earthy.
As I sit in this humble position and let go,
help me realize that I don't always have to be in control.

The bedroom too can be a place for special blessings and prayers. In the Book of Tobit, for example, Tobiah and Sarah prayed and blessed their space before they made love!

Each of the rooms in our home can be integral to a spirituality of blessing — both in how we consciously bless our special places and in our awareness of how they bless us.

REAL LIFE SPIRITUALITY

In her splendid book *Real Life — Real Spirituality*, Judy Esway, a very busy wife and mother who balances demands of a family and a career, has a chapter entitled "Making Room for Prayer." She writes of her conversion to prayer — to the conviction that prayer had to become a priority in the midst of her rush and hyperactivity. She learned that she couldn't be a superwoman or supermom and that she couldn't make her family life work without prayer. She also realized she had to make room for prayer, that she had to carve out time and space in order to honor her commitment. She writes:

I had gotten lost in all my roles. I didn't know who I was

until I started to pray. Don't get lost in busyness. God wants to spend time with the real you and wants you to spend time with the real you too.

Judy made room not only by carving out time from the hyperpace of her life, but also by creating a "prayer room." For older mothers and fathers, when children leave the nest, the bathroom need not be the only quiet private space at home. An empty room may be available. And for younger homeowners who inhabit larger houses with fewer children, carving out a blessed prayer space often only requires some imagination and effort.

When Judy's oldest son moved out of her house, she had the opportunity to develop her own "holy space." Through her decorating and placement of icons and holy books, she developed a personally meaningful contemplative space.

Since I live in an apartment, I don't have the option of an extra room. I have, however, created a prayer space in my office. On one shelf of a cabinet, I have my most holy books — the Scriptures, the documents of the Vatican Council and other favorite spiritual reading. In the center is an icon with a vigil light. On the wall is a colored stained glass mandala, a circular prayer wheel. When the time comes for my morning reading, meditation and prayer, I swivel my desk chair around from my computer, and I have my own blessed prayer space in front of me.

Some of my friends have created special prayer corners in their sleeping areas or other rooms. A small table or stone slab can serve as a prayer altar. A cross, icon or other sacred image can help that corner become a shrine. So too can a special book, photo, rock, feather or flower. Sacred objects and prayer allies come in many shapes and sizes.

Other friends have created prayer spaces in their yards or gardens outside their back doors. Among them are lovely gardens with birdbaths presided over by that lover of nature, Saint Francis. Every morning, the birds sing their praise to God. What a wonderful prayer space!

We now also know that we can make our home space healthier by bringing some of the garden inside, since volatile compounds, "VOCs," from synthetic products like rugs, furniture and tiles, can poison our homes. We also need nature in our offices. It's become commonplace to hear of new office buildings that are "sick." Green plants actually help us to breathe by cleaning our air and replenishing oxygen. When we surround ourselves with greenery, these living creatures bestow marvelous blessings.

SPIRITUALITY IN CYBERSPACE

Another home space that can be turned into a spiritual oasis is the computer desk. More and more spiritual resources are appearing on the Internet. For instance, Creighton University offers a thirty-three week on-line retreat that can be plugged into at any time! It offers instruction, Scripture readings, prayer, meditations and opportunities for sharing. Participants are urged to focus on each week's themes throughout the day. It opens with these words:

> This is the first week of a 33-week journey. We begin at the beginning — our story. Prayer is about our relationship with God. We will begin to grow in the relationship with God in the midst of our everyday lives this week by simply reflecting upon our own story. There may be times we will want to take a period for prayer to reflect upon our story this week. What is most important, however, is that we begin by letting this reflection become the background of our week.

We grow in our relationship with God by reflecting on our story. Since our story usually revolves around home, what better place to begin prayerful reflection! Now, with the Internet, we don't have to go off to a retreat house. We can pursue spiritual insights in our own house, as close as our fingertips. This is a marvelous opportunity for the increasing numbers of cyberspaced folks seeking spirituality and for all of us who are hyperpaced.

HOME BUILDERS

Maybe you've been dreaming the American Dream lately — a new house, an addition or simply a remodeling project. Homebuilders have a singular opportunity not only to consider a prayer space in the planning but also to take a spiritual approach to the building process. Homebuilders might consider creating space that would bless not only themselves and their families but the earth itself. The Environmental Defense Fund suggests maximizing energy efficiency, limiting damage to or destruction of surrounding greenery and recognizing that small can be both efficient and beautiful. Materials can be used that are environment-friendly. Such a "green house" might, for example, use Trex, a "lumber" made from recycled materials. Insulation might be fire-resistant cellulose fiber made from recycled paper. Even ceramic tile can be recycled from old automobile glass! Such concern both for the environment of the house we will live in and for sustaining the redwood forests and other dwindling earth resources can make house construction part of our practice of prayer. Rather than despoiling, building a home can be a blessing for individual homeowners and for the earth.

CONTEMPLATIVE SPACES

Here's where interior designers enter the picture of blessing space. They are trained to design space for particular usages. I asked interior designer Jeannie Beal to elaborate on the effects of different kinds of space on our quality of life and on our very spirits. Jeannie is certified by the New York School of Design and has thirty years of experience as an interior design consultant at Phoenix College. Her specialty is teaching and coaching others how to decorate their own homes, focusing on the home as a sanctuary. Like David Beringer, the architect who helped design St. Gerard's Church, Jeannie's spirituality impacts her work. Her desire to create blessed space is reflected in her latest book, *Authentic Ambiance*.

THE BLESSINGS OF INTERIOR DESIGN

I asked Jeannie how the right kind of design might affect our quality of life and, more specifically, how interior design affects the spiritual need for our space to become a blessing.

Jeannie's response was, "Designers and artists have long known that the energy of a space affects our quality of life. Pleasant, orderly surroundings make for a pleasant, orderly life. Disorder and lack of beauty make for a disordered, depressing life. As without, so within.

"Interior designers are trained to design space, first, to function well. Second, to create a harmony and balance in support of that function, it is important to notice what the space is doing to us or for us. Yes, the design of space can be either a blessing or a burden.

"As far as color is concerned, look to nature, God's magnificent creation, as your guide in how to use color. There is a vast amount of lightness of color in the sky, and darker shades on the ground. And tree trunks and earth provide quiet, neutral colors. Lighter above, darker below with neutrals to give richness. Zippy, punchy, bright colors are in small quantities, like the face of a flower or the wing of a bird. Occasionally, for a season, a tree may light up all over with radiant red-orange flowers, but notice that they're not there all year round. Nature gives us simple, healthy guides to create peaceful environments.

"Bedrooms ought to be quiet rooms for sleeping or relaxing, places for winding down. They should not be libraries, television rooms, offices or computer terminals. Psychologists warn about combining contradictory usage of space because of the stress of mixed messages. Saying one thing. Doing another.

"An example of a mixed message would be an office with a portrait of a sleeping girl. We can give similar mixed messages in the way we furnish our homes. Should a room that is designed for visiting and hospitality have telephones, fax machines or even television sets? Ideally, I think not."

"Jeannie," I said, "I read an article from the Gannett News Service, in which Joanne Ford comments on the rising popularity of 'the great room,' sometimes called the 'family room.' She quotes other designers referring to it as 'the hearth of the twenty-first century.' What do you think about that designation?"

"I would rather think that our popular 'family rooms' can sometimes be destructive examples of a mixed usage of space that has developed so fast that some of us have missed it. I fear that too many of our 'family rooms' have degenerated into passive entertainment centers, where the family has become an audience, facing toward the screen rather than toward each other. We used to be plenty of entertainment for each other, swapping stories, telling our dreams, wondering together about what God is doing in our lives, recognizing each others' value in our lives. That kind of a room carried with it the warmth of the hearth and many kinds of blessings."

I agree with Jeannie. But finding time for family visiting is a primary "home problem." With so many different and conflicting work schedules and children's extracurricular activities, many families I know seldom have family meals. Added to that, according to 1999 research by the Associated Press, the "average American" spent 4.4 hours a day watching TV. Maybe in our hyperpaced culture, just spacing out in front of the TV is all that many have the energy to do.

REFLECTION PAUSE OR JOURNAL OPTION

PONDER QUESTIONS

Does any of my space deliver a mixed message?
How does nature guide my decorating?
How much space and time can I carve out for hearth/heart
*   communication in my home?*

I also asked Jeannie, "Is there such a thing as a place having healing powers? Can we influence our space in its capacity to empower and bless us? "

"Yes," she said. "There is documented research that we are affected, for better or for worse, by our environment, whether we are aware of it or not. This applies to both work and home.

"The ancient Greeks, five centuries before Christ, knew that healing is best supported in nature. They were wise to the connection between the gods and nature and healing. When they built the temples at the Acropolis, worship was outdoors on the steps of the Parthenon, and the places for healing were right there too, facilitated by priests and priestesses.

"How often Christ healed outdoors, by a pool, on a walk, in a garden. At last, our hospitals are beginning to include healing gardens. Mayo's new hospital in Arizona even has an interior waterfall! We've become too much an indoor society, disconnected from the natural, and some think this is a major cause of illness! The least we can do is to bring plants and flowers — and their healing energy — inside, giving us the blessings of oxygen and beauty. They're not only blessings of recognition and thoughtfulness. They are life-giving."

JUMPY SPACE

Jeannie went on to say, "On a mundane level, we know that too much busy pattern and bold color in a nursery or playroom can make a normal person hyperactive and a hyper person impossible. Just last night I attended a lecture in an all-red room, with red seats, red curtains, red walls and red carpet on the floor. Next to me was a friend who normally is pleasant and gentle. She began jumping around in her chair and talking much louder and more often than usual. I could hardly wait to get out of there into the calm night air. Calmer colors and patterns are called for in many places.

It is tempting to make children's bedrooms too busy and too bright because of all the cute things available. Simplify, if you don't want nervous wrecks for kids."

FENG SHUI

"Jeannie, I've seen articles and references to an Oriental practice that has to do with design and decorating. What is that all about?"

"The ancient wisdom of *Feng Shui* (pronounced fung-shway) arrived in our land from the Chinese. They developed it as a system to bringing harmony of placement within space, aligned with the most basic laws of nature. *Feng Shui* first became popular in the United States when large international companies like IBM began using it as part of their plan for yielding success. Business has had excellent results in creating harmonious environments, and the rest of us began taking notice.

"*Feng Shui* sets forth the idea that unless you have nourishment and support from your environment your internal energy does not flow as it should. Lack of health and prosperity can be the result. Space has energy that sometimes has to be redirected. The Orientals see energy as a life force or *chi* that moves through space just as it does through our bodies.

"This correlates with quantum physics' new outlook. Yet mystics have been telling us for centuries that God is one, that everything is vibrating energy, that we are mostly made out of space, that material things are not as solid as we thought. Space, prayer and thought are all energies that have a direct effect on our health.

"When I first got acquainted with the art of *Feng Shui*, I looked upon it with a wary eye. It seemed strange and sometimes contrary to my design training and my Western sensibilities. However, after studying different authors and talking with practitioners of building design, I realized there was a great range of solutions that embraced the occupants' own sense of what was beautiful and what intuitively felt right to them.

"Heretofore, my internal sense of sculpting space had been mainly intuitive and design-driven, yet knowing the value of Eastern practices like meditation, I decided to keep an open mind. Activating a life force through principles as simple as placing your bed or desk in a better place for *chi* to flow seemed worth a try. Common sense and *Feng Shui* are usually compatible. The resting person in a bed should be able to see anyone coming through the door without having to turn around. Similarly, sitting at your desk with your back to the door can cause anxiety or restlessness.

"*Feng Shui* began to open doors for me in terms of design. The idea of developing creativity by enlivening the home's creative corner or the thought of improving health in the central living area were news to me. Prosperity and health have their own areas in a house, and these corners must have plants and other 'cures' in order for the environment to empower. Color has its own power to add. *Feng Shui* is a vast art and science, and I am only considering it briefly."

"Jeannie, I'm wondering if the coach who painted the locker rooms different colors may have known a little *Feng Shui*."

"Maybe! Just as the coach knew how to use color for power, we too can use our surroundings to empower us and to help one another. When that happens, it is a very great blessing. Winston Churchill once said that first we shape our spaces, and then our spaces shape us! To help a friend get well, we can clean up and pick up his or her room and establish order; we can bring in flowers, and we can bless the person with our own positive energy and prayer. It is environmental affirmation. It's hard to get well in the clinical, antiseptic, no-frills room of a hospital or a slovenly, ill-kept room at home. Improve the space and it will help the patient to get better.

"When we dive deeply into housecleaning and orderliness, we are not just working on the space around us. The soul itself is worked upon. Thomas Moore says, 'We work with the stuff of the soul by means of the things of life.' Create order and simplicity and harmony and balance. Let go of anything that is not either beautiful or useful."

LETTING GO

"That sounds," I suggested, "like the basic spiritual principle of letting go."

"Yes, eliminating the unnecessary creates space in which you can breathe and in which God can work. Artistic, orderly space points to that which is beyond itself, to the Creator behind all creation. When we experience such space, we are stopped in our tracks, as we say, 'Oh!' Our minds are affected by our surroundings, for better or for worse. It is good to make a beautiful place in which to live and work and love and worship and pray. Our space becomes our sanctuary.

"As we are blessed and quieted within, we are funded with power to bless others. Our cup overflows to those in need from the peace and harmony radiating within. A balance of giving and receiving occurs. Neither extravagant nor miserly with ourselves or with others, we remember that all is well. In this way the path of balance, I believe, becomes a path of blessing."

GOING HOME

All of these reflections about the blessings of home bring back memories of my own home and the neighborhood I grew up in. It was wonderful. Home was a warm, secure place in the winter, and yards and alleys proved to be great playgrounds in the summer. From time to time when I go back to my home city, I drive around the block where I once lived. Old memories come flooding back. Perhaps best of all, I notice that whoever lives where I used to live has kept up the old house, which now must be eighty years old. It is spic-and-span and well cared for. I smile when I pass by this old friend, this old house of mine. It blessed me for twenty-five years, and I am grateful.

If home is so important, it is of great value to pass on to future generations both our earthly dwellings and our larger earth home as blessings. For having such a sense of home is indeed a fundamental human need. An old storyteller once told this tale:

While walking through the woods, a traveler came upon a cabin with a note pinned to the door. It read, "If you wish, come in and rest for awhile. Feel free to build a fire, make a meal and lay down your head. Stay for an hour, a day or a week. Take what you need and be refreshed. We ask nothing of you in return but that you help make this a welcome respite for others traveling along the way. If you can, please chop some wood to replenish the woodpile. If you have extra supplies, leave what you can for those who will come after you. If you have nothing to spare, know that you are still welcome and invited to return again.

The traveler could not believe her eyes. She accepted the surprising invitation, and after being refreshed she prepared to make the cabin ready for the next traveler. She contributed what supplies she could spare, then chopped and carried in some firewood.

Upon departing, she spied a traveler in the distance, but walked on, happy in the knowledge that she had done her part and passed on a blessing in this house by the side of the road.

SCRIPTURE IMAGES AND PASSAGES FOR REFLECTION

Hebrew Scriptures

Exodus 12: 7-13 — *Blood on the doorposts*
...They shall take some of its blood and apply it to the two doorposts and the lintel of every house....

2 Kings 4: 8-17 — *The Shunammite's hospitality toward Elisha*
...You lavished all this care on us; what can we do for you?

Christian Scriptures

Luke 19: 1-6 — *Hospitality at the home of Zachaeus*
...Zacchaeus, come down quickly, for today I mean to stay at your house....

John 19: 25-27 — *John took Mary into his own home*
...And from that hour the disciple took her into his home.

BLESSING PRAYERS

BLESSING OF A HOME

O God, send your angels to bless this house:
Michael from the east to make it strong,
Gabriel from the west to make it radiant,
Raphael from the south to make it warm with hospitality,
a guardian angel from the north to protect it always.
Where angels gather

may humans here be enlightened;
may humans here grow in the Spirit;
may humans here speak wisdom;
may humans here give comfort and solace.
Bless this house, angels dear,
for whom God's love commits us here.

BLESSING OF A DOOR

In and out, in and out,
so goes our journey.
As we pass this way,
bless this door today
for it leads us out
and beckons us home.

Close it to strife;
open it to welcome.
Through this portal
guide our steps
on the way of peace,
on the way of joy.

Bless our coming;
bless our going.
May this day's key
lock in our safety,
lock out all strife
and unlock our heart's desire.

BLESSING OF A FAMILY ROOM

Tick tock, tick tock, ring, ring, up, up, move, gulp, out.
Commute, sirens, traffic, push, pull, in, out.
Go out, move, up, down, all around.
Sell, buy, learn, decide, act, hurry.
In line, out of line, on line,
press, stress, regress.
So goes our journey.
So goes our day!

Until:

This family room today:
a place to disconnect from stress.
Bless and refocus the world's blur.
Open our eyes.
Open our arms.
Open our minds.
Open our hearts.
Let us be!

BLESSING OF HOUSE PLANTS

O Divine Gardener and Artist,
you have painted the skies blue,
you have watered the earth
and have even given promise to muddiness.
You have carpeted the earth in verdant green.

May these living creatures, our plants,
breathe life into our home.
They live. They breathe. They grow.
Blessed be life!
Blessed be breath!
Blessed be growth!

Bless these plants.
They have developed from seeds.
Blessed be small beginnings.
They have been watered with care.
Blessed be attention and nurturing.
They have grown in the midst of mud.
Blessed be the fruit of fertile messiness.
They smile at the sun.
Blessed be openness and optimism.
They flower forth in beauty.
Blessed be our hopes and dreams.

THE BLESSINGS OF PILGRIMAGE

I am sending you to a land I will show you...and I will bless you.

—Genesis 12: 1-2

Through the centuries, both in the East and the West, pilgrimages have been considered a form of prayer and a source of great blessings. A pilgrim's journey recognizes hallowed places. To walk a pilgrimage path is to follow a blessing way.

A PILGRIM'S JOURNEYS — TWO PARABLES

I. A TRAVELER'S JOURNAL — 1960

Today is the day of the long-anticipated train journey to San Francisco!

2:30 P.M. I walk down the platform alongside the train — the silver California Zephyr. Steam hisses from a car's undercarriage. I search for the number of my car. I find it, step up onto a little yellow stool and enter. I go down a long narrow passageway until I find compartment C. It's nice and cozy. I stow my gear and sit watching the milling crowd outside. I can sense lots of anticipation as the people flock past my picture window.

3:05 P.M. With a gentle movement, we begin to slide through the train yard. We pick up speed as we pass by commercial buildings until we finally leave the great city of Chicago and move swiftly through the Illinois countryside. Naperville, Princeton, Galesburg all flash by. I get a sense of really getting away from home and beginning a grand adventure — all the way to the shores of the Pacific Ocean!

4:30 P.M. I wander out into the corridor and make my way to the dining car. Seated at a linen-clothed table, I write down my order for the waiter. Others seat themselves. Over a red carnation in the center of the table, we introduce ourselves and enjoy conversation over a first-class meal.

5:30 P.M. I leave the diner and head back to the lounge car. It has a dome for better viewing. So I climb the stairs, grab a seat and sit back to enjoy the scarlet-splashed sunset over the Illinois plains and its row upon row of ripening corn. When this train sees the edge of the sun again we'll be somewhere in western Nebraska — another time zone, another world. I order a drink and begin to converse with a passenger from New York.

6:15 P.M. The attendant announces that we are crossing the mighty Mississippi River into Iowa. I look out at the great river and see barges slowly making their way toward New Orleans. This is the granddaddy of all America's rivers. What a sight in the descending dusk!

8:30 P.M. I go back to my compartment, where my bed is all made up. I stretch out and begin my novel. Time slips by. Every so often I hear the clanging bells of a crossing. I look out, see the cars waiting to cross and wonder where they are going and who they might be.

10:00 P.M. I put away the novel and slip under the covers. As I lay back and relax, I am rocked by a gently swaying motion and serenaded by the rhythmic clickety-click of the wheels. I don't bother to pull down the shade. There's a full moon tonight and the moonlight lulls me to sleep.

Midnight. Passing lights outside the window awaken me. I roll on my side and peer out. A station sign says "Council Bluffs." I wonder who counseled here — then I remember: Lewis and Clark did 150 years ago as they came up the Missouri. And this is the very spot that Lincoln selected as the starting point for the Transcontinental Railroad.

Then in a few moments we cross the wide Missouri. I can see its banks below. In one evening, I have crossed the two greatest rivers in

North America! We are now in Nebraska as we crawl to a stop at the Omaha station, standing of the west bank of the Missouri. I pull down the shade most of the way and go back to sleep.

6:30 A.M. Light filters in around the edges of the shade. I pull it up. I find myself in a different world. No more rows of corn. Rather, the terrain is rolling hills with sagebrush, and on the distant horizon the faintest hint of purple peaks. We are in Mountain Time now. The Midwest is behind us. The Colorado mountains are ahead.

7:30 A.M. By the time I get to the diner, we are approaching Denver. Seated across from me is a 22-year-old lassie from Australia. I am fascinated by her tales of the outback. When I express my astonishment that she is so far from home, she responds, "Sure, don't ya know, mate, that all we Aussies try to go around the world before we get serious and settle down?" Then she tells me how her brother met his future wife from the States in Munich at the Octoberfest, while dancing on a table! With a big smile, she says, "You've got to dance on tables — you never know who you might meet there!"

"Not enough room on our table," I respond, "but I sure have enjoyed visiting with you across from this table." She is up and on her way with her young batteries fully recharged.

As I finish my leisurely breakfast, I notice we are backing into Denver for some reason unknown to me. After breakfast, I go back up to the dome car. An hour after arriving, we leave the Denver station and twist our way up the foothills toward towering peaks on the horizon. They are magnificent! A child in the car exclaims, "Mom, how are we going to get over those big mountains?" The answer comes soon enough. The silver train plunges into the great Moffat tunnel that burrows its way beneath some of the highest peaks on the North American continent. We are enveloped in black. Only the dim walking lights allow us to see at all. I sit in wonder! At some point in this tunnel we will pass under the continental divide. Right now, the streams above us flow down the mountains to the east, but when we reach a spot midway in this tunnel, the streams above us will flow west.

The dark allows me to ponder. So long ago, our ancestors trekked westward. So long ago, Thomas Jefferson sent Lewis and Clark to find a water passage to the west. When this tunnel was dug, in a way it fulfilled a dream Thomas Jefferson never really anticipated — an unlikely easy path to the Pacific.

7:50 A.M. Suddenly, the light brightens, and we burst out of the dark into brilliant sunshine, towering mountains, tall pines. A sparkling stream runs beside us. Thus begins our oddessey through the gorgeous scenery of Colorado's western slope. What a day! I am reminded of a prayer I've heard at church, "All creation gives God praise!" And I am moved to say a morning prayer, "Yes, indeed, God, maker of the mighty mountain! They are glorious — the work of your hands! Glory! Glory!" And I recall that these pillars of stone are actually dancing! That's what a physicist friend says. There is movement in them. And why wouldn't they dance? They are made up to party — dressed in all their finery. Their bodices are threaded with shimmering golden aspen and their skirts with verdant greenery. And they have the dancing, laughing streams for partners.

On this day's journey I will stay in the dome, catching a sandwich along the way. Winter Park, Granby, Glenwood Springs and the road to Aspen and Grand Junction — all are small Colorado interludes in a continuing pageant of beauty upon beauty. My dome window frames a new work of God's art with every passing mile!

7:02 P.M. I put my novel aside and take out my journal. I begin to write as twilight stretches its dark fingers between rocky crevices and buttes. I wonder, did the mapmakers use geographical landmarks to draw the state lines. For here we are in Green River, Utah, and it *is* different from Colorado. No less beautiful — but unique with its buttes and craggy outcroppings. This is the country of wide-open spaces. It is easy to imagine the Native Americans riding their ponies over this rocky land. They traveled light, leaving the land as beautiful as they found it. Not always true of the white man who pushed the natives — and all of life — to the margins. During this nighttime we will pass Salt Lake. When I think of the Mormon pioneers crossing these vast spaces in prairie schooners seeking their promised land and all the other settlers whose motto was "Westward Ho!" it reminds me that although my own life journey sometimes hits bumps and demands detours I need to keep moving on. Westward Ho! But like the Native Americans, I also need to travel light — not overburdened by the demands of this consumer society in which I seem more and more immersed.

11:00 P.M. Bedtime again. What a wonderful day! My spirit is saturated with beauty! And now the night is pulled down over the beauty so that we can discover it all anew with the dawn.

9:00 A.M. No discovery at dawn this day. Instead, a lolling about in my berth, so relaxed that I can enjoy the luxury of a couple of hours of extra sleep. When I pull up the shade, I discover we are in Nevada!

9:40 A.M. I am in the diner, and we are rolling into Reno. By the time I finish breakfast and linger over a steaming cup of coffee, we will be in California and close to Lake Tahoe.

11:00 A.M. Yesterday was the delicious cake of the Colorado Rockies. Today is the frosting — California's Feather River Canyon. We're approaching the Sierras, the last looming obstacle that stood in the way of the pioneers' westward trek. Now, the range is no longer an obstacle but rather the California gateway to the Pacific.

Noon. Lunch, and we are on a downhill roll now, breaking into the golden California hills.

3:20 P.M. Roseville — the mountains are behind us. The Pacific Ocean beckons.

5:30 P.M. Oakland. I debark the silver Zephyr, which has indeed been like a spring breeze wafting its way over the plains, beyond the mountains, toward the setting sun.

6:00 P.M. I board a ferry to take me across the bay to San Francisco. The setting sun frames the skyline of the great city of Saint Francis. It is a gorgeous sight. I hum a tune: "This land is your land, this land is my land, from California to the New York islands...." Yes indeed, but it is more than my land and your land. It is God's magnificent creation. I have been privileged to see it and walk upon it and savor its countless blessings. This journey has been more than a trip — it has been a pilgrimage!

II. FORTY YEARS LATER — A FLIGHT LOG: CHICAGO TO SAN FRANCISCO, THE YEAR 2000

Monday

9:40 A.M. Arrive O'Hare, check luggage, go through security, red light flashes with a warning signal. I forgot. Remove change. Try again. O.K. Wait for flight.

10:00 A.M. Announcement: "Incoming flight delayed. Stand by."

10:30 A.M. Announcement: "Flight has arrived; we will begin boarding shortly."

10:45 A.M. We can begin boarding now. Waiting in line, pass through tube into the bigger aluminum tube that will take me to San Francisco. Pick up a sack lunch on the way into plane.

Pilot: "Sorry, we have a delay, but we are number nine to take off."

11:10 A.M. Take off, followed by beverages, followed by movie, plane window shades pulled. I am wedged into the middle seat.

1:15 P.M. Somewhere over the Colorado Rockies — movie is over. Cloud cover — nothing to see.

I eat my sack lunch: a piece of ham and cheese on dry white bread, plus an apple and a cookie. I plug in my computer and get to work on business.

2:25 P.M. PACIFIC TIME Nervous aisle seat holder next to me asks the flight attendant, "How soon into "San Fran?" I've got a 3 o'clock business meeting."

She smiles and responds, "You mean San Francisco?"

"San Fran" — "Frisco!" What's the difference?"

She responds, "We'll be arriving pretty soon."

He is not consoled. As he turns around, he inadvertently jabs me in the ribs. He pulls out the flight phone and dials in. "This damn plane got off late; I'll get to the meeting as soon as I can." He then carries on a long conversation, disrupting my thought patterns. So I unplug my computer and wait impatiently for a landing announcement.

2:45 A.M. PACIFIC TIME Pilot announces approach to San Francisco. Low lying fog, visibility poor. A few bumps, a few white knuckles. We break through the fog — nothing but ocean below. Down, down, closer to the water. Suddenly, land appears right below us. We touch ground. There is a patter of nervous applause. We wait for a terminal jet way to open up. We are like racehorses at a starting gate. Finally, the ding tone — the sound we so eagerly await — announcing that the aircraft has come to a full stop. We are up in an instant — up, but not out. We open the overhead bins and awkwardly try to wedge our carry-ons between us and the people standing cheek to jowl with us. We wait and wait, tense, hunched over our carry-ons. Finally, there is movement, slow at first but then surging outward. We go through the tube and rush to the phones to announce our late arrival.

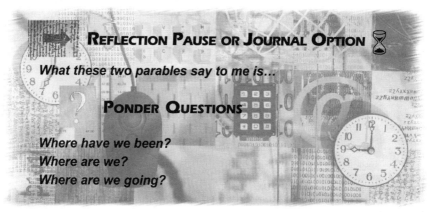

REFLECTION PAUSE OR JOURNAL OPTION

What these two parables say to me is...

PONDER QUESTIONS

Where have we been?
Where are we?
Where are we going?

THE PACE OF LIFE'S JOURNEY

When we were children, the teacher would call our name and we would respond, "Present!" Today we are propelled through space like cannon shots — Chicago to San Francisco at 550 miles an hour! And in our ever-accelerating cyber- and virtual-reality-world, we run the risk of never really being present anywhere. When we lose our sense of presence, there are no hallowed places, no special shrines. And if we fail to sense that some places are special, then no places are. No wonder we despoil our earth home of its ability to bless us! We move too quickly to receive her blessings.

Notice the words *flight, trip* and *pilgrimage.* The one-syllable *flight* and *trip* are sharp and quick in their pronunciation. On the other hand, the word *pilgrimage* contains three syllables and requires that we linger as we pronounce it. Notice how we even condense our words. "San Fran" is quicker than having to say "San Francisco." Not only does *pilgrimage* take longer to say, more importantly, it requires a more leisurely pace to accomplish. In his classic work *Leisure: The Basis of Culture,* Joseph Pieper proposes that leisure requires a contemplative attitude. He goes on to point out that such an attitude allows us to steep ourselves in the wonders of creation. A traveler goes at 550 miles an hour. A pilgrim, however, must slow down to a contemplative pace to find the meaning that lies at the heart of pilgrimage.

The great religions of the world affirm pilgrimage as a contemplative journey. It is seen as a special opportunity to make a deliberate, reflective and sacred journey and to be blessed by special places and unexpected encounters.

We can even turn ordinary journeys into pilgrimages if we are willing to be fully present and open to sacred meetings that may come our way. That was true for Susan Gallagher on a train trip to Dublin. She was so moved by the encounter that she wrote this poem:

A Chance Encounter

He lumbered down the aisle,
feet knocking against the chairs,
knees bent to steady his gait.
Stopping at her booth, he folded
into the seat and eased
his thickness onto the backrest.

Blue eyes set firmly deep
darted from table to window
to trees flashing past his vision
on the train to Dublin. He wiped
sweat from bushy eyebrows and lower lip.

"Do you read a lot?" he wondered.
"I do," she answered, smiling,
setting down the book to notice
the eyes. His hands fluttered, flecked
nothing from his lapel.

The train rounded a bend, they
leaned into the curve and slipped
into conversation. He told stories,
she listened. He cried for the loss
of his love. She held his hand.

The train clattered
into Heuston Station
and they parted.

—Susan Gallagher, Clifden, Ireland

She set "down the book to notice." Letting go of her own concerns, she was truly present to a holy encounter. She blessed his presence. He blessed hers. To travel as a pilgrim is to be open to the unfolding mystery of whatever happens. To let go of control and open up to unexpected encounters, synchronicities, graced moments, pilgrims' rewards.

CROAGH PATRICK — THE RELUCTANT PILGRIM

On July 25, 1973, my friend Larry and I were in a pub in Westport, Ireland. We had journeyed for two weeks around that beautiful island and were winding down, for we were to catch our plane the next day for our return home.

As we sat in a lovely restaurant, savoring a cup of coffee, the only dancers on the small dance floor before us were a silver-haired couple. We sat in silence. We had been together day in and day out for a fortnight, and we were in a simmering down mood. Suddenly, I broke the silence and said to Larry, "I think I'm going to dance before leaving Ireland!" He looked at me with a raised eyebrow — Larry was sometimes a little skeptical of my spontaneous urges. As the couple came to sit down at their table near us, I got up, went over and said, "Sir, may I have the pleasure of one dance with your lovely wife, if she would acquiesce?" They both did, and I found myself in an unplanned encounter/tour on the dance floor. For the first dance, you don't need to say much, but when she suggested, "Let's do one more," we both seemed to recognize that we'd reached a point of introductions. "What do you do?" and "Where do you live?" she asked. I identified myself as a pastor from the Midwest. I then asked her what she did. "Oh, I'm a psychiatrist associated with Cornell University." I blinked. Then I thought, "Oh, Oh! Here I am on a dance floor with a psychiatrist looking right into the depths of my psyche!"

After a nice conversation with her and her husband, I returned to Larry. He rolled his eyes and said, "Well, you've had your fun — now let's go out and get a snack. I saw a Wimpy's Hamburger shop down the street." It was now 11:00 P.M., but Larry was a night person, and for him the night was still young.

When we emerged into the cool night air, we were astounded to discover the streets of Westport teeming with people. We asked a Garda policeman what was going on, and he responded, "Well wouldn't you be knowin' that this is the night when the pilgrims come from all over Ireland to climb the holy mountain and pray for peace in Ireland?"

Larry's eyes lit up, and he said, "Let's see what's going on!" I was less enthused, but he had the car keys. When we reached the foot of Croagh Patrick, the 2,510-foot-high mountain, cars were parked everywhere. As we looked up, tiny dots of light were moving upward. That night, 50,000 pilgrims were streaming up the mountain where in the fifth century Saint Patrick had fasted and prayed.

Larry said, "Let's do it!"

"Do what?" I exclaimed.

"Climb the mountain!" he responded.

I gasped, "That's crazy! We have to fly home tomorrow, and we're not dressed to be climbing any mountain!" When I saw the gleam in Larry's eye, I realized he was going to climb this mountain, no matter what I said. So I fell in with him, a reluctant pilgrim on an unplanned, unanticipated adventure. Quite some time later, when we were about halfway up the mountain, I said, "Stop! I'm not going to climb another foot. You go on, and I'll wait for you and catch you on the way back." "Oh, come on." he said, "We need to find out what's at the top of the mountain." I wouldn't budge, so he went on ahead.

As I sat there catching my breath, I began to notice what a wide variety of pilgrims were passing by — young and old, boyfriends and girlfriends and some old-timers climbing the mountain "the old-fashioned way," by going barefoot!

As I sat and thought about it, I realized Larry would go back home and tell all our mutual friends of his exploit of climbing the mountain and about how old Fitz "wimped out." So I gritted my teeth and resumed the climb. The last 100 feet were the worst — over loose shale — and I had to crawl up on my hands and knees.

He would describe my arrival later in these words, "There I was by 'Patrick's Bed' with the pilgrims marching around in a circle saying their prayers. And I glanced over to the rim of the mountain and saw two beady eyes looking up over the edge, and I knew that Fitz did not wimp out after all. He made it to the top of the holy mountain."

Once there, I gradually began to feel a sense of accomplishment, and I found my cranky mood begin to mellow. Then, when the first pink edges of dawn appeared over the bay that lay right below the edge of the path, my attitude began to change perceptibly. You can always see farther and clearer from a mountaintop. When we finally began to make our descent, I could see the long line of pilgrims in a new way. There was a sense of being in a holy place and being joined to a procession of pilgrims that seemed to stretch right back to Patrick in the fifth century.

With the sunrise, it dawned on me that this place was hallowed ground. We would not arrive back at our hotel until 8:30 A.M. We had left the night before as tourists. We came back as pilgrims.

When we arrived back in the States, the experience was so vivid in my imagination that I sat down and wrote about it. My article "The Reluctant Pilgrim" was published in a Sunday supplement magazine. I had never even dreamed of writing before that experience. Since then, I've often wondered if I ever would have started writing had Larry not challenged me to forgo wimping out and to keep climbing the holy mountain.

Over the years, he and I would share that story with friends, and that unexpected pilgrimage became a kind of mile marker in our long friendship. The day before Saint Patrick's Day in 1998, my good friend Larry died of a heart attack. I told the story one more time for him during his funeral homily. We all need fellow pilgrims who are soul friends — the Celts called them *anam cara* — who challenge our souls to be steadfast in our climb toward holiness and full humanity. Larry was truly such an *anam caras* for me. In the dedication of my book *A Contemporary Celtic Prayerbook,* I wrote, "Dedicated to Larry Dorsey. He has climbed Croagh Patrick, and he now can see farther than any of us can dream!"

I know that now in my later years I refuse to give up on projects and hopes largely because on a pilgrim's path a quarter century ago he encouraged me to venture up and to keep climbing. This unexpected blessing from a spontaneous pilgrimage has truly left a lasting impression on my soul.

REFLECTION PAUSE OR JOURNAL OPTION

Recall some unplanned meeting of your own that turned out to be an unexpected blessing.

PONDER QUESTIONS

As in the song title, when did you last experience an "amazing grace?"

What is the attitude that allows amazing grace incidents to unfold in our lives?

I have made return pilgrimages to Croagh Patrick — not to climb to the top again but to climb up the first station on the mountain and pray there. There are seven stations that lead up to the summit. At the first is a lovely statue of Saint Patrick with his arms held out in blessing over the County Mayo countryside. On one visit, a group of five of us agreed to split up for forty-five minutes by ourselves. When we reassembled, Suzy, a Jewish lady from New York, had tears in her eyes. She said softly, "I am moved to tears by the holiness of this place."

SENSE OF PLACE

Why do we need to make pilgrimages to "special places"? Native American author David Abram, writing about oral cultures — and the Celts have a strong oral history — says this:

> A particular place in the land is never, for an oral culture, just a passive or inert setting for the human events that occur there. It is an active participant in those occurrences. Indeed, by virtue of its underlying and enveloping presence, the place may even be felt to be the source of the primary power that expresses itself through the various events that unfold there.

This view illustrates in a profound way the sense of reverence native peoples have for the place where they stand and where the spirits of their ancestors still hover. Certainly, the spirit of the fifth century Patron Saint of Ireland hovers at Croagh Patrick. To make a pilgrimage there is to connect with Patrick himself though the mountain and the path that he trod.

Pilgrimages acknowledge that places have unique flavors, personalities and quirks — and messages laden with levels upon levels of meaning. It is traditional for pilgrims who climb Croagh Patrick to take home a stone. The one on my mantle has two ancient lines running through it, indicating eons of evolution. This rock does speak! It remembers before the dawn of human awareness, and its story is written in its veins.

PILGRIMAGES ALLOW US TO REMEMBER

A pilgrimage to this revered place allows us to stand where Patrick stood and to remember what he stood for. Pilgrimages are about such remembering. In our post-modern world everything changes so quickly. Computer files become obsolete in a decade. Just before the millennium a computer analyst informed me that to solve the Y2K problem we had to revert to old "obsolete" Russian computer systems because our current computers in the West were so updated that they no longer remembered!

In a world where everything seems to be in rapid flux, pilgrimages remind us that history is an unfolding process and that we are connected to the events and messages that Patrick brought down from the holy mountain. For one thing, his was the first voice to condemn slavery. That old message is not obsolete. In many parts of the world it needs to be heard now just as much as it was then.

MEANING

In a more powerful way than any book or computer screen could create, pilgrimage sites connect us with meaning. Even national shrines like the Washington Monument, the Statue of Liberty and Gettysburg are all hallowed places that speak meaningful messages by their silence and enduring presence. We need their messages so that we might reclaim what is best from history as well as not repeat the worst. In this way we can be blessed and not cursed by the past.

In the last several years I have made pilgrimages a part of my vacation time. Recently, a one-day pilgrimage took me to the Statue of Liberty and Ellis Island. As we approached these sites on the ferry, I saw before me what so many of our ancestors beheld when they escaped their old countries and were welcomed here by the lovely lady bearing the torch of freedom. For those who were driven out by famine in the nineteenth century, Lady Liberty not only ushered them into freedom, she also offered them food and sustenance.

On a more recent trip, we drove to the embarkation docks of Cobh in Ireland, where my ancestors would have embarked. My cousin and I stood there on the dock and looked out at what our ancestors saw as they departed from Ireland. When they left, they would never have the advantage of returning, even for a visit. So the night before emigrants sailed off, a "wake" was held to say good-byes to kin they would never see again.

Today's native Irish who prosper have never forgotten their own famine, and whenever famine appears in our day, the Irish are among the first to offer assistance. They recall the worst of times and resolve that it should not be repeated in our time.

On that trip to Ireland I also hiked up to the ruins of a village deserted during the famine. To follow the path of my ancestors on their emigration famine walk was a religious experience for me — a true blessing. It opened up a pilgrim's concern for those throughout our world today who do not have enough to eat while we are worried about becoming more overweight. Because of the wonderful cuisine in Ireland, I actually gained eight pounds on that trip. Had it not been for the pilgrimage to Cobh, and the short famine walk, I would have returned quite blissful — but unmindful of how things once were, and should not be again. Such a pilgrimage can bless the pilgrim by raising consciousness and inspiring generosity.

Happy Times

Pilgrimages can also recall happy and joyful experiences. On a recent one-day stop in Boston, we not only walked the freedom walk and visited the graves of John Hancock and Ben Franklin, we also stopped for lunch at "Cheers" and shared happy memories of Sam, Norm and the rest of the TV sit-com gang. Such pilgrimages, and those to sites of personal, family, religious or national celebrations — even revisiting locations of favorite family vacations — can cheer the heart and soul.

Special Blessings

Sometimes pilgrimages are made for the purpose of seeking special blessings. There is a story of a couple who for many years had been childless and who deeply desired to have children. A friend recommended they make a pilgrimage to the Shrine of Saint Anne in Canada and pray there that they might have a child the next year. They did, and, sure enough, within a year their first child was born. So they made another pilgrimage the following year — and, lo and behold, a year later they had triplets! Soon after that birth, which amounted to four children in two years, they were asked, "Are you going to make a pilgrimage to St. Anne's shrine next year? The father was about to say yes, but before he could get the words out, his wife interrupted and replied, "Next year, I think we'll make a pilgrimage to Disneyland."

LITTLE BIGHORN

At the turn of the nineteenth century it was commonly a tradition to have a painting over saloon bars picturing George Custer, his yellow hair unfurled in the wind, standing amid fallen horses, taking his last stand against the "savages" encircling him. But if you make a pilgrimage to Little Bighorn, you will find a much more textured message. You can look below and see the meandering stream where the Cheyenne were encamped on a land that they and their ancestors treasured. Stand at the top of the rise and listen to the wind and see the prairie grass rustle, and you will sense there is a much bigger picture here, a larger and deeper story than the mythologized portraits of the white man's bravery. A pilgrim's path through such a vivid place as Little Bighorn opens both the senses and the heart to a greater reality. Walking "a mile in their moccasins" helps us remember some things that the white man has conveniently forgotten: the deep connection that native peoples possessed and cultivated. This is a special grace and blessing that only pilgrimage sites can bestow. Being at the action sites and standing on the holy ground has the power to flood the senses and fill the heart with the meaning held in that ground.

As we become more and more interconnected through our cyberworld, we can also, in some sense, become more imprisoned. Images and words are one step removed from real, concrete places. By journeying to special places, we allow the earth to speak, the sky to hover, the wind to whisper.

BLACK ELK'S SHRINE

Years after my first Croagh Patrick experience, when I was writing my second book *Seasons of the Earth and Heart*, which contained several Native American themes, I recalled the value of pilgrimage and how it helped me begin to write. So one day, driving across Nebraska, I decided to take a detour and make a small pilgrimage to Black Elk's shrine at a park near Blair, Nebraska. The site was dedicated to Black Elk and John Neihardt, his biographer and Nebraska's poet laureate.

Neihardt interviewed Black Elk toward the end of the native holy man's long life. As a child, Black Elk had a vivid vision that showed the sacred hoop, the holy circle of the Sioux broken. He yearned for it to be mended and mourned for its return in the sunset of his life. His vision is contained in a book that has become a classic, *Black Elk Speaks*.

The shrine to Black Elk is very beautiful, situated in the rolling Missouri River bluffs. It contains a circular path crowned by a beautiful colored tile mosaic in the form of a circled cross. There, beneath the cross, I prayed to the four directions as Black Elk would have done. Then I put my book project in the hands of Black Elk and Kateri Tekakwitha, a patroness for Native American Catholics. At that moment, I not only felt close to them but also sensed that I was standing on holy ground. I also felt that I needed their help and blessing.

Later that evening, when I opened my daily prayer book to the page for that day I made an interesting discovery. I found that the saint honored that day, unbeknownst to me, was Kateri Tekakwitha. Coincidence? Synchronicity? Maybe. But, for sure, a blessing!

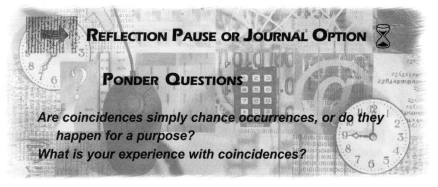

REFLECTION PAUSE OR JOURNAL OPTION

PONDER QUESTIONS

Are coincidences simply chance occurrences, or do they happen for a purpose?
What is your experience with coincidences?

OTHER PILGRIMAGES

Doing research for *Seasons of the Earth and Heart* took me to New Mexico, where I made a pilgrimage to the lovely shrine at Chimayo. There, every Holy Week, native people walk many miles to the old adobe church with the hole in its floor. As is the case with many shrines, healing powers are attributed to the site. At Lourdes, pilgrims bring home water from the font that sprang up at the spot where the village girl Bernadette received her visions of the Virgin Mary. At Chimayo, pilgrims bring home blessed dirt. Many healings have been ascribed to the faithful who use the dirt as an aid to prayer. In an age when the earth suffers so much wounding from humankind, honoring holy dirt from Mother Earth would seem appropriate and timely. I keep my dirt from Chimayo in a little vase on the shelf that I call my prayer shelf. When I later visited Tara in Ireland, the site where Saint Patrick lit the great Easter fire, I gathered a little of the old sod from there and added it to my Chimayo dirt. Besides being sacred ground upon which the tribes of Ireland were reconciled by Patrick, the earth from Tara is the soil from which my ancestors sprang. I also have a bottle of spring water from Saint Brigid's holy well — the same water that nourished my forebears. Having this water and earth in an honored place in my home shrine gives me a sense of place and rootedness. Not only are this soil and water the ancient origin of my body, they also symbolize the ancient origin of my faith and spiritual life.

LOURDES

Perhaps the most famous pilgrimage site in the Western world is Lourdes in the south of France. There in 1858, a village girl was visited by the Virgin Mary. Mary directed the child Bernadette to scoop up some soil and a spring gushed forth. She also directed that a shrine be built there. Her requests have been granted, and each year thousands of pilgrims flock to Lourdes, many of them seeking physical or spiritual healing. The grotto is lined with crutches left by cured pilgrims. A commission of doctors has long monitored the alleged healings at Lourdes, and only after much study and clear evidence has the commission declared some of these cures to be miraculous — beyond any medical explanation. The story of Lourdes and the child Bernadette was even chronicled in a famous movie, *The Song of Bernadette*. In 1933 Bernadette was declared a saint, and today her uncorrupted body rests in a class tomb at Nevers in France.

The area of Lourdes surrounding the shrine can be quite disappointing from a spiritual perspective. The street is lined with hucksters selling all varieties of religious goods. However, on entering the grounds of the shrine itself, the atmosphere changes dramatically. The site is filled with reverent pilgrims. Many sick and suffering are brought from far and wide.

Each spring, two dear friends of mine, Jeannie and Jack, journey with other Knights of Malta and act as stretcher-bearers for a sick person. Once beyond the commercial hubbub of the city, it is the sick who take first place at the shrine. The grotto area is a different world, a sacred place, a different zone. The sick, who in other places are closeted away, are lifted up and dipped into the blessed Lourdes water that flows from the spring exposed by Bernadette. Their presence makes the Magnificat come alive: "You have raised the lowly to high places" (Luke 1: 52).

Forty years after my own birth and baptism I made a pilgrimage to Lourdes and allowed myself to be briefly submerged in the flowing spring water, as many pilgrims do. It's a religious experience that demands a trust and a letting go — especially since one is surrounded by so many persons with such a variety of maladies bathing there at the same time. However, this trust is an essential characteristic necessary for any spiritual seeker or pilgrim. To make a pilgrimage is to make a prayerful journey with no rewards or results guaranteed. The true pilgrim may seek to have specific needs met but is open to whatever God chooses to grant. The pilgrim trusts that there will be graces and gifts, but the giving is in God's hands. This seems to be the attitude of many of the sick who are brought to Lourdes, and it's an attitude that's contagious. Only a minority is actually healed, but most everyone there seems to be gifted with blessings of consolation and renewed hope.

Each evening at Lourdes a candlelight procession winds through the grounds and toward the grotto where Mary visited Bernadette. The pilgrims chant "Ave! Ave! Ave! Maria" and gather round the shrine honoring Mary, who did not have the normal expectations of a teenage Jewish girl realized. Instead, she received other graces and replied, "Be it done unto me according to thy will." That seems to be the prayer of many Lourdes' pilgrims, sick or well. There is an abiding trust that God will give what is needed most. Thus, everyone at Lourdes comes away with a blessing.

THE CHARTRES LABYRINTH

A more ancient French pilgrimage site is the great twelfth century cathedral at Chartres. One of its many unique features is a labyrinth etched into the Cathedral floor that dates to 1220 A.D. It is a circular maze, a series of passageways leading to a central core. According to Alex Champion, an expert on labyrinths, it may have roots in a Cretan design from a thousand years before Christ. It is designed so that pilgrims can wind their way from the labyrinth's outer perimeter to its inner core. In one sense it's a metaphor for the pilgrim's lifelong journey from birth to death that takes many twists and turns along the way. In another sense, the labyrinth is a prayer-wheel. Christian pilgrims to Chartres in the Middle Ages would make the journey on their knees — in a spirit of prayerful penance. Perhaps this seems extremely austere. However, in an age like ours — which seldom sees a genuine admission of fault, and the most one can expect is an acknowledgment that a mistake has been made — admitting one's sins on one's knees might be a practice worth reclaiming. Many pilgrim journeys historically have been about doing penance for the righting of wrongs.

HOLLOWED AND HALLOWED GROUND

On one of my visits to Chartres, I stood on the spot where a church has stood since the eighth century and in the portal of a doorway that dates to 1145. Just then, through the door passed an ancient pilgrim clad in black, with a beard down to his waist, a pilgrim's staff in hand. He was like a vision out of the Middle Ages. Maybe he was! He looked as though he had been walking since the twelfth century. I glanced down at the stone blocks beneath his feet. They were hollowed out by the footsteps of thousands of pilgrims over hundreds of years. Once again, I felt blessed to be a part of more than a millennium of uninterrupted prayer.

ROOTS OF PILGRIMAGE

Pilgrimage is one of the oldest forms of prayer. If we look into the Hebrew Scriptures, we see the great exodus event — out of bondage, across the Reed Sea, across the desert, up to Mount Sinai and on to the Promised Land. This was a pivotal sacred journey for the chosen people. In our time, devout Jews make a pilgrimage to the Wailing Wall, returning to the foundations of the Jerusalem temple destroyed almost 2000 years ago.

Whereas their pagan neighbors often had a spirituality that was cyclical, the Hebrews followed a path with a destiny. In the New Testament, we see Jesus following this pilgrimage tradition. We find him on the road before being immersed in the Jordan and then again journeying deeper into the desert. He healed and taught on the road before eventually traveling up to Jerusalem for the climactic events of his passion. Jesus walked a blessing path. Jesus was a pilgrim. And even after his death it was out on the pilgrim road that Jesus accompanied the two disciples and finally revealed his risen presence to them at an inn on the way to Emmaus.

From the earliest days of Christianity, pilgrimages to Jerusalem and other holy sites have been a significant spiritual exercise. And from the fourth century — when Helena, the Roman emperor's mother, went to Jerusalem to seek the true cross — through the Middle Ages' culture of the Canterbury Tales, pilgrimage has been a spiritual way of life. Moreover, most of the great religions of the world have recognized the value of pilgrimage as a special opportunity to make a deliberate, sacred journey and to be blessed by special places. Islam, for example, requires a pilgrimage to Mecca at least once in a lifetime. And a pilgrimage to sacred temples and shrines is an important expression in Hinduism, Buddhism and other Eastern traditions.

PILGRIMAGE TODAY

Because of my writing, I have had occasion to travel far and wide and make many pilgrimages. Not many of my readers have opportunities for such extensive travel. And most of us usually travel not by foot or by train but on swift-flying planes. Nor do most people ever have the opportunity to travel to a foreign country on pilgrimage. But everyone has special places nearby that could offer a wonderful pilgrimage experience. The Black Elk shrine was only thirty miles from my home. Pilgrimages are about slowing down from our hyperpace and spending time in an out-of-the-way place. And "out-of-the-way" need not mean far away.

Perhaps Americans' most common occasion for a pilgrimage is Memorial Day. On that holiday we prayerfully visit graves of loved ones and tend them with care. Where I grew up, the people of Italian descent used Memorial Day as an opportunity not only to visit the gravesites of loved ones but also to visit with kinfolk they might not otherwise see. They would bring camp chairs and a picnic lunch and have a family gathering. This very ancient form of pilgrimage probably has its roots in the pre-Christian practice of leaving food offerings at Roman tombs.

When did I last spend some quiet time looking through family albums containing pictures of departed loved ones or friends?

When did I last visit the quiet and peace of a cemetery and spend some time remembering?

A visit to a nearby cemetery, retreat house or natural place of beauty can provide an opportunity for prayer. We can reflect on the meaning of our life and recall God's blessings we share with living and departed relatives and friends. Such opportunities offer a significant pause in the whirlwind of daily rush and stress. A cemetery visit slows us down — whether we walk in or are carried in! Also, many "walks" for good causes, such as the CROP Walk for the Hungry, are modern pilgrimages that can become prayer experiences of love and service.

Perhaps we also need to bring the notion of pilgrimage into some of the short trips that take so much of our busy time. For instance, we might create pilgrimage prayers for soccer moms or little league dads as they make their frequent treks. Samples of such prayers and pilgrimage blessings are found at the end of this chapter.

BLESSINGS OF PILGRIMAGE

From my own and others' experiences of pilgrimages, there are a great number of blessings that can result from prayerful journeys:

♦ The pilgrim slows down, moves according to God's time. A pilgrimage is a conversion from "road rage" and "road rush" to an unhurried, thoughtful pace.

♦ The awareness that we are pilgrims can sensitize us to walk with care and reverence upon the earth, both for the earth's sake and for the sake of all the other creatures that will come after us in the journey of life. To walk with awareness and reverence is to walk a "blessing path."

♦ A pilgrimage reminds the pilgrim of a destiny beyond the day's immediate worries and anxieties.

♦ A pilgrimage is an experience of the senses that influences the imagination and leaves lasting images.

♦ A pilgrimage remembers and brings to the present other pilgrims who have endured and reached their destiny.

♦ Hallowed places and sacred shrines possess spiritual energy. There is a unique blessing of energy in places such as Lourdes and Chimayo.

♦ Sometimes pilgrims can bring spiritual energy to a place that needs to be reclaimed; a place that has been cursed can now be blessed by pilgrims' feet. When I walked through Dachau in silence with a young Jewish woman, it was an act of reclaiming the dignity of that place through gestures of silence, repentance and reflection on the depths of human depravity. Today, many pilgrims flock to Medjugorje in Croatia. Perhaps Medjugorje and all the blood-smeared Balkans need pilgrims more than the pilgrims need to visit a holy site. For the very earth there cries out for exorcism.

♦ A pilgrimage challenges our trust and endurance. And often, pilgrimages seek healing. So does the earth beneath the pilgrims' feet.

♦ Perhaps the greatest blessing of pilgrimage is an increased sense of awe and respect — respect for the journey, for fellow pilgrims who all need healing and for our beautiful earth home in which we all live on borrowed time. Whether our spiritual journey is inches in a sickroom or miles on a foreign footpath, a prayerful pilgrimage can restore hope that we can arrive at the holy place beneath our feet and at last be at home.

Scripture Images and Passages for Reflection

Hebrew Scriptures

Exodus 12: 40-41 — *Exodus from Egypt*

This is a night of vigil, for God led them out of Egypt....

Exodus 40: 34-38 — *God's presence with the pilgrim people*

Then the cloud covered the meeting tent, and the glory of God filled the dwelling.... Whenever the cloud rose from the dwelling, the Israelites would set out on their journey....

Hebrew Scriptures

Matthew 4: 1-17 — *Jesus' journey into the desert and into his public ministry*

Then Jesus was led by the Spirit into the desert.... When he heard that John had been arrested he withdrew to Galilee. He left Nazareth....

Blessings for Nearby Pilgrimages

Blessing for an Internet Spiritual Journey — using websites for spiritual journeys. Here at a few possibilities:

- **http://web.lemoyne.edu/~bucko/jesuit.html** — *links to retreat centers as well as Jesuit services worldwide, including the Dublin Jesuits' site at:* www.sacredapace.ie
- **http:www.creighton.edu/CollaborativeMinistry/ cmo-retreat.html** — *spiritual retreat reflections*
- **http://www.cbn.ie/WESTPORT/** — **virtual pilgrimage up Croagh Patrick**

Blessing for a Pilgrimage On-Line

O God, let me approach this screen
    in another mode,
    with a different mood.
Like Peter's vision upon the sheet
    may this screen be a revelation.

May this pilgrimage
    on the information highway
    lead me to rest stops along the way
    as I sit back to be refreshed.

Once my hands have played the keys
    may they let go of control.
May my spirit let go of grasping
    and may the blessings that come to me
    seep deeply into my soul.

Lead me to quiet pastures,
    to refreshing waters.
Bless this journey.
    Bless this screen.
    Bless the Spirit it can reveal.

Blessing Prayer for Pilgrimages by Soccer Moms

Hear, O God, soccer moms and grandmas
    as we prepare for another day at the soccer field.
Bless the driving.
    Bless the playing.
    Bless the kicking.

They run around in circles for fun,
    yet unless you slow me down,
    the running in circles I do
    will not be fun for me.
Bless my stopping.
    Bless my sitting.

Bless my needed time outs.
They kick the ball with gusto,
    always aiming.
Bless me when I feel kicked.
    Bless me when my efforts seem aimless.
    Bless me when I am tired out.
Let me find true rest,
    not just more stress,
    at the old soccer field.

Blessing Prayer for Little League Pilgrimages by Dads and Grandpas

Another day, another game
    in the great American pastime.
Let it be a pastime,
    not a stress time.
This is a game of leisure:
    no fast breaks,
        just breaking pitches,
    no sudden death overtimes
        just lots of time for stretches.
Bless the kids;
    let them play.
Bless the coaches;
    let them coach.
Bless the parents;
    let us relax.

Blessing for a Young Mom's Pilgrimage to the Mall

Today we go for a stroll, just baby and me,
    credit cards at home.
Bless our strolling.

Bless our gazing.
Bless our browsing
at windows filled with "goods."
Praised be beauty!
Praised be abundance!
Praised be a stroll
where I do not have to buy.
Let me sit down at the mall
and people watch,
each one more dear
than any price-tagged item.
Yet let me look at baby
as more precious than all these goods.

Blessing for a Cemetery Pilgrimage

Before going to the cemetery, consider taking out the family album and recalling old faces and memories.

At the cemetery:

This is holy ground.
This is sacred space.
To this earth they have gone.
From here they will arise.

I bring a heart of gratitude
for those I now remember: _____.
I sense your presence,
souls who are dear to me.
I remember your kindnesses,
which still nourish my soul.
Blessed be your rest.
Blessed be your peace.
Blessed be our reunion,
when time is done.

BLESSINGS OF CREATIVE EXPECTATIONS

We have been born anew to a living hope. —I Peter 1: 3

THE PARABLE OF THE CHURCH COMMITTEE

As the committee huffed and puffed, it seemed to take one step forward and then two steps back. Each of us had our own ideas, and the process of trying to reach any kind of consensus was messy, not clear-cut and direct. That was my impression as we labored to agree on the final plans for our new church. One would think that the Holy Spirit would just take hold of the project and guide it smoothly to completion. After all, this was to be God's house. However, the Holy Spirit seemed content just to brood over our decision-making just as He/She had brooded over the first creation.

The two final tasks for our design committee remained: to choose the color of the carpet in the sanctuary and to consult with the artist who was to produce the Christ figure that would look down upon us from the sanctuary wall. We had engaged in our discussions for two hours. Marge held out for blue carpet. "It's so cool!" she would exclaim — I did not quite know whether she meant cool as in "with it" or cool as in "cold."

John, who operates a greenhouse, sure enough wanted green. Mary Ann who has red hair and flashing eyes, broke in with, "The people who are going to use this church need a 'wake up call'! They are too complacent. We all are. The Gospel ought to wake us up — not just with words from the pulpit but with the atmosphere of the sanctuary itself. Why not put in red carpet? After all, it was Christ's blood that was shed for us!"

"No, no," said Marilee, "red is just too much! We need some peace when we come to church — and no red brick wall either. When I enter a church with only brick walls in the sanctuary, it reminds me of that brick wall in the Saint Valentine's Day Massacre."

Round and round we went. It was like unraveling the strands of a ball with no cover. The more we unwound, the messier the whole process seemed to become. As I sat there bemused, I recalled an old adage that somebody had once told me, "You know what a camel, that ungainly, stupid-looking, cantankerous creature, is the product of? It's the result of a committee!" As I was thinking this, Al suggested that we take a break.

When we returned with coffee cups in hand, Al said, "I have another suggestion. Let's take a few moments in prayer and see if we can come up with some kind of compromise." So we prayed for three minutes, which seemed like an eternity. Betty, our architect, reopened the discussion by saying she had of another thought. "What if we considered burgundy. It has a touch of red to it, but on the color wheel when you mix red and green you get brown. Burgundy would not be as bright as red or as earthy as brown. Well?"

After what seemed like an interminable pause, Mary Ann said, "I kind of like that suggestion. It still has some red in it." And John responded, "Yes, green and red results in brown, but brown would be too stolid even though it is an earth color. Burgundy could be a good compromise. Other heads nodded. One problem solved, one more to go: the Christ figure for the sanctuary.

"What do you think?" asked Betty.

Mary Ann responded immediately, "I want the traditional crucifix with lots of blood on it! That's what our people are used to! They need to see the blood and recognize that Jesus is a suffering victim on the cross!"

Marilee sat with her arms crossed and shook her head, "No!" As everyone knew, she had recently been abandoned by her husband of nineteen years. She had been "traded in for a new model." Marilee was silent now, as she often was during the meetings, but the perceptive architect, Betty, looked at her and asked, "Marilee, how do you feel about the traditional depiction of a Jesus as a bloody victim?"

"I don't like it. I don't want to be a victim, and I don't really care to be reminded over and over that Jesus is a victim!"

Now, Father George interjected, "But he was, Marilee!"

"Yes, he was," said Marilee, "but only for three hours, not every moment of his life. Why do we always, every time we come into church, see him as a victim? I think victimhood is something to pass through — not to linger over." There was a long silence.

Then Betty spoke, "Well, you know, many new churches are placing an image of the Risen Christ instead of the suffering Christ in their sanctuaries. Often he is depicted with his arms extended in blessing."
"I like that!" responded Marilee. "We need his healing and blessing more that we need to be transfixed with his victimhood."

"But Marilee," sighed Mary Ann, "the crucified Christ is so traditional in our church. Many people won't readily accept a departure from that image."

A long silence ensued. Tradition and creativity were in a wrestling match, and it seemed to be a draw. Finally, Father George made a suggestion. "You know, it's almost eleven o'clock. We've all been here for three hours. Why don't we adjourn for the night? Let's sleep over our discussions. We can put this project under our pillows. Sometimes the best ideas come in our sleep. So, let's get a good night's rest and see if we can come to a conclusion tomorrow night." Heads nodded yes. "Seven P.M. tomorrow then?" Chairs began to shuffle, their movement indicating, "Good idea."

And so we gathered the next night at seven o'clock. We prayed, and then we discussed again. Out of a mishmash of ideas, something began to surface. John said, "You know, I tossed and turned all night, and when I woke up this morning, I had a new idea: Why not have two Christ figures? We could have a suffering figure for Lent, replaced by a glorious, risen Christ the rest of the year?" What had seemed an insurmountable problem last night came to a solution as all the committee members began to nod and then smile.

John's solution to the problem of the Christ figure is a parable. In real life, however, I had a similar experience when we approached a final decision about the kind of figure we would have at Saint Gerald's Church. At Easter, the suffering, nailed, pierced corpus high in the sanctuary of that new church in the suburbs of Omaha comes down off its cross and is replaced by a joyful, smiling, risen Christ beckoning all to come to him.

How we got there is a story that I know very well. Being on the design committee for three years prior to the construction of the new church gave me a unique opportunity to share fully in the creative expectations of a parish community. When it came time to consider the sanctuary design, my co-pastor, Father Larry Dorsey, and I conferred with our committee and met with the artist responsible for creating the Christ figure that would be so prominent in the new church.

I remember the scene and the ensuing conversation vividly. Engaging the blessed talents of the sculptor was only half the equation that would lead us to a new creation. The other half was entering into the disorderly but exciting process of creative expectation and brainstorming. This demanded an awareness of available gifts and blessings, entering into the often chaotic process that prepares for creativity, creating something new out of the messiness and eventually opening to the transforming effect of the new creation. Blessings! Messiness! Creativity! Transformation!

All good efforts start with blessings. The blessings in our project first took the form of the unique artistic gifts and talents of sculptor John Lajba. He had just finished sculptures for the Western Heritage Museum, and we wanted him to create a Christ image that, down though the years, would portray our heritage as a hope-filled Resurrection People.

We encountered the artist in a very messy place — his studio. Bits and pieces of his work were scattered around. If one did not know what creative juices flowed there, one might have mistaken it for a small junkyard. But that is usually the way it is with artists — gooey clay and messy pallets. In the midst of that messiness lies the pure gift of creativity.

We shared ideas from our design committee, and at some point Father Larry said, "We want a smiling, welcoming Jesus — a Christ figure that greets everyone who enters our church and makes each person feel welcome and loved!" After more discussion, I chimed in and said, "Let's make him a removable Jesus!"

The sculptor and our architect, David Beringer, looked puzzled. "What do you mean, "a removable Jesus"? Confusion and messiness were meeting in our process.

So I explained, "Well, Jesus hung on the cross for only three hours. That was more than enough. And three days in the tomb was plenty. From then on, and right now, he is the triumphant, risen Jesus. Let's have two corpus figures, one a suffering Messiah that we can place on the cross when Lent comes. But let's have him removable, replacing him with the risen figure at Easter and keep him that way the rest of the year."

Almost a year later it came to be. The new church was completed. It was ready to be dedicated and the risen Jesus smiled from its sanctuary. Before the official dedication, a public open house was held. Invitations appeared in the newspapers inviting everyone interested in this new church building to be a guest and to tour the new space. Hundreds of people came, many of them strangers who had no connection with the parish.

A few days after the open house Father Larry received a letter. The writer said, "I was curious when I saw your invitation in the newspaper. I have been 'out of the church' for some thirty years. But out of curiosity, I decided to come and take a look. When I walked into the church, I stood still. The figure of the welcoming, smiling Christ seemed to be looking right at me. That experience of a smiling Savior has invited and moved me to come back 'home' — to return to church once again!"

CREATIVE EXPECTATION

Honoring blessings and talents, working through messiness, creating and, finally, transforming the beholders — this is the path we are called to trod. When we bless what is hidden and latent, we express hope and affirm creativity. The smiling, risen Christ was hidden in the disarray and dustiness of the artist's studio. Nonetheless, we blessed and hoped in John Lajba's hidden talents. We were not disappointed. And the hidden Christ who became the smiling face had a creative power of its own — the power to move hearts.

In his beautiful book *Anam Cara,* John O'Donohue writes, "Creative expectation brings you healing and renewal." It can also bring significant transformation. As such, it is truly a blessing. Creative expectation is a positive way of looking at and foreseeing new possibilities, whether the medium is the sloppy pallet of the artist, the messy kitchen of the cook or the chaotic discussions of a committee meeting. This creative expectation affirms goodness, believes in potential, expects and hopes for something good to emerge from messiness. Thomas Aquinas once wrote that "potency and act divide being in such a way that whatever exists is either pure act (God) or composed of potency and act as its first intrinsic principle." Today, process theologians go farther than Thomas by claiming that in some sense the Godhead him/herself continues to develop through the ongoing creation story, which is still being written!

CREATIVE EXPECTATION — HOPE

All created things have a blessed potential. Creative expectations thus contain a blessed hope in the power of potential. To act and live with creative expectation is to walk the winding blessing path of hope that leads toward a new horizon. Yet, when we journey in hope we cannot now possess what lies beyond – we only lean toward it. Hope is ultimately about tomorrow, and the future always contains content that we cannot comprehend now.

This future-aspect of hope is difficult to accept in our hyperpaced and consumer-driven society. In our "Now Culture" perhaps hope is the least considered of the three great virtues of faith, hope and love because we don't have time for hope! Hope always demands some kind of waiting. The best creativity is not instantaneous. When instant results are demanded and expected, there is no wiggle room for hope! And because expectations that things must happen immediately inevitably cannot be met, it's no wonder there's so much anger and such a glut of cynicism in contemporary society.

THE CREATIVE EXPECTATIONS OF THE KINGDOM

For the Christian, Jesus offers creative expectations through his parables about the kingdom of God. These parables are always about potentials being realized in unexpected ways. In the Gospels there is always reason for hope, even when possibilities seem slim. A tiny, insignificant mustard seed is planted, and it springs up into a mighty bush where all the birds of the air come to nest. A little bit of yeast permeates a mass of dough and lifts it up. Very often in the parables about the kingdom of God, we are surprised that something very great and far-reaching results from something hidden and small. If Jesus were walking through our cities today, he would surely use modern parables to give us hope and to plant creative expectations. He might say, "The kingdom of God is like the Internet. Good seed as well as bad are sown there. Weeds as well as beautiful yellow poppies grow up along the Information Highway. Rather than cutting everything down in the spring — the good with the bad — it would be better to wait until fall, when the good can be kept and the bad thrown away."

In the parables about the kingdom of God that contain an essential element of the teaching of Jesus, the kingdom is always in process. It has not yet fully arrived, but there are amazing breakthroughs that show it can and will come. There is always reason to hope because the future is pregnant with possibilities.

Doris Donnelly, speaking to a national assembly of women about hope, put it this way:

> ...when our backs are up against the wall there is a fact and a possibility that is not yet in, (we need to see)... that there is a way around our troubles and that the boundaries of the possible are wider than they may seem.... Keep hope alive because as the First Letter of Peter reminds us, "We have been born anew to a living hope" (I Peter 1: 3).

To keep hope alive is to have creative expectations.

REFLECTION PAUSE OR JOURNAL OPTION ⧖

In my own experience, the parable of the mustard seed teaches me...

PONDER QUESTIONS

What is my experience of big things happening because of small moves?

What is the connection for me between hope and creative expectations?

DASHED HOPES

Sometimes hopes are dashed. Perhaps one of the most memorable images of our times is the picture of little John John Kennedy standing at his mother's knee and saluting as his father's casket passed by. JFK Junior was born in Camelot and raised in grief, yet he seemed to possess all that we would hope for in an aspiring prince. He possessed the inward grace of his mother, the alluring vigor of his father and the cultured presence of both. The future lay before him. Perhaps intuitively many people thought: "Here is someone who could give us hope again, who could restore dignity to politics. Who knows what he might become?" Then in an instant, all these hopes fell from the sky.

In moments like these, hope is squeezed, almost crushed, by despair. The death of the young is like a bud filled with promise being cut away and left to wither. Fate can be cruel. It often intervenes and cancels out our expectations. But if the loss is great, how equally powerful are the memories. They linger and have a fertile power of their own. Tiny seeds of new hope can be planted. What John Kennedy, Jr. might have been allures us — reminds us to treasure our own now-moment of potency. This very moment is a blessing that has future potencies both in this world and in the next. Hope leans forward out of despair. Hope is most alive when it faces into the gale of chaos and moves us forward.

Jesus of Nazareth lived only thirty three years, and yet his memory empowers us to live our lives in joyful hope.

Blessed be memories. We are enlivened by goodness.
Blessed be hope. We are anchored in its depths.
Blessed be forward motion. We move from dead center.
Blessed be tomorrow. We bless the future.
Blessed be the beyond. We are open to new possibilities.
Blessed be endurance. We bend but do not break.
Blessed be affirmation. We say "yes" in the midst of naysayers.
Blessed be positive thinking. We circumvent prophets of doom.
Blessed be risk taking. We dare to imagine what no one has foretold.
Blessed be creative expectations. We turn fractured energies into
    synergy.

To sustain these blessings depends on our mind-set. Hope either shines or is absent in the prism of our attitude. We have a choice to focus on the depth of the pit or to look up and out toward the stars. Sometimes we have to hunker down, wait in silence, step back, regroup, look around and discover that others are there before we can summon the energy to even look up and out. But if we get stuck in the pit, we never see glorious possibilities. How we eventually choose to see is our choice — and it's an important life-stance.

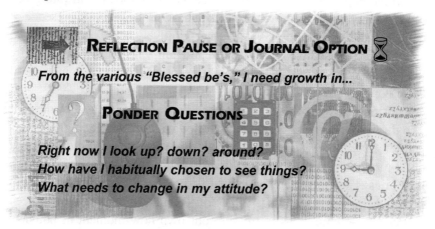

REFLECTION PAUSE OR JOURNAL OPTION

From the various "Blessed be's," I need growth in...

PONDER QUESTIONS

Right now I look up? down? around?
How have I habitually chosen to see things?
What needs to change in my attitude?

CREATIVE EXPECTATIONS FROM THE INTERNET

When little Kelli was born on August 2, 1999, she could not breathe. She was immediately placed on a ventilator. For weeks, her parents kept vigil. Finally, a pulmonary specialist performed an exploratory operation on her tiny lungs.

When the surgeon emerged from the operating room, he had the sad duty of telling Kelli's parents that her lungs were the worst he had ever seen. Her lungs had been trashed by some mysterious cause. After the operation, Kelli's condition was critical, and her parents did not expect her to live through the night.

This is when I received a call to go to the hospital to pray with the grieving family. As we prayed, we asked for whatever was best for Kelli. At the end, the parents asked me, "What are we to do?" I was silent, for I had no answer. Finally, I responded, "Perhaps at this time you must follow your heart." Kelli's grandmother added, "Your heart will find the right way."

That night, Kelli's grandmother went home and got on the Internet and started searching the net for any hospital or research center that might focus on Kelli's unique situation. Kelli did make it through the night and the next night, and many more.

Many weeks later, the grandmother called and told me what had ensued. They had found a hospital in St. Louis that had a great interest in Kelli's case. Now 2½ months old, Kelli was on her way to St. Louis to await a double lung transplant. She even had her own web site now (www.ctaz.com/~vtach/kellineal.htm), providing an opportunity for others to contribute toward her expenses and to communicate about her situation. And they did, from as far away as Japan!

Through the generosity of two parents who mourned the loss of their infant, Kelli found a donor for two new lungs. Two days after the operation, Kelli was taken off the respirator and began to breathe new life. Fractured family energies had turned into synergy. The Internet had become a safety net.

THE BLESSINGS OF SILENCE

When we are confronted with tragedy, we are stopped in our tracks and struck with silence — at least for a moment. Often, the most we can utter is a moan from the depths of our being. The dashing of hopes affects us very deeply. One of the graced aspects of coping and of growing is the blessing of silence and reflection.

> The Spirit helps us in our weakness; for we do not know how to pray as we ought, but that very Spirit intercedes with sighs too deep for words (Romans 8: 26-27).

"Too deep for words"? Perhaps. But if we stop long enough in silence and reflect deeply enough, we can all open our hearts to the words of the poets. For it is the poets who ascend the heights of joy and plumb the depths of tragedy. Life usually goes its merry way until tragedy streaks through the sky like lightning — and we are startled, then silenced. It is in such silence that the poets would speak to our souls.

In his poem "Musée des Beaux Arts," W.H. Auden writes of a "boy falling from the sky" and how such a tragedy precludes our going about our daily business unaware of suffering all around.

> About suffering they were never wrong,
> The Old Masters: how well they understood
> Its human position; how it takes place
> While someone else is eating or opening a window
> or just walking dully along.

In days of old, it was easy to be ignorant of tragedies far away. With today's technology we are instantly informed of tragedy as it happens everywhere. How does our soul respond?

Silence and Soul Work

In the face of tragedy and sorrow, we need silence in our lives in order to ponder deeply, to become aware, to do soul work. Soul work is like garden work. Just as the gardener must slide the spade deep into the earth and turn it, so too our souls are spaded deeply by life's tragedies. And sometimes the field of our life experience needs to lie fallow and be watered. We cannot control everything, even if we'd like to.

When we enter into the silence and solitude of prayer, we become aware immediately of how much we are surrounded by extraneous noise and distraction. When I sit in silent prayer, I hear the hum of the air-conditioner (at this very moment I hear a watering hose outside of my door). The roar of airplanes fills the horizon. Traffic starts and stops on the street outside. Sounds of machines fill up our office space. In the humdrum of my human experience, someone "opens a window." Others "walk dully" by. Everywhere I go, TVs blare their siren songs. And in my rushing hither, thither and yon I become accustomed to this commotion as reality, as if it is the only reality.

I can become caught up in noise and frenzy and even in the excitement of tragedy. I can even be like a thirsty man running round and round a well, yelling, "I need a drink," never stopping to sit down and draw the water from the well of silence that is right at my side and lies right at the heart of who I am. Tragedy — and all of life — demands silence, rest, contemplation and even sleep. As Aeschylus said in *Agememnon*:

> He who learns must suffer. And even in our sleep pain that cannot forget falls drop by drop upon the heart, and in our own despair, against our will, comes wisdom to us by the awful grace of God.

The well is dark and deep, and it is precisely beneath the surface of my rushing about that the nourishing waters of hoping, coping, compassion and creative expectations surge. And if I am yelling or talking all the time, I shall never sip this life-giving water or allow wisdom to drip down upon my soul. Our mouths and tongues are just too busy.

The main gift that flows from tragedy in our lives ought to be compassion. We begin to realize that we are all in this human situation together. Whether it is a glamorous personage like a JFK, Jr., or Princess Diana, or the street person we pass on the sidewalk, we all have hopes, we all have dreams, we all experience tragedies. Compassion goes beyond coping. Compassion can alert us to possibilities of receiving and bestowing blessings — being present to others, standing by others, praying for others in their grief.

TECHNOLOGIES

In the event of great tragedies, our technologies can aid us or distract us from noticing what is important and responding in a blessing mode. At a time like the death of Princess Diana or John F. Kennedy, Jr., television gives us instant and blanket coverage. There is a thin line between cultivating compassion and becoming voyeurs mesmerized by the important people who gather at tragedies or by the technical details of the tragic incidents: How fast was Diana's car going? Was the driver inebriated? Why did JFK Jr.'s plane stall? How long was its descent into the sea? There is a thin line between being a reflective viewer and a curiosity seeker. Too many details can turn us from being silent mourners into scientific sleuths.

Still, the images, if received in silence and reflection, can be powerful in eliciting inner soul work. The image of young John Kennedy, Jr. saluting at his father's funeral or the image of Princess Diana holding a child with AIDS — these are soul food. How these famous people encountered human suffering in their own lives and acted with great grace and empathy might well move us to become more compassionate and more helping in the circumstances around us. We can begin to think creatively about how we can respond and not "walk dully along." We can have creative expectations. A picture does speak a thousand words if we allow it to touch our souls.

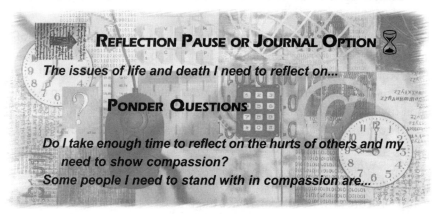

REFLECTION PAUSE OR JOURNAL OPTION

The issues of life and death I need to reflect on...

PONDER QUESTIONS

Do I take enough time to reflect on the hurts of others and my need to show compassion?
Some people I need to stand with in compassion are...

CELL PHONES

We need a spirituality of creative expectations and blessings for all of our modern forms of technology. They ought to serve our growth and not stunt our spirit. For example, we need to bless our cell phones so that they really connect us to each other in a fruitful way rather than disconnecting us from reality.

What a wonderful gift they are when we are caught in traffic; they enable us to let our hosts know that we are OK and will be just a little late. For my friend Mary, driving back late at night to Dublin and running out of gas on a remote road, having a cell phone brought friendly help. Others' lives have been saved when they used a cell phone to alert 911. They can be marvelous tools in so many ways.

It is also true that noise and busyness have reached a penultimate level in the proliferation of cell phones. Go to a quiet restaurant and enjoy the ambiance of a candlelit table, and you may well find a cell phone ringing at the next table. Usually it's not calling a doctor to an emergency but, rather, allows idle jabber about some inconsequential item that could well wait until tomorrow. Cell phones now ring in church, in movie houses, in libraries and at graveside services. They can be abrasive and intrusive.

Even worse, they can disconnect us from what we should be doing and paying attention to, like driving an automobile — a complex vehicle that needs careful maneuvering through potentially dangerous traffic. Recently, I was called to the hospital room of a badly injured young woman. She had just returned from surgery where they had removed her spleen. She was in critical condition. She had stopped at a stop sign, and her car was plowed into by a driver so completely immersed in his conversation on his cell phone that he didn't notice she had stopped.

When used creatively and in important circumstances, cell phones are great blessings. When abused, their consequences are not only rude interruptions for those around us, but they may even be accomplices to tragedy and death. We need to bless our cell phones and to develop our own rules for the road in using them.

A Daily Blessing for a Cell Phone

Hello again, companion on my journey.
    You are my friend — not my master!
    You are like an angel at my side.
May I exercise restraint
    and only dial from the side of the road.
May my answering be brief,
    my road attention alert.
O God, bless your presence.
    O God, bless this road.
    O God, bless my arrival.

Some of the greatest tragedies are those that so easily could be avoided. When technology helps us to be safe, what a marvelous blessing. When we misuse a gift, we actually curse the instrument that was meant to be our friend.

Teens — Speed and Tragedy

Tragically, next to accidents, suicide is the leading cause of death among teens. Young people have been programmed by our hyper-culture toward speed and to believe that everything ought to be instantaneous as it is wished or sought. This can contribute to an attitude that all is lost when a particular significant thing is lost. Adults need to model hope and teach teens patience with their own creative expectations. When winning at all costs, having great success and achieving all goals quickly are demanded of teens, it can actually set them up for a fall. Life can begin to seem hopeless when there is failure in some area where much is expected of them. We parents and teachers need to bless our young, to let them know that, yes, we want them to succeed but that initial failures are not the end of the world. Too many teens are led to believe that failure does end their world. In fact all age groups in our "Now Culture" need models of hope and mentors of creative expectations.

MODELS OF CREATIVE EXPECTATION

In Omaha, where I spent most of my pastoral life, I had the privilege of being in close proximity to some wonderful models of creative expectation. I remember as a young altar boy meeting Father Flanagan. It was shortly after the filming of the movie *Boys Town* that his "no such thing as a bad boy" statement became famous.

Father Flanagan was not a Pollyanna. His life and actions revealed he was both a realist and a dreamer. He believed in potential. He believed in creative expectation. He was walking a Creative Expectation path that was marked by four important road signs:

1. Bless and affirm inherent goodness.
2. Have creative expectations even in the midst of messiness.
3. Trust that a new creation can emerge.
4. Transformation can follow.

To walk this four-lane spiritual path is to walk a blessing path. Father Flanagan knew how to bless! Over the years, Father Flanagan's dream has grown into a little city that is an international model for youth care and transformation. Living out the charism and dream of Father Flanagan, Boys Town has expanded with satellites spread across the United States and has developed creative new models of youth care for the changing problems of a new millennium. Their hotline for troubled youths (1-800-448-3000) has recorded over two million calls!

Today's clientele differs from Father Flanagan's original orphans. Father Val Peter, the current, dynamic successor of Father Flanagan describes many of Boys Town's incoming youth as victims of drugs, alcohol and parental abuse. When these youths graduate with their heads held high, creative expectations have been fulfilled. Their stories are Easter stories too, for they have risen up out of cold tombs to lead new lives. Boys Town has always worked, and still does, because it has remained true to the charism and creative expectations of its founder and has been willing to expand and adapt to changing needs.

When Father Flanagan started Boys Town, he started on a shoestring and a prayer. He was working with homeless men and orphaned boys and was simply not equipped to extend his ministry to girls. But Boys Town has been an expanding dream and a growing tree whose branches today reach out far beyond what Father Flanagan's resources allowed.

Boys Town now enrolls girls. A young woman was recently elected its mayor! In accepting girls, Boys Town has doubled its creative capacity for transformation! Joan Chittister recently said that "when half of humanity is ignored then all of humanity becomes half-souled, the church half-graced and the world half-developed." Today Boys Town serves 33,000 young people at 14 different sites in 18 different states. Half of those served are young women.

Attending a reunion twenty-five years after the admission of girls, several from that first class commented on Boys Town's blessings. Diana testified, "It saved my life." Joni said, "It was truly a blessing. Everyone needs the right environment to flourish and become the person they were meant to be." Joni is now completing her studies for a master's degree in counseling. As a counselor, she hopes to help other young people just as Boys Town helped her. "I think I have an understanding — I have a lot to offer someone who is struggling. Kids just sometimes need a little extra help and guidance to become who they were meant to be."

"That's what we hope for," replied Father Peter. "I ask our alumni and alumnae to make a promise that sometime in the future they will help a youngster that has lost her or his way. That's how the world gets better." And that is a creative expectation.

These days, Boys Town is going full speed toward full development of the potential of both sexes and continues to move ahead on a path marked Creative Expectations. Father Flanagan must surely smile down upon this blessing path.

A GHETTO MODEL OF CREATIVE EXPECTATION

Not too many miles from Boys Town there is a parish in North Omaha's ghetto, not as well known as Boys Town, but rich in imagination and fine-tuned toward developing creative expectations. For twelve years, Father Jim Scholz worked with a dedicated team in improving Sacred Heart grade school. Recently, of its 142 students 141 were black and 83% of the children weren't Catholic.

Sacred Heart school recognizes that a quality education leads to jobs and social stability. Like Boys Town, Sacred Heart has developed a model that can be shared with others. Mutual of Omaha invested $100,000 as seed money in Sacred Heart's curriculum-model: "Employability in the Mainstream." This allowed Sacred Heart to share and pilot this model with 2500 students at other school sites, both public and private.

"Employability" teaches basic skills to grade-schoolers that are important for anyone who wishes to find success in the workplace and in life. Lessons cover such topics as dependability, goal setting, business English, money and banking and how a business works. Lessons in life-skills include table manners, resolving conflict, phone skills, and teamwork. This program won a "Points of Light" award presented by the George Bush administration. In the fall of 1998 it began to be marketed nationwide under the name "Life Skills: Building Blocks for Success."

When Sacred Heart representatives hear from teachers modeling this program at various sites, the comments are very positive. A teacher from an ethnically mixed urban school in Denver testified, "This program makes sense, and it fits our students and their needs perfectly!"

That Sacred Heart should be so creative is no surprise, for those who staff Sacred Heart are very creative people. They very much hold the spirit of Father Flanagan. They recognize blessed potential. They inject creative expectations. And the result is motivated students with good growth and job potentials. Staff and students alike believe good things can happen in the ghetto.

The school's promoter, Father Scholz, was an artist whose photography has been displayed and admired at various exhibitions. But perhaps his greatest artistry was to provide vision for Sacred Heart. Yet his vision was no idle dream. He was very successful in drawing business and industry into collaboration in the inner city. His successor, Father Tom Fangman has continued fulfilling that dream. To develop the talents of these young black children is not just a good idea; it is right and just. And corporate leaders are to be praised for realizing that developing the hidden potential of these children is also good business.

One of Sacred Heart's longtime supporters is John Keneflick, retired Chairman of the Union Pacific Railroad. He is honorary chairperson of Sacred Heart's C.U.E.S. — "Christian Urban Education Board." Other acting chairpersons have been outstanding lay people with business know-how. With leaders like these, C.U.E.S. is receiving support and help from 265 businesses and 20 foundations! The success of Sacred Heart is one beautiful example of grass roots solutions to big problems. There are other "Points of Light" happening throughout the country — getting successful people involved in giving young people a real chance to have creative expectations and helping motivate them to prepare for a productive job in the future.

These motivators are like the one who searches for the pearl of great price in the parable of Jesus. From small beginnings and with lots of creativity such helpers are finding youngsters in the ghetto who are pearls of great price, and they are helping to bring them forth to shine and radiate.

The efforts at Boys Town and at Sacred Heart flow directly from the heart of the Judeo-Christian tradition. In fact, the whole Judeo-Christian tradition has given birth to reverence for creativity and for creative expectations. And so, it is fitting that Jews and Christians of many denominations have been very supportive of Boys Town and of C.U.E.S.

HEROES OF IMAGINATION

Daniel Boorstein, in his epic work *The Creators — A History of Heroes of the Imagination,* shows how the Judeo Christian tradition from Moses to Saint Augustine gave us a prophetic vision of the human as a creator made in the image of a Creator God. Rather than history simply being a recycling of previous events, the Judeo Christian heritage gave history a linear but often indirect path toward a destiny. In fact, it is sometimes said that God writes straight but with crooked lines. If this is so, it means we are never in complete control of the unfurling of events. At the same time, if we are made in the image of the Creator, we do have an inbred role in creating something new, whether with troubled youth in the ghetto or in our personal lives. We can, by our very humanness, have creative expectations. These expectations in every age open new vistas and untapped possibilities. The human ability to cocreate is mysterious and marvelous. As Daniel Boorstein says:

> Mystified by the power to create, it is no wonder that man should imagine the artist to be Godlike. In the West, belief in a Creator-God was a way of confessing that the power to make the new was beyond explanation.

The creative exclamation *Aha!* phonetically resembles *Awe.* Creativity is, indeed, awesome, whether it is forming a child in the womb or splitting an atom. The whole story of human history is an unfolding of human creativity and imagination. And in human hands is held the responsibility of using this creative power for weal or woe.

Wendell Berry, Kentucky farmer and poet, reminds us that in creating we deal with a mystery bigger than ourselves. In *Standing by Words,* he tells us that the wider and deeper the radius of our vision, the wider becomes our circumference of mystery:

> ...some possibilities must not be explored; some things must not be learned. If we want to get safely home, there are certain seductive songs we must not turn aside for, some sacred things we must not meddle with.

When we think about this, it seems pretty obvious. Just because Hitler had a "bright idea" for a well-designed shower and oven system at Auschwitz does not mean he had to follow the creative expectation for carrying it through. As technology continues its rapid development, we increasingly need to address moral questions regarding its production and our use of it. If we are to be true to our Judeo-Christian heritage, we need a spirituality of technology to ensure that the maze of scientific discoveries and creations is a blessing path.

MOSES — MODEL OF CREATIVE EXPECTATION

In the Western world, we have many mentors who have modeled creative expectations that have resulted in countless blessings for humankind. One of the earliest and greatest was Moses. All those who would bless thereafter would have their roots in Moses, including David with his blessing psalms and Jesus with his beatitudes.

God required Moses to cultivate high creative expectations. Indeed, Moses needed an unfaltering hope that he would lead his people through an arid desert to a new and different land flowing with milk and honey, a land of promise and untold blessings.

God challenged Moses to set out on an epic journey. Moses was to have creative expectations about crossing the Reed Sea, about receiving water from a rock, about finding food in a forlorn desert, about molding a grumbling people into a community, about delivering commandments to a people who at that very moment were worshiping a golden calf. Most of all, God asked Moses to have creative expectations about a land flowing with milk and honey — a land Moses would not enter. And at the climax of this arduous journey, worn out from all these challenges, Moses would have his arms propped up by companions so that he could give a final and hopeful blessing to the Hebrew warriors. Like so many before him, Moses would not live to see the fruit of these creative expectations. But until the end, he journeyed in the footsteps of his ancestors with undaunted faith and hope. Saint Paul in the letter to the Hebrews expressed this kind of creatively expectant yearning that is based on firm faith and a steady hope:

> By faith, Jacob, when dying, blessed each of the sons of Joseph, "bowing in worship over the top of his staff.... By faith, Joseph, at the end of his life, made mention of the exodus of the Israelites and gave instructions about his burial. By faith, Moses was hidden by his parents for three months after his birth. By faith, Moses when he was grown up, refused to be called a son of Pharaoh's daughter, choosing rather to share ill treatment with the people of God than to enjoy the fleeting pleasures of sin.... By faith, he left Egypt, unafraid of the king's anger; for he persevered as though he saw him who is invisible (Hebrews 11: 21-23, 27).

The faith that Paul writes of is a trusting faith, a faith of creative expectation.

TRUST

Scripture scholar Gerard Von Rad, in his book *Wisdom in Israel*, indicates that the wisdom literature of the Old Testament identifies this steady faith and hope as deep trust that God is at work among God's people.

Trust in Yahweh with all your heart
and do not rely on your own insight (Proverbs 3: 5).

One might add: Trust in Yahweh and have creative expectations about blessings. Von Rad indicates that the authors of the Book of Proverbs took it for granted that God was at work in human history. As the author of all life, God was to be trusted to care about God's people. Because of this trust in God's care, human life possessed the ability to be open and receptive to blessings.

It is precisely from Moses and our Jewish roots that our understanding and use of blessings emanate. Moses was steadfast in trust. And even though the Hebrews often wavered on their Exodus journey, God still blessed them abundantly. In the end they always blessed Yahweh. The Hebrew word for blessing is *berakhah*, a word that has roots in Sumarian hymns. The Sumarians used the word *bulug*, which referred to barley that had soaked in large vats and was about to burst forth. They then also applied the term to their deities to connote that which breaks all boundaries or limits. It suggested a quality of overabundant fertility or fruitfulness. And that is how the Hebrews understood the abundant blessings that Yahweh, the one God, bestowed. Through their *berakhah* blessing prayers the Hebrews tried as best they could to bless God. They saw such prayer as a dim human mirror reflecting back in deep gratitude the mercy, the beauty of the law and the abundance that God bestowed on them as a people.

The *berakhah*, like most of Jewish prayer, is both a declaration of dependence and an expression of gratitude and praise to our Creator for the many gifts with which we are blessed. While such prayer begins with the self, it moves us away from self-centeredness and from an unreflective routinization of life. Too often we take the world for granted. The *berakhah* is a specific way of awakening us from our limiting assumptions about life and of responding to each of God's gifts with awareness, awe and gratitude.

THE SABBATH

The Exodus event led by Moses liberated the Hebrew people. In the process it allowed them to bestow on all of us a marvelous blessing. We have received the gift of God's rest that refreshes us after our labors and enables us to access deep inner wellsprings from which fresh creative expectations arise. One historian has called the Sabbath the greatest gift of the Jewish people to Western civilization!

At the core of the great commandments that Moses brought down from Mount Sinai was "Remember to keep holy the Sabbath day." We have not remembered. We have forgotten. The Shabbat, so sacred to the Jewish people, has probably also been the day that has suffered the most from modern technology and our consumer culture. Whether it is the Jewish Saturday or the Christian Sunday, the practice of setting aside one day for rest, quiet, contemplation, learning and prayer has been decimated by our hyperactive culture. It's been squeezed out by our need to be on the move, to cram as much activity as we can into each of the twenty-four hours of every day. If leisure is the basis of culture as author Josef Pieper claims, then in our disregard for the Sabbath we in the West have lost touch not only with a reality of great religious value but also of great cultural value. The change in pace that the Sabbath offers allows the field of human imagination to lie fallow. Without Sabbath rest, the fertility of the creative powers of our imaginations dries up.

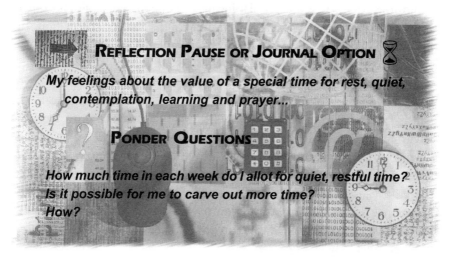

REFLECTION PAUSE OR JOURNAL OPTION

My feelings about the value of a special time for rest, quiet, contemplation, learning and prayer...

PONDER QUESTIONS

How much time in each week do I allot for quiet, restful time? Is it possible for me to carve out more time? How?

A BLESSING PEOPLE

Much later in Israel's salvation history, after the destruction of the temple, which was the official center of worship and sacrifice, only the synagogue, the home and nature remained as holy places for prayer. The rabbis now emphasized the importance of *berakhah* — the blessings.

Blessing became integral to Hebrew prayer. Blessings filled the rhythms and cycles of all of Jewish life. *Renew Our Days*, a current book of Jewish prayer, gives this rationale for the importance of blessings:

> By reciting blessings we learn to recognize the divine current that is present in our world. Blessings transform the ordinary into the extraordinary. Ordinary time becomes sacred time, awareness of others is reverenced and gratitude for the gifts of life grows deeper.

CREATIVE EXPECTATIONS — A SACRED TRUST

As we journey into the twenty-first century, some 3300 years after Moses and 2000 years since Jesus Christ, we cannot forget that the twentieth century saw the creation of some of the most marvelous inventions as well as some of the most brutal and devastating weapons of war. Electricity, automobiles, airplanes, spacecraft, computers, scientific genetic breakthroughs and other technological advances all showered tremendous blessings on us. On the other hand, poison gas, atomic explosions, germ warfare, the Holocaust, "ethnic cleansing" and other abuses of creativity also sprang from mankind's fertile imagination. In the twentieth century more humans were slaughtered than in any previous century and much more damage done to the earth.

What are our creative expectations for the new century? Might we hope for creative solutions to intractable problems — the Middle East, Northern Ireland, the division between the first and the third worlds, environmental despoliation? If we can imagine war at its worst, might we also imagine peace at its best? Will the ever-expanding potential of women help bring about a better balance in our creative process? This is indeed a cause for hope; after all, women have had intimate hands-on experience in the human procreation process. They are physically and psychologically closer to the creation of new life. Women more naturally "expect creatively."

To have a blessing mentality and a reverential attitude about creativity is a major challenge for the new millennium. It involves a spiritual quest for the inheritors of the Judeo-Christian tradition, in which humankind is understood to be made in the image and likeness of the creator God.

Scripture Images and Passages for Reflection

Hebrew Scriptures

Isaiah 40: 1-5 — *Comforting expectations*

Comfort, give comfort to my people....

Isaiah 55: 9-13 — *Creative renewal*

...just as from the heavens the rain and snow come down and do not return until they have watered the earth, making it fertile and fruitful...so shall my word be....

Isaiah 61: 1-4 — *Hopeful expectations*

The Spirit of God is upon me...and has sent me to bring glad tiding to the poor.... They shall rebuild the ancient ruins....

Chriatian Scriptures

Romans 15: 13 — *The God of hope*

May the God of hope fill you with all joy and peace....

Colossians 1: 3-6 — *Hope bearing fruit*

...Just as in the whole world the Gospel is bearing fruit and growing, so also among you....

Acts 2: 17 — *Creative dreams*

...I will pour out a portion of my Spirit upon all flesh. Your sons and daughters shall prophesy, your young men shall see visions, your old men shall see dreams.

Millennial Expectations

Blessed be the gift of time.
Blessed be the promise of a new millennium.

In the year of our Lord, let this day be:
a time for dreaming,
a time for hoping,
a time for imagining,
a time for expecting,

a time for creating,
a time for growing,
a time for healing,
a time for befriending,
a time for connecting.

Bless our days and bless our nights.
Bless the unfolding of all our years.

Blessing in the Midst of Tragedy

Faith, hope and love,
but the greatest of these is love!
When tragedy strikes,
our departed loved ones
travel very light.
Their love is all that is carried
into the afterlife.

Faith is for the living.
Hope is for the living.
Tears and sighs are ours.
Bless our faith at this hour of history.
Bless our hoping,
Bless our coping.
Let us stand together in love.

Ritual Blessing for a Task Group Meeting

Leader:

We arrive with scattered thoughts and desires.
We gather together from scattered places,
We've rushed and pushed to be here.
Lead us now to the well of silence.
Lead us to the kiva of darkness.
We now close our eyes...
We dwell within....
We seek peace...
Shalom!

A Period of Silence
Leader: We come back now to the light.
Leader or all:

Blessed a little by stopping.
Blessed a little by relaxing.
Blessed a little by breathing.

Let us now see a little differently.
Let us now listen a little more closely.
May the Spirit of creative expectations
...breathe between us,
...breathe among us,
...breathe around us.

The sum can be greater than its parts.
Our hope can surpass all our doubts.
Our creative expectations can be fulfilled.
...Let it be so!
...Let it be so!
...Let it be so!

A Blessing for a Couple Hoping to Expect

And now you will conceive in your womb and bear a son (Luke 1: 31).

Jesus, you pitched your tent
in the womb of Mary,
lingering there for nine months.
Mary waited in creative expectation,
allowing great fruit to emerge
in its own time.

Allow our womb to be hospitable.
Allow us to relax and await a visitor,
...nothing to fear,
...nothing to fret.
If it is within God's wisdom,
...let it be!
...let it be!

THE BLESSINGS OF TRANSFORMATION

When (Christ) has gathered everything together and transformed
everything…God shall be all in all.

—Pierre Teilhard de Chardin, *The Phenomenon of Man*

PARABLE – JOE O'MALLEY'S TALE OF TRANSFORMATION

Joe O'Malley was a grizzled veteran reporter who did the night shift for
a New York paper. He covered muggings, drug raids and burglaries.
His sources were often the habitués on the street and in the bars.

After ten years of writing about the miseries of society, he sat down
with his editor and told her, "I feel burned out. I need a change of pace."

His editor, her glasses slipping down on the bridge of her nose,
took a good look at Joe and responded, "Yeah, maybe you do. Tell ya

what, we're supposed to do a feature on 'Transformation.' How about if I give you that assignment?"

"Well, yeah...I guess so. But what is transformation?"

"That's for you to investigate and write about. Find out yourself. Go check it out. Start small and then go big. Search high an low, and you'll find something."

The first thing he did was to check his dictionary, which told him:

> Transformation: a change in form, appearance, nature or character. Transform: to change in form, appearance or structure; metamorphose. In physics: to change into another form of energy.

Joe closed the book and muttered, "Physics-schmiseks! What does that mean? Change in appearance? Is changing diapers a transformation? I'd better do some interviews."

And that's what Joe did. He scratched around, did interviews and took notes until it all became kind of a jumble in his head. One night, after one too many drinks at Moloney's Bar, he went home with a scattered mind and dropped into bed. In the middle of the night he had a dream:

A voice spoke to him. "What about transformation?"

"Yeah, that's what *I* want to know. What about it? And just who are you?"

"I'm the voice of the muse, Joe. Every writer has a muse, you know."

"Well, maybe. Only right now, I'm not musing so well, and I'm not very amused. So, tell me, how do I find out about this transformation thing."

"Do what your editor said: Start small and then go big."

"Yeah, but how do I do that?"

"You asked for it, Joe. Hold on — and away we go, Joe! You want small? I'll show you small!"

Small, indeed. Joe found himself the size of the bug in the midst of other bugs. Only the other bugs had headlamps! They were shining all over in the midst of the darkness. "Whoa! Am I on the freeway?"

"No, not at all, Joe. You're on the grass, under a tree in Iowa with a lot of other bugs!"

"What kind of bugs? Who are these crazy bugs with headlamps zooming all around me?"

"Lightning bugs, Joe. Some call us fireflies."

Then a chorus of bug voices cried out, "Sing with us: 'Glow little glow worm, glitter, glitter!'"

Joe could only groan, "Is this the D.T.s or what? This is wild!"

"No," said the muse, "this is Iowa and these are bugs. And this is how you start small. Ask them about transformation."

"OK, OK." He stopped one of the fireflies and asked, "What do you know about transformation?"

The bug in front of him thought hard — so hard that the glow on his dome began to dim. "Actually, quite a bit. We're the bright guys of the bug world you know. To start out, I came from an egg — but not an ordinary one. I even had a little glow on as an egg! Two weeks later I had my coming out as a larva on the underside of a leaf, and I glowed. That's why we're sometimes called glowworms. But that's not the end; it's just the beginning. All summer long I glowed and ate, glowed and ate. When the winter winds began to blow, I dug a foxhole in the earth and pulled the soil over me for a blanket. Then in spring, I put together a little dome and crawled inside to await what you are looking for — a transformation. In the winter, I was buried; and then in the spring, I arose and broke out into a new flying creature. What's a transformation? It's when I emerge from that cocoon and have wings. I'm a different creature now. My light has a new radiance, and I can fly and flash a hello to worthwhile females. And to predators, my flashing light says, 'Bug off! I want you to see me, because if you try to eat me you'll get real bad indigestion.'"

"Well," said Joe, "how did this all come to be? How did you get this flashing light power?"

"Hey, I'm a firefly, not a philosopher. But sometime way back, some intelligence emerged in my ancestors — call it what you want: a DNA code, an unfolding, a creative expectation — that brings light out of darkness. Pretty neat, isn't it?" As the firefly spoke, other airborne relatives were making swoops and dives and buzzing around Joe's head.

Joe was getting a little uncomfortable in the bug world when the muse said, "Joe, we've got to search high as well as low for transformation. Let's take flight and set our sights higher." With that Joe and the muse catapulted right up through the midst of fireflies that were darting and flashing all around, making blurs of light in the Iowa night.

Then, whoosh-zoom-zing. Joe was off flying through the sky, back toward New York, his muse leading the way. "Search high and low; start small, then look big. That's where we're headed — high and big."

All of a sudden Joe was eyeball-to-eyeball with a great bronzed-faced lady. She smiled and said, "Joe, what took you so long? Didn't you know I've been carrying the torch for you for a long time? Don't you know me, Joe?"

Astonished by her formidable appearance, Joe replied, "I don't know. You are awful big and threatening — like an amazon!"

"You're too close, Joe; move back some. You've spent so much time in our city's bars and grills that you may never have really seen me — like some guy living in the foothills and never seeing the mountains."

When the muse and Joe moved back a few yards, Joe recognized her — Lady Liberty with her torch held high. "So, Joe, you want to know about transformation. Let me tell you. I've got a high perch here, and I can see transformation every day. Each dawn and each twilight, the radiant light and the fertile dark do a dance together, and there is transformation from light to dark and back again. The holy dark is my friend. It gives me the opportunity to let my torch shine. And the radiant light of day is a blessing that through the years has let me smile and welcome the immigrants, 'the refuse of foreign shores.' And what about them, Joe? What about their journeys, their transformations? You have an Irish-sounding name. Do you know that at the time of the famine in Ireland, when people were fleeing from their homeland, they would hold a wake for those departing because they knew they would never be seen again? And some of the boats that held them became 'coffin ships' because so many died on the way. Those who survived came with nothing. Their breath and their mere existence were all they had, but they experienced even those basic realities as great blessings.

"And look at this great city across the river. It has sprung from the hopes of immigrants — Europeans, Asians, Africans and now from many Hispanics and South Americans. Transformation often means big things happening from tiny beginnings. Transformation means letting go and allowing new possibilities to emerge. Transformation evolves from creative tensions. Transformation means letting radiant light emerge in the holy dark.

"And listen, Joe, transformation for our time also means that our world as we have known it is at the dawning of a new millennium — an era of transformation. I think you and the muse ought to talk to the new kid on the block, who might have a lot to say about transformation."

"And who is that?" asked Joe.

"I know," said the Muse, and off they went — over the city's tall buildings, through office canyons — alighting finally before the biggest computer Joe had ever seen.

"Hello!" said Big Blue. "What can I do for you? How about a game of chess?"

"No, no games," said the muse. "We're searching high and low for transformation. We've searched big and small. And you are the last expert we'd like to quiz. Tell us about transformation."

"Ah, Transformation. Let me spin that around in my memory. Well, I simply didn't exist a hundred years ago. Nobody talked about me. No one knew me. I just wasn't. And here I am — right here — from nothing to something. No, not just something — I now hold almost everything inside of me. I've got it all! How about that? Not only am I a chess champion, but I'm increasingly becoming a transformer. My brain has the capacity to transform you. What do you think of that?" Joe and the muse looked at each other.

"You know the bugs you saw in Iowa? I know all about them. Just type in bugs.com, and I'll tell you more about bugs than you'd ever want to know."

"We've gone the bug route; no thanks," said Joe.

"Well, Joe," said Big Blue, "I also know all about you; I have all the data. I know your bank account, your preferences, even your liking for Moloney's Bar. Listen, Joe, alcohol is a small kick compared to what I can do for you. You can get hooked on me. Search me. Spend more time with me. Go steady with me, Joe, and I will embrace you, hold you, keep you! Do you know that just one typical search engine on my Internet can put you in touch with 50,000 porn sites! Or if you even want to get into hating, right now I have 250 hate web-sites — and that's growing.

"On the other hand, if you want religion, I've got it. If you want great art, I've got it. So, what do you think about me transforming you? Do you think I have the moxie? Why do you always have to be a human? Maybe you need to be transformed from being human into something else. Look at the fireflies. They're worms turned into high fliers. Just think, you can have it all with me. I can become your brain, and your hands can become my hands. The new day has arrived when all I need is your touch or your voice, and all you will need is my bright face in front of you. I think this is a very good idea. I am smarter than you. I certainly know more. Indeed, I see my future role being in the transformation business. I'll be the transformer, and you'll be the transformed, recreated to my image and likeness. I think this is a great idea. I'm bored to death with chess."

By now, even the muse was perplexed. He whispered to Joe, "When that day comes, I wonder where that will leave you and me?"

At that moment, Joe turned over and woke up. With a furrowed brow he sat up and wondered, "What does transformation mean for me? Maybe I am the final person I need to interview."

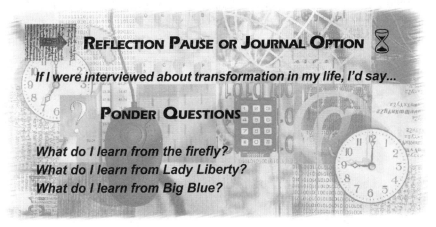

REFLECTION PAUSE OR JOURNAL OPTION

If I were interviewed about transformation in my life, I'd say...

PONDER QUESTIONS

What do I learn from the firefly?
What do I learn from Lady Liberty?
What do I learn from Big Blue?

TRANSFORMATIONS

Transformation is defined in physics as a "change into another form of energy." In spiritual writings transformation often refers to a conversion or moving to a new level of growth. In both cases, new energies are released. If we reflect on our spiritual lives, we can trace transformations through various life phases. At the core of our transformations is a blessing given by God. This primary spiritual blessing is the gift of grace. For we cannot move or be or pray without first knowing the gift of God's gracious power. Then, quite often we pass through a period of darkness or creative tension before we undergo transformation and something new is created. We can observe this process in the growth patterns of the larger society as well as in our own life experience. In each case, transformation often results from tiny beginnings.

THE MUSTARD SEED AND THE BUS RIDE

The kingdom of heaven is like a mustard seed that someone took and sowed in his field; it is the smallest of the seeds, but when it has grown it is the greatest of shrubs and becomes a tree (Matthew 13: 31-32).

Once upon a time, there was a small black lady who rode the bus to work every day. Where she lived, it was tradition — in fact, it was the rule — that she should sit in the back of the bus. That's the way it had always been; that's the way it was and that's the way it would always be. But then, one day, this formerly unknown and unassuming black lady named Rosa had a better idea. When the bus driver demanded she get up and give her seat to a white male, she said, "No!" She even spent a night in jail because of it. It was really a very tiny, seemingly inconsequential act, and yet what mighty results were borne from that simple deed by Rosa Parks. It was a small thing, but it took great courage. And because of her better idea new energies were, indeed, released. From that tiny seed energies would sprout and spread to bring about a major transformation in society.

THE YEAST AND THE BASEBALL PLAYER

The kingdom of God is like yeast that a woman took and mixed in with three measures of flour until all of it was leavened (Matthew 13: 33).

Once upon a time, only white men played major league baseball. That's the way it was and ever would be. Then the Brooklyn Dodgers had a new idea — an unheard-of idea — and hired a black baseball player named Jackie Robinson. Nobody had thought of it before, or at least no one had mustered up the courage to do it. When Jackie Robinson ran out onto the field in a Dodger uniform, the baseball ground shook and new energies were released — energies that would transform baseball — and ripple throughout society.

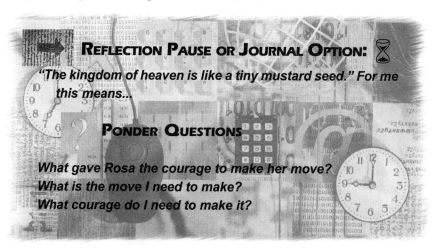

REFLECTION PAUSE OR JOURNAL OPTION:

"The kingdom of heaven is like a tiny mustard seed." For me this means...

PONDER QUESTIONS

What gave Rosa the courage to make her move?
What is the move I need to make?
What courage do I need to make it?

The Weeds and the Cigarettes

The kingdom of God may be compared to someone who
sowed good seed in his field; but while everybody was asleep,
an enemy came and sowed weeds among the wheat, and then
went away (Matthew 13: 24-25).

Once upon a time, everyone was asleep to the dangers of the tobacco
weed; it was considered clever and very sophisticated in the United States
to smoke cigarettes. All the important people smoked. The president
smoked. Celebrities of stage and screen invariably had a cigarette in hand,
whether on or off camera. It was the thing to do. It was as natural
as...breathing. In fact, in a way, it was breathing.

Then a wise Surgeon General had the courage to contradict the
prevailing wisdom that smoking was beneficial for everyone involved.
He unmasked smoking as a curse rather than a blessing. He felt strongly
that a warning should be placed on cigarette advertising and campaigned
vigorously for it. When the Surgeon General's warning finally appeared
on each pack of cigarettes, a slow revolution began.

It has gained enough momentum so that today in the United States
smoking is forbidden in many public places. The ensuing extensive
anti-smoking publicity through the years, culminating in lawsuits against
cigarette companies, has so raised awareness about the health-damaging
effects of cigarettes that a major social transformation is well underway.

More and more people have begun to realize that a cigarette is a
weapon that takes the lives of smokers. Even more, it is a weapon turned
upon those non-smokers who have been forced to breathe secondary
cigarette smoke. To realize how extensive is the anti-smoking transformation
that has occurred in the United States among adults, one need only to
travel in Europe. There, even highly civilized and cultured people fill the
air in most public places with a pall of cigarettes smoke. Pall is a fitting
word, for it commonly refers to the covering placed over coffins at funerals.

The Republic of Ireland — which at this writing possesses cutting-
edge technology and one of the finest education systems in Europe, and
whose GNP is racing ahead of the rest of Europe and even the United States
— remains in the dark ages as far as smoking is concerned. For a people
who so highly value their sense of freedom, the prevalence of smoke in
most public gathering places signals the pervasive and subtle enslavement

of a nation to nicotine addiction. Yet no matter where it lingers, the pall of cigarette smoke covers us in darkness. Often the darkness has to become stifling before there is a move to new creativity and to transformation.

In all cases of social transformation there is a justice factor. It was unjust to consign blacks "to the back of the bus." It was unjust to reject black ballplayers. And it's unjust to inflict the hazards of cigarette smoke on non-smokers and children.

PERSONAL ADDICTIONS AND SPIRITUAL TRANSFORMATIONS

> Again, the kingdom of heaven is like a merchant in search of fine pearls; on finding one pearl of great value, he went and sold all that he had and bought it (Matthew 13: 45).

Freedom from drugs or alcohol is indeed a pearl of great price! Spiritual programs that enable people to move out of various addictions require the individual addict to recognize the power of a higher being, to pass through darkness or rise up from rock bottom, to create a new way of living and to be transformed in the process. We all know stories of great transformation, perhaps in the lives of friends, relatives and neighbors who have changed destructive tendencies into new healing and growing patterns. These transforming energies are truly pearls of great price! They are blessings retrieved from the dark.

If one pays attention to the Internet, sometimes a restless stirring for transformation buzzes through cyberspace, such as this litany from an anonymous sender:

> The paradox of our time in history is that we have taller buildings, but shorter tempers.
> Wider freeways, but narrower viewpoints.
> We spend more, but have less.
> We buy more, but enjoy it less.
> We have bigger houses, and smaller families.
> More conveniences, but less time.
> We have more degrees, but less sense.
> More knowledge, but less judgment.
> More experts, but more problems.
> More medicines, but less wellness.
> Some of us drink too much, smoke too much,

spend too recklessly, laugh too little, drive too fast,
get too angry too quickly, stay up too late,
get up too tired, read too little, watch TV too much
and pray too seldom.
We have multiplied our possessions,
but reduced our values.
We talk too much, love not enough and hate too often.
We've learned how to make a living, but not a life.
We've added years to life, not life to years.
We've been all the way to the moon and back,
but we have trouble crossing the street to greet a neighbor.
We've conquered outer space, but not inner space.
We've done larger things, but not better things.
We've cleaned up some of the air, but polluted our soul.
We've split the atom, but not our prejudice.
We write more, but learn less.
We plan more, but accomplish less.
We've learned to rush, but not to wait.
We've higher incomes, but lower morals.
We have more food, but less appreciation.
We build new computers to hold more information,
to produce more copies than ever,
but we have less communication.
We've become long on quantity, but short on quality.
These are the times of fast foods, and short conversation,
tall people, and short characters,
steep profits, and shallow relationships.
These are the times of the end of the cold war,
and the beginning of domestic battles.
We have more leisure, but less fun.
More varieties of food, but less nutrition.
These are the times of quick trips, disposable diapers,
throwaway morality, one night stands,
overweight and underweight bodies,
and pills that do everything from cheer, to quiet, to kill.
It is a time when there is much in the showroom,
and nothing in the stockroom.

A time when technology can bring this letter to you.
And a time when you can choose either to make a difference
Or just to hit the delete button!
— Author Very Wise but Unknown

New Millennial Transformational Energies

When the century turned, we looked back upon significant world transformations, like the collapse of Communism, a rising tide of new democracies, the emergence of the space age and the whole development of new technologies. Quantum leaps have been made toward an appreciation of women's dignity and giftedness. At present, women equal 46% of the workforce. (And they are beginning to break through the glass ceiling into top management. One such success story is Donna Dubinski and her promotion of the Cyber-Palm Pilot.)

Moreover, there is a deepening sensitivity regarding the human interconnection and our relationship with Mother Earth. As the new information age dawns, there is a corresponding greater awareness of the ongoing evolutionary process and its potential for transformation.

From Lightning Bugs to the Stars

We now realize, as never before, that we are a part of the evolutionary process — that from the lightning in the sky to the lightning bugs in an Iowa field there is transformation. The lightning bug does, indeed, enter into a profound transformation. In fact, as we observe the natural world, transformation goes on everywhere. The fact that we humans have some say in our personal transformation often obscures how we are part of a larger and interconnected transformational process. In a dialog with theologians at Notre Dame University, physicist David Bohm explained an insight from quantum physics that each part of creation, including the human element, is at a deep level connected to the whole of creation. We are all part of something bigger, mysterious and hidden. He indicated that when we fail, as it were, to know the forest from the trees it leads us to fragmentary thinking.

> ...the widespread and pervasive distinctions between people (family, profession, nation, race, ideology, etc.) is preventing human beings from working together for the common good, and indeed, even for survival. When man thinks of himself in

this fragmentary way, he will inevitably tend to put his own separate ego first, or else his own group. He cannot seriously think of himself as internally related to the whole of mankind and therefore to other people.

Bohm pegs the odds very high when he speaks of survival. Likewise, in his book *Quantum Theology,* theologian Diarmuid O'Murchu calls for the transformation of our masculine thought patterns, which presume we can control everything. He suggests that we need to cultivate an attitude of letting go instead of playing God, acknowledging humbly that we are a part of an unfolding evolutionary process more sublime and mysterious than we ever dreamed. Looking at the course of evolution, he compares extinction to Calvary and transformation to resurrection.

Walking on Water

Peter said, "Lord, if it is you, command me to come to you on the water." Jesus said, "Come." So Peter got out of the boat, started walking on the water, and came toward Jesus. But when he noticed the strong wind, he became frightened and, beginning to sink, he cried out, "Lord save me!" (Matthew 14: 28-31).

Our unfolding, mysterious transformation is often as tenuous as Peter's staying above water. When out of fear Peter felt the need to take control of his walking on the water, the dynamic interaction of his connection with Jesus was broken, and he began to sink. To gracefully walk the path of transformation requires a faith that allows us both to focus our attention on the divine and to let go, acknowledging that we are not in total control.

For Peter, in a moment of fear and doubt, the dynamic interaction revealed in quantum physics broke down. It is interesting that in other verses the Gospel tells us Jesus went to his hometown but could work no miracles there because of the people's lack of faith. This indicates how important that dynamic interaction was even in the miracles of Jesus. The attitude of the recipients was crucial. If they were open and trusting, if they let go of their own need to control — then his grace and power could truly be transforming. If they were not open, trusting, and willing to let go, however, then part of the dynamic interaction was missing, and nothing could change — even in the face of divine willingness. Blessings can fall on deaf ears and empty hearts.

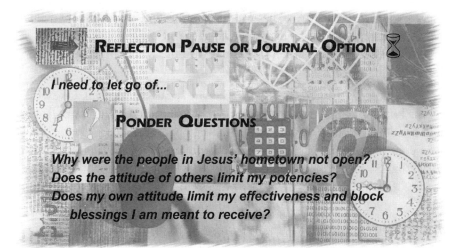

REFLECTION PAUSE OR JOURNAL OPTION

I need to let go of...

PONDER QUESTIONS

Why were the people in Jesus' hometown not open?
Does the attitude of others limit my potencies?
Does my own attitude limit my effectiveness and block blessings I am meant to receive?

At the dawning of this new millennium, in some religious quarters, there is a lot of doubt, fright and need to take control of the future. Some prophets of doom even predict an imminent end of the world. Yet from the most mature Christian perspective, we are never guaranteed that the waters will always be calm. What we are guaranteed is that Christ will be with us in the calm waters and in the storms. Ultimately, the most faithful and trusting Christian response to the mysterious unfolding of evolution is the confidence that God is present within this unfolding. Had Peter held firm to this "life preserver attitude," he would have continued to walk on the water. The bottom line of this Gospel story is total trust in a gracious providence.

QUANTUM GROWTH

This view does not make us robots. We still have the inner freedom to grow or not. In *The Quantum Society,* Danah Zohar and Ian Marshall suggest that the crucial factor that allows us to have a say in the larger unfolding and transformation of reality is our attitude. They propose that we need to modify our rugged individualism, pointing out how quantum physics shows that everything is interrelated. For a mechanistic, atomistic society of selfish individuals, each pursuing his or her way in isolation, to be transformed into a quantum society with a vibrant sense of emergent, creative community requires a transformation of personal attitude.

It is precisely in the area of the formation of attitudes that technology is a mixed blessing. Without personal discernment, the movie screen, the TV screen and the computer screen all inadequately shape our view of reality. Virtual reality easily becomes our inner reality. The screen becomes "the real." Quite often the glut of images portrayed in the media cultivate an illusion of male power, dominance, control, violence, separation and fragmentation — the very images that writers like Bohm and O'Murchu say lead to extinction rather than transformation.

THE INTERNET AND THE SEA

Again, the kingdom of heaven is like a net that was thrown
into the sea and caught fish of every kind; when it was full,
they drew it ashore, sat down and put the good into baskets
but threw out the bad (Matthew 13: 47-48).

The Internet *is* like a net thrown into the sea! So are the networks of television and all the rest of contemporary media. Like the fishers in Matthew's Gospel passage, we need to sort through the contents of the net. We need to discriminate with respect to what we see and make critical judgments about media's messages. This sorting out is a process of forming our attitudes that amounts to spiritual discernment.

DISCERNMENT QUESTIONS
FOR THE HYPERPACED AND CYBERSPACED:

How much time a day do I spend in front of a screen at my work?
How much E-mail traffic do I have to handle?
Is this easily handled or is it an overload that causes stress?
How do I feel at the end of the day?
How many calls do I handle on the cell phone on the way home?
Is my journey home peaceful or stressful?
How do I feel on arriving home?

How much time do I spend in front of a TV screen at home?
How much of that time is spent on action or adventure?
How much of that time is spent on sports action?
How much of my time is spent on soap operas?
How much is spent on comedy?
How many news broadcasts do I need?

When I view violent episodes:

Does it offer a catharsis, a necessary cleansing
   of my own violent tendencies — or
Do I become fixated and require more and more stimulation?

Do I fall asleep while watching? Is that good or bad?
Do I have any conversation while watching?
When I turn the TV off, how do I feel? relaxed and peaceful?
   re-energized? ...something else?

How much time do I spend in front of a computer screen at home?
Do I feel enriched and at peace with myself when I leave?
Do I need a spiritual discernment about the revelations
   from these answers?

Scripture says the fruits of the Spirit are: "love, joy, peace, patience, kindness, generosity, faithfulness, gentleness, and self-control (Galatians 5: 22).

The bottom-line questions: Do my answers to the above questions indicate that the various screens — computer, TV and movies — provide real relaxation, peace and re-energizing? Or does their overuse diminish the fruits of the Spirit in my life? Do the 8,000,000 pixels of light being beamed into my face enlighten my psyche or dim my spirit?

THE PARABLE OF THE HIDDEN TREASURE

The kingdom of heaven is like a treasure hidden in a field, which someone found and hid; then in his joy he went and sold all that he had and bought that field (Matthew 13: 44).

When we look at the inner dynamics of our spirit, we discover a great hunger. But what do we hunger for? Our discernment can identify us as either junk collectors or connoisseurs of great treasures. Cream does rise to the top. Over time we come to know some TV dramas as quite valuable. The really good ones become syndicated and retain their allure even beyond the lifetime of their performers. But entertainment is like panning for gold. We have to sift through a lot of grit and silt to find the treasures.

Such treasures "hidden in a field" of media mediocrity usually offer us a catharsis through their violence, or laughter from their comedy, or images of courage, love, joy, peace, patience, kindness or generosity from their dramas. We need, however, to discern the great treasures from among the many junkyard selections to be found on all the screens that illuminate our lives.

Illuminating Screens

Paul says we see dimly as in a mirror,
   but are we not face-to-face with radiant light?
Eight million pixels lighting up a small TV screen,
   computer screens shining in our faces,
   movie screens illuminating our cave of dreams.

John says true light enlightens everyone;
   Moses veiled his face because of the light.
Peter, James and John fell to the ground,
   blinded by the glow of transfiguration,
   stunned by the transforming light.

What are the screens that illumine our lives?
   Are we dazzled, bamboozled, snookered and fooled?
   Or are we consoled, refreshed, relaxed, renewed?
Do we have within our human psyche
   a screen that filters silver from dross, gold from silt?

Our Human Treasure Hunt

Our hearts are made for treasure. We are treasure seekers, and where our hearts are, there is our treasure. Indeed, the Internet pours out a vast array of treasures. It is like a torrent, a rushing stream cascading out of our screens, some of its waters, clear, fresh, life-giving and some of its waters polluted. In its depths are glittering specks of gold. Yet in an addictive exposure to the constant gushing we may run the risk of being drowned.

The Internet Cornucopia

Never in the history of mankind has so much material treasure been dangled in front of viewers' eyes! Now that we can buy directly from the Internet, a whole cornucopia of consumer items spills out from our screens. All the allure of the shopping mall now extends itself right into our living rooms. In the quest for riches we can even gamble on the Internet, placing our bets directly through the computer. All of this appeals to our innate need to search for treasure.

Again, this glut of images challenges us to discern. Where is our treasure? Does someone or something deserve our time, our attention and concern more than the glittering screen that now speaks to us all too often with the voice of a huckster, the lure of a con man?

Prayer for Cyberspace Treasure Hunters

Our hearts are made for treasures
buried in fields and mountains,
sunk in mysterious seas,
cached away in the depths of hearts
needing to be discovered
or perhaps only opened.

O God, deliver me
from the plastic control of credit cards
and from checkbook frenzy.
Help *me* to be a top consumer item
for those who hunger and thirst
for my care or my simple presence.

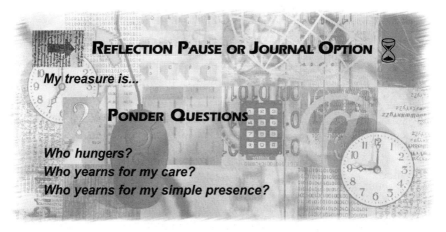

Reflection Pause or Journal Option

My treasure is...

Ponder Questions

Who hungers?
Who yearns for my care?
Who yearns for my simple presence?

The twenty-first century spread of the computer throughout our offices and even our homes has opened the door to a cultural transformation that might be compared to the advent of the automobile in the twentieth century. It signals a societal shift whose final results are still difficult to measure. The decreasing cost of computers will only serve to speed up this process.

In the early 1900s Henry Ford had a better idea based on creative expectations. Instead of automobiles being driven just by the elite, he set out to mass-produce automobiles for the common people. He paid the workers on his assembly lines enough wages to be able to purchase their own Model T Fords. Automobiles then needed paved roads and a whole spectrum of services. A new world was created based on the automobile. Suburbs appeared. Interstate travel became common. What had been rare and novel prior to Henry Ford became a controlling factor in the way people lived in the United States. Yet this cultural phenomenon brought mixed blessings; along with mobility there came urban sprawl and unhealthy air pollution.

WHAT THE FUTURE MIGHT HOLD

The computer world is moving so fast that what is written about it at this moment will seem like ancient history by they time it is read. However, the present course would point to the computer's increasingly pervasive influence in our daily living. Will "Big Blue" totally transform us to his wishes, or will we determine the direction that transformation will take? It took radio 38 years to reach 50 million people. It took television 13 years. It took the Internet 4 years. U.S. Internet business totaled $4.3 billion in 1998. It is expected to reach $1.3 trillion by 2005. According to an August 1, 1999 article in the *Scottsdale Tribune*, an estimated 500 million Internet connections are expected globally by 2005.

FUTURE MIXED BLESSINGS AND CURSES

Household appliances will quite likely be computerized soon. Computerized robots will do more and more work, including some housework.

Political guru Dick Morris further predicts that the Internet will revolutionize the political process. People who vote will get the information they need to make educated choices and will have the opportunity to interact directly with politicians. The campaign will come "home."

In the religious arena, the power of virtual imaging will open up more and more opportunities for generations raised with virtual reality to search for spiritual meanings and insights on the web. Religious images that have been held captive and localized in church stained glass windows or trivialized by being co-opted by advertising now are set free on the web. Such images do have a power of their own. Many of the young have never lit a vigil light or held a rosary. Yet regardless of where they are viewed, sacred images carry meaning and spiritual energy. On beholding an icon of Christ or the Madonna before flickering vigil candles — even on a video — the power of the religious image flows into the viewer's imagination. That is true even for many young people who have never stepped into a church.

In his insightful book *Virtual Faith: The Irreverent Quest of Generation X*, Tom Beaudoin writes about a new religious community of the X generation coalescing on the web. Religious communities, particularly of Xers, are beginning to thrive in virtual space. In that arena, faith and life mingle at all hours of the night — with less reservation than one finds in the coffee hour after most religious services.

Some observers of the religious trends in America, such as Quentin Schultze, author of *Internet for Christians*, foresee more and more Christians in the new millennium worshipping in virtual congregations, held together only by the Internet screen. They indicate that many Christians will become cafeteria churchgoers, plugging in or plugging out as to what suits their fancy. They will see no need to assemble in some mixed assembly where the old and the young, the poor and the rich might come together on common ground.

At present, the Alta Vista search engine finds the word *Christian* on 7 million pages, *Jewish* on 1 million, *Islam* on 500,000, *Buddhist* on 250,000 and *Hindu* on 230,000. One thing is certain, as far as information is concerned: The Internet is the most significant advance for the proliferation of religious information since the invention of the printing press.

Religious information, however, is not the same as experience. Observers like Rabbi Gerald Zelizer admit that the Internet does offer a cornucopia of religious information, but he is skeptical that it can provide adequate religious experience:

> ...religion includes the donning of costume, the taste and scent of foods, the sound of song, and touching and embracing on sacred occasions. Cyberspace religion is limited to mostly sight and some sound. While the Internet certainly provides ample religious information, it conveys limited religious experience. It is, after all, "religion lite."

Children will see the Internet as integral to their learning, just as previous generations saw the blackboard. Even if parents choose not to have a computer at home, their children will have Internet access in schools, libraries or friends' homes.

It is also proposed that extramarital affairs will blossom on the Internet. Already, Peggy Vaughan, a relationships expert from La Jolla, California, who has her own website at www.vaughan-vaughan.com, describes on-line affairs as "commonplace and typical!"

With fewer and fewer people in motion on their jobs and more and more stationary in front of screens, snacking becomes pervasive. In a *New York Times* article, Dirk Johnson suggests that already:

> In some offices, desks and cubicles look almost like food pantries — chips, nuts, rice, cakes, fruit — all placed within easy reach of a telephone and computer keyboard.... This practice of all day grazing, meanwhile, has largely replaced the old-fashioned business lunch, for which workers actually leave the office.

In the twenty-first century, as the number of elderly mushrooms, chat rooms will become a boon for widows and widowers, allowing them to allay their loneliness by electronically connecting with other people. Listen to the testimony of one such widow:

> Margie Crandall's husband Lynn died and she was looking for something to occupy her time so she wouldn't spend the day crying. So she entered the widows and widowers chat line. "They asked me if I had been in the room before and I told them, "No." They asked me if I was widowed, and I said, "Yes." And they asked me how long, and I said it was a year that day. All of a sudden, everybody just started to give me hugs. A cyberspace hug is when chat rooms put your name in parentheses. It's just a wonderful group. It just changed my life!

From birth to death — computers will monitor everything. Already, a burial service in my community offers cyber-connected mourners the ability to sit in on the cremation of a relative or friend!

One of the greatest blessings to result from the Internet is our ability to be in instant communication with people all over the world. When I was in Ireland, I met with a group of writers in the small village of Clifden.

One poetess shared a beautiful poem about meeting a widower on a train. When I returned to the United States, I E-mailed her for permission to use it in this book. Through the Internet, a chance meeting on a train in Ireland is wafted across the seas and ends up in this book. We are, indeed, living in the global village prophesied by Marshall McCluhan. But McCluhan also issued a warning about the hyperpace of cyberspace and the danger inherent in the increasing velocity of communication and living.

HYPERPACE AND CYBERSPACE

In *The Global Village: Transformations in World Life and Media in the Twenty-First Century,* McCluhan foresaw excessive use of the computer speeding up cognition and mixing reality and virtuality so much that the user — body in one place, mind floating in cyberspace — might fall into a virtual-reality schizophrenia:

> What may emerge as the most important insight of the twenty-first century is that man was not designed to live at the speed of light. Without the countervailing influence of natural and physical laws, the new video-related media will make man implode upon himself.

Too much hyperpace and cyberspace could lead to a personal collapse.

There are now cases of people experiencing toxic overdoses through excessive downloading from the Internet. So it would seem that living in hyperpace and cyberspace raises questions about our human capacity for such instancy. This, in turn, forces us to ask how we are to maintain our unique humanity and our personal human touch when we are wired to the speed of cyberspace. This question has deep spiritual implications. We are not angels who move even faster than light. We will need to discover our limits before we overdose on microdots.

RELATIONS WITH MACHINES

The day may not be far off when we can create robots that look like humans, and even feel to the touch like humans. We may have them for personal servants. Will we even have them for bedmates? If so, will this enhance our humanity or degrade it? Can we manufacture love and relationships? Is this where our future treasures lie? If so, we had best be careful that instead of blessing us our technology might transform us into the ultimate self-centered narcissists.

A Better Transformation

In his book *Geo Justice*, Jim Conlon suggests, perhaps with tongue in cheek, that transformation happens only on two occasions, when we fall in love or when we have a nervous breakdown. He goes on to suggest that our twenty-first century culture may go through a nervous breakdown, which could lead to a breakthrough into a transformed culture that is more human and earth-connected.

More than electronic connections, we need human connections. Neither a keyboard nor a screen can ever take the place of the touch of a human hand that communicates the love we need in our joy and the consolation we need in our grief. There would seem to be certain basic human interactions no technology can replace: the hand of a friend upon our shoulder at times of pain and loss, the magic of a child's kiss, the joy of holding a baby. More than looking at microdots, we need to see, hear, smell and touch the natural world lest we become occupants of a tower of Babel — cut off from the essentials that nourish our soul. We need soulfulness, which no machine can adequately provide. And we need a connection to creation. We cannot well survive as independent operators disconnected from the earth, oblivious to the movement of the tides or the changing of the seasons.

Far Out

Nonetheless, electronic communication does enable us to go *far out*, to leap into the sky, as it were, and bounce messages off satellites. Our communication abilities have taken a quantum leap forward, enabling us to extend ourselves far above, far out, far beyond what a few generations ago would never have been dreamed possible. This electronic capacity can transform human communication in new and exciting ways and can greatly enhance the potential for interconnection among diverse cultures and distant peoples. It can facilitate breakthroughs in human understanding. It can be a great aid to illumine human acceptance of diversity while at the same time cultivating unity among peoples of the global cyberspace village. It can thus result in a deeper reverence for human dignity, acceptance of those who are different and compassion for those who suffer. This kind of communication transformation can truly be a blessing that moves us ahead in our strivings to be deeply human.

Far Down

There is also another transformation that is brewing at the dawn of the twenty-first century: intercommunication *far down*. It takes place in the world of quantum physics, in the world of the ancient shamans, in the world of a mother who is the earth. This is the world that reverences the feminine. This is the earthy world of interconnectedness that is deeply rooted in the essence of matter. In the process of this *far down* communication we realize that the material world speaks to us and that we speak for it. And in this process we gain a reverence for the earth upon which we stand.

To enter this world demands a new way of thinking, a new attitude, a new experience of reality — a vital transformation of our human worldview. Not all of this earth-connected attitude is entirely new, but it is an attitude that — in our Western way of looking at creation as subject and object — we have forgotten.

At the dawning of the cyberspace age, we may be in a "nervous breakdown" regarding some of our ways of perceiving space. But evolution and creativity assures us that out of breakdowns and chaos new energies can and do arise. In a dialog with his spiritual mentor, theologian Thomas Berry, physicist Brian Swimme spoke of insights that have made the universe come alive for him. These new understandings helped make the universe his primary reference point. He now sees gravity as a "divine allurement." He now agrees with Thomas Berry that the universe is the first and most fundamental revelation of God. The universe has become his first and best teacher. This has been a new perspective for him as a human, as a scientist and as a religious seeker.

Since the dawning of Newtonian physics, have we not culturally considered the universe, earth and all material things as objects for us to conquer? Have we not even looked upon our earth with a certain disdain — as controllers and conquerors of the inert matter beneath our feet? Thomas Berry responded to Brian Swimme's amazement in these words:

> The switch out of an attitude where the human is the center of everything to a biocentric or cosmocentric orientation where the universe and Earth are the fundamental referents is THE radical transformation that we are presently involved in. It is disruptive. We are so quickly confused because we are accustomed

to forgetting Earth and cosmos to concentrate on the human world. But when you begin to grow in this larger way of living, you will discover new freedom, and a vast vision of being that makes the struggle worthwhile.

ULTIMATE TRANSFORMATION

Another prophet, distinguished Jesuit paleontologist and theologian Pierre Teilhard de Chardin, a serious student of evolution, proposed that Jesus Christ did more than simply enter into the exterior human world. In a real sense, Teilhard suggests, the incarnation of Jesus inserted his presence deep down into the evolution of our material world and the universe itself. In *The Phenomenon of Man,* he said that Jesus is the Cosmic Christ...

> ...in the heart of matter, assuming the control and leadership of what we now call evolution.... And when he has gathered everything together and transformed everything...as St. Paul tells us, God shall be all in all.

Teilhard sees the universe fulfilling itself. In that finality, Jesus Christ coincides with the fulfillment, the Omega Point. The vision of Teilhard is filled with hope and trust, confident that the ultimate transformation will be the work of the Cosmic Christ. And what is the energy that Jesus brings to this future unfolding? Teilhard believes it is the energy of Christian love, which, once fully unleashed, will lead to an ultimate transformation of all things.

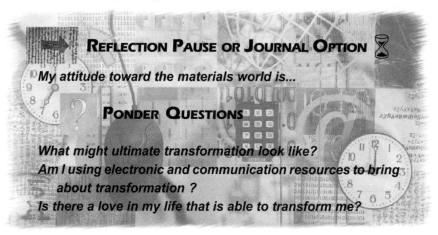

REFLECTION PAUSE OR JOURNAL OPTION

My attitude toward the materials world is...

PONDER QUESTIONS

What might ultimate transformation look like?
Am I using electronic and communication resources to bring about transformation ?
Is there a love in my life that is able to transform me?

SCRIPTURE IMAGES AND PASSAGES FOR REFLECTION

Hebrew Scriptures

Psalm 80 — *Prayer for restoration*

> ...Stir up your power, come to save us
> O God of hosts, restore us.
> Let your face shine upon us,
> that we may be saved....

Jeremiah 31: 1-14 — *Israel's rejoicing at her restoration*

...Again I will restore you, and you shall be rebuilt, O Virgin Israel; carrying your tambourines, you shall go forth dancing with the merrymakers....

Christian Scriptures

Romans 12: 1-2 — *Transformation through the renewal of our mind*

...Do not conform yourself to this age but be transformed by the renewal of your mind, so that you may discern the will of God, what is good and pleasing and perfect.

Matthew 17: 1-8 — *Jesus' Transfiguration*

...Jesus took Peter, James and John and led them up a high mountain.... And he was transfigured before them, his face shone like the sun and his clothes became white as light.

Colossians 1: 15-20 — *The Cosmic Christ*

...In him all things were created in heaven and on earth....He is before all things and in him all things hold together....

1 Corinthians 15: 51-52 — *Transformation in the Resurrection*

...We will all be transformed....in an instant, in the twinkling of an eye....

BLESSINGS FROM ABOVE AND BLESSINGS FROM BELOW

Blessed be the transformation from fireball to the planets.
Blessed be the transformation from gas in space to solid earth.
Blessed be evolution — the unfolding of rich potentialities.
Blessed be creative expectations — hope mixed with potency.
Blessed be the Cosmic Christ, who rules from pole to pole.
Blessed be the Spirit hovering over chaos.
Blessed be angels, God's messengers of the spiritual.
Blessed be the moon, which moves the tides of our feelings.
Blessed be the sun, which blankets us with warmth.

Blessed be gravity, the *allurement* binding us to earth.
Blessed be the earth, which holds and molds us.
Blessed be dancing molecules, electrons and quarks.
Blessed be speech, song, story — voices of the earth.
Blessed be electricity, which lights up our stories.
Blessed be the Internet and virtual reality.
Blessed be television and the alpha state of relaxing.
Blessed be E-mail and the instant written word.
Blessed be the cell phone that can rescue us in trouble.
Blessed be creations — natural and human —
that bring us closer to the Source of all blessings.

PRAYER FOR BOOTING UP THE COMPUTER
— FOR A PRAYER PARTNER

It is suggested that regular computer operators form prayer partnerships and that they use the booting up moment at the beginning of each day as a pause for prayer. Many computer users are agreeing with one or several other users of cyberspace that each time they turn on their computer they will take that moment to remember and pray for their prayer partners.

Before I travel on the information highway,
in this moment of waiting,
I pause to remember _____ in prayer.
Bless their (his/her) booting.
Bless their (his/her) working.
Bless their (his/her) journeys.

As we enter cyberspace,
may we hold each other
in our heart space.

LITANY FOR TRANSFORMATION

Blessed be transformation!
Blessed be transformations that move us:
from the fireball toward earth. Blessed be!
from the darkness of caves toward mountain vistas. Blessed be!
from tribalism toward a global village. Blessed be!
from the evolutionary process toward the Omega point. Blessed be!
from scatterdedness toward quantum connection. Blessed be!
from boredom toward enchantment. Blessed be!
from male domination toward a sacred letting go. Blessed be!
from female subjugation toward fulfilled potential. Blessed be!
from being observers toward being participants and partners. Blessed be!
from a static, frozen worldview toward dynamic insights. Blessed be!
from conquering the earth toward being at peace with earth. Blessed be!
from numbness toward compassion. Blessed be!
from deafness toward hearing the cry of the poor. Blessed be!
from ecological imbalance toward eco-justice and balance. Blessed be!
from cynicism toward creative expectations. Blessed be!
from raw sex toward nuanced and intimate sexuality. Blessed be!
from passive screen viewers to active real life doers. Blessed be!
from hyperpace to a human-pace. Blessed be!
from shortsightedness to farsightedness. Blessed be!
from being stuck to dancing with creation. Blessed be!
Blessed be!

THE BEATITUDES:
UPSIDE DOWN BLESSINGS

Blessed are the poor —Matthew 5: 3

A PARABLE — THE PRINCE WITH THE MUDDY FEET
or SWIMMING UPSTREAM

What if Jesus came to Colorado? ...I imagine myself in the mountains tubing down the Colorado River. Spray is flying. Rocks loom up ahead. We bounce and twirl. It's an exciting ride. But I am secure in my life jacket, and I laugh and holler with the rest of my companions. We are well stocked with food, and our beer cooler is lashed securely to the side of the rubber raft. And all in all, we are having a great time. We are indeed blest.

Then the river calms down some and spreads out before us. We have left the most exciting and dangerous rapids, and we have come out OK.

Now, as we drift more lazily downstream, content and basking in the twilight glow, we see a figure swimming upstream toward us. The current is still strong, so he must exert lots of energy as he approaches. We yell and warn him, "You're swimming into danger. Downstream is the only safe and sensible passage." But he does not heed us. The distance shortens between us. Ever more leisurely, we continue to drift downstream in the opposite direction of the summer. Suddenly, we hear a voice and we look toward the bank. There stands a striking figure — some kind of mountain man — and he is surrounded by a lot of poorly dressed campers who seem to be squatting along the bank. At the water's edge children in tattered clothes squint their eyes as they look toward the swimming figure.

The wild-looking mountain man shouts, "Look! There is the Lamb of God!" Yes, he is pointing directly at the man swimming upstream. A cloud comes over the horizon. Just as the swimming man passes our rafting tube, a voice rolls through the canyon: "This is my beloved Son!" At that moment an eagle swoops down from the sky and flies over the head of the swimming man. Soon he is beyond us. Exerting great effort, he continues to swim upstream but now veering toward the motley crowd on shore. As we begin to move out of hearing range, he struggles out of the water. Someone in our raft exclaims, "Look at him — what a handsome figure! He looks like a prince!" Another laughs and responds, "Yes, but a prince with muddy feet!" Then the children run up to greet him. As he puts his arms around the first to reach him, we can just barely hear him say, "Blessed are the children! Unless you become..." and his voice fades out of our hearing range.

We are left to wonder who this man is. He seems to have had it all backwards and upside down. No one swims toward the rapids! All conventional wisdom points downstream, away from the rapids. Prudence says to go with the flow! And why would he team up with that ragged rabble on the shore? It all seems crazy.

ANOTHER IMAGE OF THE "PRINCE WITH MUDDY FEET"

This is the second imaginary picture of a "Prince with Muddy Feet" (see Chapter 2) — swimming against the stream and associating with grungy people on the shore. At this very moment, I have just finished a lovely lunch and a nice nap. As I honestly ask myself where I find myself in this parable, I have to reply: in the raft floating downstream.

REFLECTION PAUSE OR JOURNAL OPTION

In this parable I would find myself...

PONDER QUESTIONS

Is swimming upstream always a crazy direction to go? What do you think are the words that we miss when the man on the shore meets the children?

THE BEATITUDES

The richest 225 people in the world have a net worth equivalent to the annual income of the poorest 2.5 billion people in the world.
—*Money Magazine*, March 2000

The world's most famous sermon was delivered by Jesus from the Mount of Beatitudes and on the Plain. Luke's latter version is more pointed, directing our attitudes toward the poor themselves. Scripture scholar W.D. Davies writes that Luke sees Jesus always as "the friend of the poor, the sick, the outcast, and the women of the first century." He suggests that Luke's Gospel and beatitudes might well be summed up by the words inscribed on the Statue of Liberty:

> Give me your tired, your poor,
> your huddled masses yearning to breathe free...
> Send these, the homeless, tempest-tossed to me.

Matthew's mountain version of the beatitudes is directed more toward the middle class. These beatitudes challenge us to find a spiritual poverty.

THE BE ATTITUDES

And what are these "beatitudes" found both in Luke and in Matthew? They are blessings. In the fourth century, when Saint Jerome translated the Scriptures into Latin, he used the Latin word *beatus*, meaning blissful. In our day, John Powell calls these blessings *Be! Attitudes!* Richard Rohr calls them "the happy attitudes." But in his book *The Ladder of the Beatitudes,* Jim Forest says "happy" is not good enough. Being blessed means you aren't lost, that you're on the right path, the path the Creator intends you to be on. But the beatitudes suggest that what you recognize as a blessing may look like an affliction to an outsider.

THE BEATITUDE BLESSINGS AND "YES, BUTS,"

True enough. We might call them the "upside down blessings," for they often seem to be the opposite of conventional wisdom — what we consider normal, proper, and fitting. We might also call them the "Yes, But Beatitudes," for, if we are totally honest, we usually hedge our bets with them when we hear them. Don't we sometimes say within ourselves, "Yes, but." I know for myself at various times in my spiritual journey, I have said these "Yes, buts":

Blessed are the poor in spirit, for theirs is the kingdom of heaven.
(Yes, but God does bless those who work hard, and some poor people just don't seem to care.)

Blessed are those who mourn, for they will be comforted.
(Yes, but we should put on a happy face. Mourning is a private thing we do when we personally lose something. We cannot carry the grief of the world on our backs.)

Blessed are the meek, for they will inherit the earth.
(Yes, but let's be practical. God allows prosperity for those who work hard. Property rights are also important and need to be honored.)

Blessed are those who hunger and thirst for righteousness, for they will be filled.
(Yes, but we should not be religious fanatics.)

Blessed are the merciful, for they will receive mercy.
(Yes, but death row inmates showed no mercy to their victims.)

Blessed are the pure in heart, for they will see God.
(Yes, but we don't want to be Pollyannas, naïve about life. Moreover, a lot of people just don't get the other half of this Beatitude: They dress poorly, live in unkempt shacks and smell to high heaven. Isn't cleanliness next to Godliness?)

Blessed are the peacemakers, for they will be called children of God.
(Yes, but we also have to be willing to defend our strategic interests — such as oil and national security. Don't we even call some of our strategic weapons "Peacemakers"?)

Blessed are those who are persecuted for righteousness sake, for theirs is the kingdom of heaven.

(Yes, but if we have proper self-esteem and try to get along, we will not place ourselves in a "victim" position.)

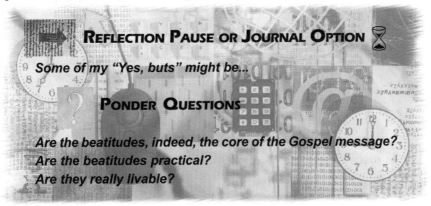

REFLECTION PAUSE OR JOURNAL OPTION

Some of my "Yes, buts" might be...

PONDER QUESTIONS

Are the beatitudes, indeed, the core of the Gospel message?
Are the beatitudes practical?
Are they really livable?

It is interesting to note that Jesus begins each of these phrases with a positive blessing. Even in Luke's more-stark account of the beatitudes, in which each beatitude ends with a jarring challenge, "but woe to those" who do not observe them, Jesus still starts with a blessing. The reason these beatitudes are so jarring is that the culture in which we swim and live has its own set of beatitudes. It counts as blessing to have no pain, no cost and no changing of the status quo. In fact, our cultural beatitudes enshrine the status quo. These beatitudes point us downstream, toward seeking the American Dream in the new millennium in our own promised land. They might read this way:

THE NOW CULTURE'S BEATITUDES FOR THE NEW MILLENNIUM

(The poor in spirit?) Blessed are the prosperous, for prosperity is a sure sign of God's favor.

(Those who mourn?) Blessed are those who ignore pain and think self-actualizing thoughts.

(Those who hunger?) Blessed are the high achievers who never want or hunger.

(The meek?) Blessed are those with high self-esteem.

(The righteous?) Blessed are the "saved," who are secure in their "rightness."

(The merciful?) Blessed are those who aren't limited by having "bleeding hearts."

(The pure of heart?) Blessed are the clever, street-wise and street-tough.
(The peacemakers?) Blessed are sacred guns in our homes that keep the peace.
(The persecuted?) Blessed are the assertive and aggressive, who never let themselves become victims.

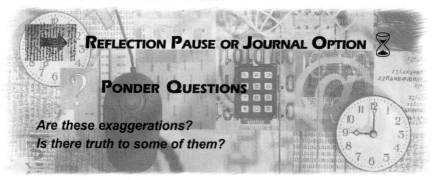

REFLECTION PAUSE OR JOURNAL OPTION

PONDER QUESTIONS

Are these exaggerations?
Is there truth to some of them?

TV GOSPEL VALUES

Too severe a commentary on the "American Dream"? Perhaps. Yet aside from its devotional content, does not American TV evangelism sometimes infer that God wants you to have prosperity and that God blesses your path by making you rich rather than poor? Blessed are the good people, for we shall know them by their place in life. Like cream, they always rise to the top! They are the "saved," the favored and anointed of God! As for the rest — the unbelievers, the homeless, the sick without insurance, the lowest of the low? Those lacking basic necessities of life? What about them? As Pat Robertson of the 700 Club said:

> It isn't compassionate to take somebody's money and give it to somebody else! The government does not owe grants of money to any group in our society.

THE BLESSED PROSPEROUS ONES

Yet if the "American Dream" is a sure recipe for blessedness, why do we have more violence than any other industrial country? And in all of our frantic efforts to achieve success and security, why are we too often bored, depressed and hungry for something more? Commenting on the American cultural scene in *Alone But Not Lonely*, Donna Schaper writes:

> In many ways we are all the same, both very full, and very busy, and very empty and very worried. Our loneliness comes

from this strange mix which is simultaneously "too much and too little...." Being needy inside the experience of "too much" is standard American fare. We have it all, but we are still needy and lonely.

If that statement rings true, and if we resonate with any of the "Yes, buts," then we are likely aware of our dissonance with the blessings suggested by Jesus. His "blessing path" seems to go in a strange direction when we really examine it. His path seems a little crazy — a detour from our well-ordered and secure everyday world.

Blessed are the poor in spirit for theirs is the kingdom of heaven (Matthew 5: 3)

This is how Jesus begins his beatitude sermon. And just who are the poor in spirit? In his challenging book *Jesus' Plan for a New World — The Sermon on the Mount,* Richard Rohr tells us that Scripture scholars think the first audience Jesus wanted to reach with his beatitudes were precisely the *ptochoi,* the Greek word meaning "the very empty ones, those who are crouching." And who are the crouching ones in our day? Here is a true story from our time and our North American continent about some empty and crouching ones.

FILLING THE EMPTY YELLOW BUS

Does this sound like a "blessing path" to you: a yellow school bus going its normal route up a muddy path to a stinking garbage dump? Can you imagine a school bus going to a dump to pick up children sitting atop heaps of trash? Like Jesus swimming upstream, such an idea sounds strange and implausible. However, children living in a stinking, fetid dump swarming with flies is a reality.

Barry Forbes, a newsman wrote about American supporters of Nuestros Pequeños Hermanos, an orphanage in Micatlan, Mexico, who witnessed such a reality firsthand. A Phoenix Channel 5 film crew, including anchor Jane Thomson and cameraman Gilbert Zermeno, was on the bus that detoured into a garbage dump.

They were in Mexico to film an orphanage and its mission to the many outcast children on Mexico's streets. In the local culture surrounding Nuestros Pequeños Hermanos Orphanage, children in families are loved and cherished. However, there is no room in this society for orphans. Their plight in some ways resembles that of ancient lepers — outside the gates and unwanted.

In a *Mesa Tribune* article, Barry Forbes would later describe the unexpected detour of the orphanage's school bus into the garbage dump of Micatlan this way:

> On the way from visiting the orphanage, driving back to the hotel, cameraman Gilbert Zermeno spotted what appeared to be a shimmering white gravel pit, perhaps half a mile off the rough barely paved Mexican highway. A couple of blocks wide. Maybe 50 feet high. Backing up as far a one could see.
>
> Zermeno asked the bus driver to turn toward the pit. The road up was slippery, but the stench saturated them long before the bus ever ground to a halt. The white gravel pit turned into a kaleidoscope of light and dark colors amid ever-shifting, wind-driven pieces of fluttering paper. It was an immense city garbage dump. And it was "home" to hundreds and hundreds of people.
>
> Camera in hand, Gilbert Zermeno was first off the bus, stepping straight into slimy mud. There were lean-tos everywhere, individual huts of paper and cardboard, sticks and stones — maybe 80 square feet of living space per family. The shack floors weren't even dirt, just compacted trash. Other "living quarters" were simply burrowed into hillsides of stinking junk.
>
> Filthy children in rags displayed faces devoid of expression, blankly staring into the camera lens. They were "combers" rummaging through each new load of garbage for cans, bottles, food — anything to help make it through one more day.
>
> Multitudes of flies harassed the kids' faces, noses, mouths, ears — but the children appeared oblivious. Seemingly, not once in their young lives did these poverty-stricken, luckless tikes ever experience anything akin to a bath.... A few minutes later, the bus pulled out. On board, there was total silence. Tears quietly freely spilled.

When the expedition of Americans later told their story to Father Phil Cleary, who has directed the orphanage for 15 years, it was new information to him. He was already kept fully busy caring for the 950 children in the orphanage. But he knew that the orphanage had to respond.

A plan took shape. The orphanage would offer to send their school bus daily to the dump, pick up the "dump children" and transport them to the orphanage where they could join the orphans in their school. Since the dump children were not orphans, they would be day students at the orphanage school and would return to their parents every night. But before this plan could be implemented, the orphanage children had to be consulted about bringing strangers into their school homerooms. The orphans offered openhearted acceptance to the plan. Not only would they welcome the new children, but they would help them clean up every day upon their arrival. Later, the parents of the dump children also accepted the offer of the orphanage.

On Monday, March 8, 1999, the first busload of 35 dump children arrived at the orphanage for an orientation. They were filthy, some covered with lice and came with scared expressions on their faces. After being welcomed by the orphanage children, they were accepted lovingly as schoolmates. They were given clean clothes and went through medical and dental check-ups. They were to return the next day to begin classes. When the bus pulled up the next day, there were 51 eager "garbage kids" coming to be blessed by the delousing of their bodies and enlightening of their minds.

Later that year, some of the kids from the orphanage who had welcomed the "dump kids" were themselves welcomed in Arizona when they made a journey to raise awareness about abandoned children. Various families opened their homes to the children. When they were about to leave, a 13-year-old from one of the host families, Tommy Keeley, stood before a microphone and said, "Knowing these other kids has touched our lives in a very special way. I had no idea that kids with so little could be so happy. I didn't know that they were going to be kids just like me. It is obvious that their lives are full. They have God, friends, and now a family at the orphanage, and a bright future because of Nuestros Pequeños Hermanos." To learn more, see www.nphamigos.org.

From "Fate" to Blessings

In *The Ladder of the Beatitudes*, Jim Forest speaks about the Greek word *makarios*, a blessing word meaning "sharing in the life of God, the ultimate joy." Living in blessed *makarios* means no longer being subject to "fate" but rather living with a bright future.

Surely the road to the orphanage in Micatlan is a wide blessing path, filled with *makarios*. It's a way toward the dignity that the poorest of the poor deserve. Each smiling face on that path radiates the inner beauty of children who have been blessed and who in turn heaped blessings upon others. All of this came to be because of a few people — some compassionate newspersons, a caring orphanage director and especially its founder, Father William B. Wasson, who saw a need to open doors to the desperate and abandoned. The blessing path to that door has kept widening over time until today there are almost 1000 orphans who live within the confines of hope, love and dignity at Nuestros Pequeños Hermanos.

Recently, the mission of Los Hermanos began to be helped immensely by the use of technology, especially the video camera. Suffering children seem so far away until their plight comes into our home viewing areas. Then they become the crouching ones, the empty ones who are our neighbors. Once aware of the plight of millions of orphaned children in Central and South America, opportunities open up of us to offer financial adoption and ongoing support to such outreaches as Los Hermanos.

NPH provides a **wide beatitude path** that blesses the poorest of the poor as well as their benefactors. However, there are countless little ways in our daily experience that also allow us to recognize the dignity of those who may be a rung down on the status ladder. Such recognition and acceptance of the poor close at hand can bless and open our hearts to a greater appreciation of Jesus' first beatitude.

A Narrow Path of Blessing

I am sitting in the Quilted Bear, a posh restaurant in swanky Scottsdale. The booths are padded and so are the patrons. This is former vice president Dan Quale's local hangout, a comfortable place for Scottsdale's elite to muse about what has been and what still might be.

I am joining a writer friend, Susan, for breakfast. It is 7:30, and I'm a bear at the Quilted Bear. I feel like a snoozy grizzly just barely sticking its nose out of a hibernation cave. Not a morning person, I sit hunched over, waiting for my first quick fix of morning coffee. A busboy approaches, but I am unaware of him except for some peripheral movement sensed out of the corner of my left eye.

Susan, sitting across from me, has one of those beautiful faces that can light up a room. As the barely noticed busboy pours our water, Susan looks up at him, bursts into a morning smile that would make the sun blush and exclaims, "Well, good morning! How are you today?" Finally, I look up beyond the hand that is pouring the water, noticing the face of a tall, smiling Hispanic boy. He looks very surprised and very gratified.

The next time he returns to our table, I look at him more carefully. He is ungainly, somewhat awkward. No doubt about it, he is just a teen, and at the bottom of the pecking order in this stratified, upscale, watering hole for the well-fed and comfortable. As he approaches our table, he hums a little tune and carries a smile along with his water jug. A simple smile from Susan has lit up his day.

The Wide and Narrow Paths

If we reflect on history and our wider world, we can discover from time to time well-known figures who have confounded the odds and turned some of the surging throughways of society in a blessing direction — toward reconciliation, healing and peace. Such figures move in a counter direction from what we would normally expect from people of their background. Often they surprise us by beating the odds and ushering in blessings that common wisdom would never expect. People like Father Phil Cleary, the director of the orphanage at Los Hermanos, or Mother Teresa or Rachel Carson have played out the spirit of the beatitudes on the world's wide screen. We might well call their mighty efforts **Blessings on the *Main or Wide* Path.**

But we might also look into our common, everyday experience. We might call the surprising blessings that we encounter there as **Blessings on the *Backstreet or Narrow* Path.** Little events of our ordinary hyperpaced and cyberspaced lives — like Susan's simple smile — can transport us directly into the realm of the beatitudes.

More often than not, on walking this blessing way we march to a different drummer and express the beatitudes on the narrow path. But as we work through the rest of the beatitudes in the remainder of this chapter, we can discover Beatitudes Blessings lived out on both these paths.

Blessed are those who mourn, for they will be comforted (Matthew 5: 4)

Blessings on the Wide Path

The close of the old millennium witnessed three funerals that demanded worldwide attention. People wept openly. Reverent, silent, sad crowds lined the funeral cortege routes. They came to mourn the princess, the heir to Camelot and the wizened little nun of Calcutta. When all was said and done and when the last wreath had faded, some cynics proclaimed that the weeping for celebrities had been overdone, a maudlin display of emotionalism.

However, there is another way of looking at it. We seem to live in a culture that denies death and can too easily overlook the sadness of dashed dreams. Sometimes things are going so well personally that we find no need to weep.

Our hyperpaced culture moves so fast and our attention span is so limited that we can walk around well coifed and clothed and seemingly walk right over those who weep at our feet. When asked, "Why do you pick up the abandoned off of the Calcutta streets," Mother Teresa responded, "Because they are there!"

"Because they are there!" "There" can be in the sweatshops where much of our clothing is made. When we don't have Mother Teresa's vision, we can walk over and around the children of many third world countries. They need to be mourned, not walked over. Indeed, every stunted and abused child is to be mourned. That's why Bob Ortega, a former Wall Street Journal reporter, wrote his book *In Sam We Trust: The Untold Story of Sam Walton and How Wal-Mart Is Devouring America.* Ortega wanted to expose some of the sweatshop conditions child workers face in many of the factories that supply Americans with designer clothing and sports equipment. Bob Ortega mourned at what he saw of the children in the sweatshops:

> I looked extensively into the use of child and sweatshop labor worldwide. It's not so easy to dismiss this issue when you see, firsthand, children bent over their sewing machines; when you sit in a dirt-floored shack in Guatemala talking to 11- and 12-year-old girls who work up to 90 hours a week, who are beaten if they work too slowly, who are locked into the factory at night until they meet their quotas and who can afford to eat nothing but rice, tortillas and beans.

After the flap about sweatshops producing some of the clothes TV's Kathie Lee was hawking, a new awareness opened up regarding the sweatshop origins of a lot of our clothing. The White House created a

Fair Labor Coalition of retailers, manufacturers and human rights groups to try to improve sweatshop conditions overseas. As of this writing, Wal-Mart has still declined to take part.

Mary Ann is a typical soccer mom. Things are going well for her. Her two-worker family lives in a comfortable neighborhood. Life is good. Her neighbors are young, and everyone she knows seems to be rising on the success ladder. There is not really anything going on directly in her life that requires any mourning.

But she is a soccer mom who wants to know the score. When she read an article about soccer balls being stitched by poorly treated children in Pakistan, she looked at the source of the soccer balls being bought by her child's team.

Mary Ann now reads more than just the ads from Sunday's paper. She has discovered that there are more than 300 Internet sites under the heading: **sweatshops expose.** She wants to be discriminating. For example, she read that when Levi Straus was caught using child labor in Bangladesh in 1994, it agreed to open a school for the children, pay them what they'd have earned if working in just conditions and would offer them jobs when they were older. When she learned that, she smiled with approval. "Improve their conditions and open a school," she thought. "That's great — a corporation changing course and acting responsibly." So the next time she needed jeans for the kids, she bought Levis.

Maybe there is a Mary Ann in your neighborhood. The "narrow" story of Mary Ann reveals how through discriminating purchases we can lift gloom and grief from the shoulders of exploited children. By such conscious "mourning," we can bless not only our own children but also the children of the third world.

Blessed are you who are hungry now, for you will be filled (Luke 6: 21)

BLESSINGS ON THE WIDE PATH

David Beckmann, a Lutheran pastor and president of Bread for the World at the beginning of the new millennium, proclaimed that "because of the resurrection we have hope in a world that more often fosters despair." Bread for the World was organized to make democracy work for the hungry. It is intended to be a citizen's lobby on behalf of world hunger.

As an example of its work, BFW members and partner organizations spearheaded a yearlong campaign to have the bill "Africa: Seeds of Hope" passed in Congress and signed by President Clinton. It mandates the U.S. Agency for International Development to come up with a comprehensive plan to provide microenterprise development assistance in drought-stricken sub-Saharan Africa.

Moreover, thanks to BFW, the means to do something about World hunger and starvation are on-line! At **www.bread.org** one can click on the Congress Link, then *Guide to Congress*. It shows congressional voting records and the latest legislative updates. As an expression of solidarity with the hungry, you can also send E-mail messages to your members of Congress. Such solidarity opens us to grace and places us squarely on the blessing path.

BLESSINGS ON THE NARROW PATH: The UN Hunger Blessing Path

John is 73 years old, still vigorous and an active worker. As a hobby, he makes clocks, and he finds time to surf the net in search of "hidden treasure" — but not the kind of treasure you might ordinarily expect. John seeks out spiritual resources and opportunities to spread blessings. When he finds these resources on the net, he spreads the word. He came into our office one day exclaiming, "Check this out! I just found an on-line site where all you have to do is just click in **www.thehungersite.com** to actually supply a cup of rice for a hungry child!" If you click on, here is what appears:

> Make free donations of food to hungry people while viewing an animated world hunger map. Every 3.6 minutes someone in the world dies of hunger. Three-fourths of the deaths are children under 5. When you click in, sponsors pay for 1 1/4 cups of rice, wheat, maize or other staple food to a hungry person, adding to over 50 tons weekly. Your donation was paid for by sponsors who are listed on screen.

By such a little act we can genuinely and deeply reverence the dignity of those on the lower rung. Whether it is a "free donation" or the financial adoption of an orphan, the rewards of this narrow blessing path are joy to the one who blesses as well as the one who is blessed.

Blessed are the meek, for they will inherit the earth (Matthew 5: 5)

BLESSINGS ON THE WIDE PATH

Webster does funny things with the word *meek*. On one hand it is defined as "humbly patient or submissive, spiritless or tame." On the other hand it could mean "gentle or kind." Rachel Carson was not tame, submissive or spiritless, but she was gentle and kind to the earth. She was filled with a lively spirit that wanted to bless the earth, not curse it. Due to her vision, and that of other kindred caretakers who love the earth, our children may have a slim chance to inherit a friendly earth rather than a toxic enemy.

Rachel Carson became an ecological prophetess through her 1962 book *Silent Spring*, warning of the havoc of pesticides, poisoned food and polluted streams. When she finished testifying before Congress, Senator Gruening of Alaska remarked, "Miss Carson, every once in awhile, in the history of mankind, a book has appeared which has substantially altered the course of history.... Your book is of that important character."

Rachel Carson died in 1964, but her words are more pertinent than ever for the new millennium. Almost four decades after her warnings, Diarmuid O'Murchu writes in *Reclaiming Spirituality* that the "evidence is now overwhelming" that our human abuse of the earth is placing more stress on the "cosmic" womb than it can sustain, and we are ignoring this reality. And this is despite the fact that the earth groans in agony and seeks our attention with global warming and drastic changes in weather.

Wendell Berry, a prophet following in Rachel Carson's footsteps, points his finger directly at some of the worst abusers of the earth, the worst polluters of the air, the most ignorant of their folly — and he points at me and at you! He writes that he cannot think of any American living the normal American lifestyle who is not contributing in some way to the "destruction of the earth."

"INHERIT THE EARTH"

In our day we need to ask what "inherit the earth" means. Is the earth some inert family heirloom possessed by humans? Or does "inheritance" mean the opportunity for us to be in earth's family and to receive from parent earth a gift of dwelling in a fertile place. Rachel Carson's book warned us that if we poison the earth we cease being kind and meek toward the earth, and the inheritance we give future generations is an alienation from the very source of life. If being meek means standing down from the hubris of "mastering" the earth and, rather, loving the earth and letting the earth bless us, then, indeed, blessed are the meek!

Blessings on the Narrow Path

He left home at age 18. He went on a spiritual vision quest. When he did not find what he was seeking in Chicago, he hopped a train to Dubuque, Iowa. That night, he slept in a boxcar. The next morning he walked the 20 miles to the Trappist monastery of New Mellery. His name was changed from Ed to Brother Bernard. He would never return home again. For the rest of his life he would live a simple and meek life, sleeping every night on a straw mattress, getting up in the middle of the night to chant prayers. And beyond the prayer times, his work was simple. He cooked meals for visiting guests. He worked close to the earth, growing roses, putting up preserves, even coming up with a recipe for whiskey jelly! He truly was blessed by his meekness toward the earth and is a model of blessing for those of us with small backyard gardens. He truly did inherit the earth — and in the end, as we all do, he rested in the earth.

Today the birds come and rest on his simple cross. In the guesthouse, the visitors still enjoy his whiskey jelly. And in the monastery fields, his brother monks are meek and gentle with the earth, turning all their fields over to organic farming.

Because *meek* in its best sense means neither tame nor spiritless, his brothers who have succeeded him join with other people of the soil in protesting the pollution from excessive harmful run-off from nearby confinement hog sties on their corner of the earth.

Blessed are those who hunger and thirst for righteousness, for they will be filled (Matthew 5: 6)

Blessings on the Wide Path

Imagine the old soldier, sitting in his study amidst the trophies of a lifelong military career. The evening shadows fall. A narrow shaft of light brightens the eastern wall. That wall tells the story of a lifetime of military service and much more. There is his framed degree from the

Virginia Military Institute. What might have been his dreams of future victories in those youthful years?

There are pictures on the wall from Argonne in France, from the combat of his youth and the carnage that was World War I. A picture of his first wife is there — she had died just nine years after that war — and of his second wife and of a son who was killed in World War II. There are also many pictures of various military stations between the two great wars.

Then there's the picture of him as a Five Star General, as Chief of Staff of the United States Army. As a veteran of the two great wars, his wall displays all the medals and honors to show for them. Finally, there are pictures of his last post, not as a general directing war, but rather as a civilian, as Secretary of State — a seeker of righteousness and the peace that might flow from his military career.

The old soldier had every right to scan that wall and recall many military triumphs, for it was he who had commanded the great victors of World War II: Eisenhower, MacArthur, Bradley and all the rest. But above all of those prizes is an award that would seem out of place for a lifelong soldier — the Nobel Prize for peace inscribed with his name, George Catlett Marshall!

He knew history very well. "To the victor belongs the spoils!" He knew the bloody history of wars. He remembered how the Romans crushed Carthage, aware of how after that victory the Romans plowed under the ancient city — actually pouring salt on the ground so that no living thing could grow there. And George Marshall didn't forget how the victors after World War I rubbed the German peoples' noses into the ground with the Versailles treaty, which attempted to turn an industrial nation into a pasture land, rubbing salt into the soil of the German fatherland. It was precisely in that defeated and demoralized German soil that Hitler's National Socialism would take root. George Marshall remembered.

His shining achievement took exactly the opposite direction of previous warlords and conquerors. History shall remember him always as the major architect of a plan that rescued from chaos both the victors and the vanquished of Europe. It was a plan that eschewed vengeance and promoted renewal out of the ashes of a prostrate Europe. The Marshall Plan assured the nations of Europe that if they would meet and cooperate and then propose their needs for rebuilding, the United States would underwrite their recovery.

George Marshall had to speak with the voice of a prophet, calling the American people to generosity and reconciliation even with their wartime enemies. In proposing the Marshall Plan, he acknowledged the challenge:

> ...the people of this country are distant from the troubled areas of the earth, and it is hard for them to comprehend the plight and consequent reactions of the long-suffering peoples and the effect of those reactions on their governments in connection with our efforts to promote peace in the world.

The Marshall Plan would prove to be a wide blessing path. But it demanded courageous trailblazers. Marshall, an appointee of a Democratic administration, worked hand in hand with Republican Senator Arthur Vandenburg to call Americans to their better selves. Their vision forged a trail of peace. Whereas Versailles planted seeds of a second war, the Marshall Plan brought the blessings of a rebuilt Europe and a solid alliance of friendship and cooperation between the United States and Europe, which now is stretching into a new millennium. We all have reaped the blessings of a righteous enterprise called the Marshall Plan.

BLESSINGS ON THE NARROW PATH

Jeanine had two lovely grade-school daughters involved in sports at her local parochial school. She was idealistic in her expectations. However, when she began to attend games, she became more and more aware of the pressure put on children to compete and to win. Angry-faced parents taunted referees and coaches and screamed at their children for not living up to parental sports expectations. As she faced into soccer rage, she was amazed and disturbed. Her personal experience began to validate what she was reading — that unpleasantness and undue pressure results in 73% of kids quitting their childhood sports by age 13.

As another parent remarked: "The kids drop out because it ceases to be fun, and the pressures put on them by coaches and parents don't make it worthwhile."

Moreover, parental acrimony is not confined to the playing fields. Sometimes school boards become battlegrounds for parents' personal, and often hidden, agendas.

Jeanine was a busy soccer mom like so many others in the hyperpaced world of childraising. However, when she reflected on the state of childhood sports, she saw a need for more balance — another word for righteousness, the right proportion of things. She could not be a soccer coach. That was not her gift. But she could act responsibly. She decided to toss her name into her local school board election. To try to balance thinking and priorities is to walk a narrow blessing path of righteousness.

Blessed are the merciful, for they will receive mercy (Matthew 5: 7)

BLESSINGS ON THE WIDE PATH

Joyce Hutchison's name appears next to Joyce Rupp's on the cover of a lovely book titled *May I Walk You Home?* It is *subtitled Courage and Comfort for Caregivers of the Very Ill*, and the cover pictures two companions walking through a field toward home.

Joyce Hutchison knows the way home. When she was only 29 years old and her husband Gary was 34, he was diagnosed with cancer and was informed that he had only six months to live. In reality, he fought a battle with the invading cancer for twenty-four years. Joyce was there at his side walking through fields of sorrow and of joy, over a road that sometimes had ruts and sharp turns, peaks as well as valleys. But it was always a road of shared hope.

Joyce's personal experience with Gary helped her to cherish working with the dying as a hospice nurse. If we need companions for our journey through life, then surely we need companions for our journey through death. As Joyce describes it:

...hospice caregivers do all they can to assure that the physical, emotional, spiritual and mental needs of the patient are attended so that the dying one can journey home with peace of mind and heart.

Hospice is a work of deep and genuine mercy. Yet we live in a hyperpaced culture that demands instant relief from any bother. It is also a throwaway culture. If something does not serve an apparent purpose, we throw it out. This attitude can carry over into human relationships. We can mask our impatience with sickness and our unwillingness to wait for life to take its course, resorting to the euphemism "mercy killing." Hospice is in the opposite direction of mercy killing. Hospice is a path of standing by, not throwing away.

Our hyperpaced culture urgently demands that we speed up all human processes. What may look like "mercy" in killing is often only expediency. It is easier for caregivers to decide and determine the exact moment of death. It is also usually much less expensive to kill than to wait. It is much less bother to those around the patient who are impatient. All these utilitarian values will become more and more alluring in the new millennium when the numbers of elderly mushroom, and the dying become more and more of a bother for younger generations.

However, hospice promotes "merciful dying" rather than "mercy killing." The dignity of the dying person, even when he or she can no longer perform or produce, is the primary concern of hospice. Hospice honors each moment of life as precious. For as Rabbi Heschel proclaims, "Just to be is a blessing. Just to live is holy!"

Surrounded by love and care, perhaps medicated to relieve pain, and borne up by the prayers of loved ones, the hospice patient receives the deepest and truest mercy. In 1999, the United States Post Office honored hospice with its own stamp. Its inscription reads, *Hospice Care*, and it pictures a path toward a home. Above the home hovers a golden butterfly with red wings. What a fitting symbol for the path of blessing that is mercy.

BLESSINGS ON THE NARROW PATH

Throughout his life Larry Dorsey had opposed the death penalty, while most of the persons he knew supported it. Then, one morning he received a call that savagely ripped apart his normal day's routine as well as his peaceful heart. The police wanted him to come and identify the body of his beloved niece, a lovely teenager dear to her family and her many friends.

At her high school, she had rebuffed the advances of a roughneck boy. Thereafter, the boy began to stalk her. He learned that sometimes she would stay overnight when she was babysitting the 9-year-old daughter of a single mother who worked nights.

In the middle of what became a night of horror, this boy and an accomplice cut the telephone lines to that house, broke inside, raped and beat Larry's niece and murdered her. Sleeping in another part of the house, the little girl heard nothing and was not noticed by the intruders.

In the morning, after waiting on the front steps until the police completed their initial investigation at the crime scene, Larry was ushered into the room to identify his beloved niece. The last time he had seen her she was smiling and praying at church. Now, he and her parents would have to take her to church to be buried. He would later say, "That morning was the worst of my life."

For the rest of that horrible day, he remained very quiet, and that evening he took a long walk by himself. I could only imagine his wrestling with demons of revenge, hatred and despair. Wouldn't most of us have been besieged by some of those feelings? At some point during a long conversation after he returned, he remarked quietly, "I am still against the death penalty."

He would never waiver from that opposition for the rest of his life. There was no reasonable doubt that the two young men accused of his niece's death were the actual murderers. Still, in many cases across the country, we are beginning to discover through new DNA evidence that some people is prison were not the perpetrators of the crimes for which they were convicted.

If Larry were alive now, he would likely nod his head as if already aware of that fact. But beyond that evidence, he was steadfastly against the death penalty because his very deepest values and feelings always leaned in the direction of mercy rather than vengeance, revenge or retribution. His beatitude, even in the midst of the most stinging tragedy, will always be for me a model of the blessing of mercy.

Blessed are the pure of heart, for they will see God (Matthew 5: 8)

BLESSINGS ON THE WIDE PATH

This beatitude is not about cleanliness or ritual purity or sex. It is about a heart turned in the right direction — a heart without guile. It is about an undivided heart that is God centered. It is about a heart from which all the other beatitude-blessings radiate outward in a circle of love.

Dorothy Day was a woman with such a heart. If pure of heart meant super cleanliness, she would not qualify. After all, she lived among the poorest of the poor, who often were odorous and unclean. If pure of heart meant never having any sexual experiences, she would again not qualify because in her youth she had a couple of torrid love affairs and eventually lived in a common-law marriage.

There is a saying that the first third of our lives is occupied with seeking and taking hold, the second third with having and possessing and the last third with giving back and letting go. Dorothy did indeed spend the first third of her life seeking, but once she found the treasure she sought, she skipped the phase of having and possessing and spent the rest of her life giving back and letting go.

During the first thirty years of her life, Dorothy Day wandered over many roads. She sojourned through a non-religious upbringing with an agnostic father. She then went to the University of Illinois, later becoming both a nurse and activist. Jailed in 1916 for joining women suffragette demonstrators at the White House, she later traveled to Europe. Then she became a scriptwriter in Hollywood, having a couple of intense love affairs and an abortion before becoming friends with some famous folks on Broadway, including playwright Eugene O'Neill. Her path was never boring, yet she was unfulfilled.

In her thirties, she underwent a religious conversion that coincided with the birth of her child and that set her on the path of the beatitudes. The rest of her life was beautifully marked by giving and letting go. She gave her heart and soul to the poor, opening houses of hospitality that still endure today. She became a peace activist and in her lifetime would be jailed thirteen times for peaceful demonstrations. When asked once whether her advocacy for the poor was heroic, she replied, "Not at all." For her it was just common sense, just living out the Gospel. When asked about the search for meaning in a materialist culture, she responded, "Ask for God's guidance. And be open to hear the words of Jesus to 'feed the hungry and clothe the naked.'" Born in 1897, Dorothy died in 1980 in New York City. At her death, the President of Notre Dame University described her role in life as one who "comforted the afflicted and afflicted the comfortable." Having tasted fully even the less savory aspects of life, she was filled with the vision of God and embodied the beatitude of purity of heart.

Blessings on the Narrow Path

The pure of heart are sometimes those whose hearts are broken! Take, for example, Gina, who had a long-running, passionate relationship with Francis. There was so much that was good in it, and so much that was good in both of them. Yet the deeper and wider their communication went the more she realized that there were some core values, some deeply held "heart convictions," they would never share. She saw that lacking an agreement on these essential values would create real problems in the raising of children. Sometimes, in the process of becoming *pure*, or *real* in the deepest sense, hearts are torn. Sometimes hearts must be plumbed to their very depths. Perhaps this is why the psalmist wrote,

> Indeed, you love purity of heart,
> then in the secret of my heart teach me wisdom (Psalm 51: 6).

For Gina, the deepest wisdom meant a heartrending decision not to marry Francis and to move on.

I once knew another bride-to-be. At noon on the very day of her 2 o'clock wedding, she appeared at my door in jeans, hair in curlers, and announced to me, "When I was just washing my hair, I realized deep in my heart that this marriage is just not going to work."

So we put a note on the church door for arriving guests, who would read it and quietly return to their cars. Eventually, this bride would meet someone else and enter a happy marriage. Both of these young women honored what was deepest in their hearts. Looking within, they saw rightly and with the purest vision. In a very real sense they possessed wisdom of the heart. For as Antoine de Saint-Exupery writes in *The Little Prince*, "It is only with the heart that one sees rightly. What is essential is invisible to the eye."

Blessed are the peacemakers, for they will be called children of God (Matthew 5: 9)

BLESSINGS ON THE WIDE PATH

"Remember Pearl Harbor!" was a battle cry. The memory of the sneak attack that ushered the United States into World War II was an incentive for Americans to respond with fury against Japan. It is hard to deny that some sort of revenge was desired by many Americans.

Admiral Bull Halsey, one of the heroes of the war, vowed that when victory came, he would ride the Emperor's white horse right through the streets of Tokyo. Embarrassing the emperor was a very appealing thought. It sounded like something that General MacArthur, the proud and imperious commander in the Pacific, might say.

When the war ended, it was MacArthur who accepted the Japanese surrender on the battleship Missouri and entered Japan as its conqueror and administrator. Yet he did not humiliate the emperor as one might have expected. At the same time, he succeeded in introducing democracy and woman's suffrage to a land that had never known either. The autocratic MacArthur, who might have assumed an emperor's role, instead gave away power to the people of Japan. In doing so, he assured that warlords would not control its destiny in the future.

In his last years, MacArthur addressed the U.S. Congress and ended his talk with these words, "Old soldiers never die. They just fade away." Historians may not judge his decisions in the Korean War favorably. However, his peacemaking in Japan was a blessing that MacArthur bequeathed to history, and it has not faded away.

BLESSINGS ON THE NARROW PATH

As we rode into one of the most Protestant towns in Northern Ireland, it definitely showed its colors. There was an orange arch at the entrance to the heart of the city, commemorating the marches of the Orange Order. Many of the buildings were painted red and had the Union Jack of England proudly displayed.

Our tour guide, Mick Moloney, was a Catholic. He explained to us that he deliberately brought his tours through this town. Indeed, everyone we'd meet in the hotel would be a Protestant and a loyalist to the English crown. Mick went on to tell us that the people who run the hotel are nice people and that they needed to see we are too. He encouraged us to interact. For Mick, coming to this place was one small but important way of establishing personal, human relationships. He felt this would have to happen over and over before peace could finally come to Northern Ireland.

Another unheralded but effective group called "Project Children" takes little steps toward peace by bringing both Protestant and Catholic children from Northern Ireland as visitors to the United States. The children stay in the homes of families from a denomination other than their own. There they meet on human, not sectarian, ground. Of the over 20,000 visitors, upon their return to Ireland none have joined any sectarian group that fosters hostility across religious lines! Through such grassroots, one-on-one efforts, the beatitude of peacemaking is truly felt and fostered.

Blessed are those who are persecuted for righteousness sake, for theirs is the kingdom of heaven (Matthew 5: 10)

BLESSINGS ON THE WIDE PATH

Imagine a distinguished United States ambassador, Peter Peterson, clothed in a spotless white linen suit, sitting in his sixth-floor office of the U.S. Embassy in Hanoi. The year is 1999. Across from him sits the Communist Party Secretary DuMoi. They are recalling the infamous Hoa Lo prison called the Hanoi Hilton that held countless U.S. flyers shot down and captured during the Vietnam War. It also held Vietnamese during the previous French occupation of Vietnam. The most improbable thing about this whole scene is that *both* the ambassador and the Communist Secretary are alumni of that same prison dungeon!

Flash back to September of 1968. Pete Peterson is flying his 67th combat mission over North Vietnam when he is hit by enemy fire. His aircraft goes down, and he makes a rough landing. He has broken bones and is in great pain as he sees angry Vietnamese running toward him. With his revolver in his hand, in his agony, he considers evading their wrath with one shot to his head. But only for a moment. He lays down his pistol and lets them surround him.

Thus began six years of survival for Pete in the wretched Hanoi Hilton. They would be years of deprivation and of torture. They are movingly recalled in the superb documentary *Return with Honor*. That's all that Pete and the other prisoners had to hold onto — their honor — along with their prayer, their memories of loved ones and the tapping signals they sent to fellow prisoners. They also had good reason to hate their captors and tormentors, for they lived in the harshest of conditions and were cruelly treated as a matter of standard prison policy.

In an interview with David Kotok of the *Omaha World Herald*, Ambassador Peterson recalled his final release from the Hanoi Hilton:

> When I walked out of there, I was a pretty angry person. I had hated for a long time. Day and night my life was really hate. And yet, when I walked out, I had the presence of mind to thank the good Lord — and I left my hate at the gate. While the imprisonment was dreadful, I learned who I was. I really knew who I was when I came out of there.

He went on to relate that it took a long time to overcome his anger completely. After rejoining his family and resuming his Air Force career, it took lots of effort over a long period of time for him to finally let go of his rage.

For twenty years, there were no diplomatic relations between the U.S. and Vietnam, until Peterson — the Viet vet and former prisoner of war went back as an ambassador of peace to the people and the very city of Hanoi that had imprisoned him. Because of his willingness to go back as an ambassador and reconciler, Peterson has been highly praised by both Vietnamese and United States officials. The man of war became the ideal ambassador of peace. Senator Hagel of Nebraska, himself a Viet vet, testified to that:

> The emotional scar Vietnam left on our culture, on our generation, on our society is still so deep and wide, I don't think you can do it any other way than to put someone like Pete Peterson in Hanoi.

BLESSINGS ON THE NARROW PATH

We live in a unique age, in which our neighbors, our friends and our relatives are as close as a phone call, as immediately present as E-mail. Never in the history of humanity has communication been easier. Yet we also experience great separation and alienation.

Pete Peterson and the other captives were a long way from home and forced to be out of physical contact with their families. However, their spiritual connection with loved ones sustained them. We may be close to those we know and to family members, and yet sometimes we choose to be distant. We even have it within our power to persecute, to punish, to get even with persons who once were close but now are estranged.

John and Louise were approaching their eighties. They could no longer even keep up their small house. So their son-in-law, who was very handy, finished off the upstairs part of his house and moved the old couple in so they might enjoy their few remaining years in comfort and without concern for keeping up a house.

Their son Peter and his wife would come to visit. They would walk around the house to the backdoor entrance that led upstairs to the elderly couple's apartment. However, Peter was not on speaking terms with his sister, who lived below. So every visit involved circling around and avoiding his sister. Who knows how it all started or who was at fault originally?

When we consider persecution, it does not have to be as far away as the Hanoi Hilton or Tiananmen Square. Persecution is often very close. It exists in many families. For us to realize that even our silence can be a form of persecution is a valuable insight. Yet to endure family persecution with patience and hold onto a desire to reconcile is indeed a blessed attitude. To take active steps to lessen little persecutions and to bring about reconciliation is even more blessed and holds the capacity to radically transform us.

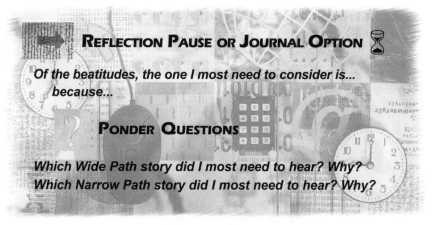

REFLECTION PAUSE OR JOURNAL OPTION

Of the beatitudes, the one I most need to consider is... because...

PONDER QUESTIONS

Which Wide Path story did I most need to hear? Why?
Which Narrow Path story did I most need to hear? Why?

THE BLESSED BEATITUDE PATH

What then are the blessings for those who walk the beatitude path, and how shall we even know that we are on this path? The blessings that come back to us from this holy path are many:

...a deep sense of gratitude for blessings all around
...a heart that sees rightly
...a healing of relationships
...a generous spirit
...a positive attitude that brings deep joy
...giving more daily affirmations than curses
...a release from stressful, hyperactive striving
...freedom from the cultural bondage imposed by ads and media
...an emptying of ego and a filling up with love
...a sense of community with all creation
...an attitude of openness to God and God's ways

And how shall we know that we are on this right road? When we press against the winds of the usual and experience the tension that exists between the ordinary and the extraordinary, these are hints that we are leaning in the direction of the beatitudes. Beatitudes are all about surprising courses of action. When we surprise ourselves by holding onto things with a light touch or by letting go of more than we ever dreamed we could, we are on the road paved by the Sermon on the Mount. We know we are on the right road when we experience deep joy in simple things. We know we are on the right road when they say of us, "Look at how they love one another!"

Finally, when we make the resources of technology, such as the cell phone or the Internet into instruments of blessing — rather than letting them make us slaves to hyperactivity, greed and lust — blessed will be our path through hyperpace and cyberspace.

BEATITUDES ON THE LINE AND THE WEB

Blessed are the poor in spirit — Friends of Orphans, call 1-800-528-6455. Another site where keying in can help Habitat for Humanity and other worthy causes: www.freedonation.com.

Blessed are those who mourn — Over 300 websites:
In a search engine, type in sweatshops expose.
Also, www.lchr.org/sweatshops/faq.htm.

Blessed are those who are hungry — Bread for the World:
www.bread.org.

Blessed are the meek — www.rachelcarson.org
or homestead@rachelcarson.org.

Blessed are those who hunger and thirst for righteousness — In a search engine, type in 1947 Man of the Year: George C. Marshall.

Blessed are the merciful — www.teleport.com/~hospice.

Blessed are the pure of heart — In a search engine, type in Illuminating Lives: Dorothy Day.

Blessed are the peacemakers — In a search engine, type in: A Father's Prayer by General Douglas MacArthur.

Blessed are those persecuted — foto.org.

Scripture Images and Passages for Reflection

Hebrew

Isaiah 11: 1-9 — *Blessings from the Root of Jesse*

A shoot shall sprout from the stump of Jesse
And from his roots a bud shall blossom.
The spirit of God shall rest upon him...
There shall be no harm or ruin on all my holy mountain....

Jeremiah 31:1-14 — *Rejoicing at the blessings of the rebuilt Israel*
...Shouting, they shall mount the heights of Zion; they shall come streaming to God's blessings.... Then the virgins shall make merry and dance, the young men and old as well....

New Testament

Luke 16: 1-13 — *Parable of the dishonest steward*
...And the master commended that dishonest steward for acting prudently....

Luke 4: 18-19 — *Jesus' mission, from Isaiah*

The Spirit of God is upon me
And has anointed me to bring glad tidings to the poor....

Morning Blessing Prayer

O God, make my tools of technology
into instruments of your peace today.
May my cell phone connect me to blessings
but disconnect me from trivia.
May my automobile move me to safety,
past road rage and road rush.
May my E-mail enrich me with connectedness
but also give me the wisdom to empty the trash.
May the Internet open up the world to me

but not snare me into addiction.
Through sights, sounds, movement and competition
move my spirit on angels' wings.
When day is done, may I come home again
out of stress into peace and joy.

EVENING BLESSING PRAYER

Blessed be slowing down:
  Deliver me from today's hyperpace.
Blessed be stopping:
  pausing along God's way.
Blessed be being:
  "Just to be is a blessing."
Blessed be simpflying:
  Deliver me from polluting.
Blessed be imagination:
  dreaming better dreams.
Blessed be creative expectations:
  I think I can — tomorrow!
Blessed be attention:
  being present to those I love.
Blessed be transformations:
  tomorrow better than today.
Bless this day! Bless this night!
  Deliver us from any fright.

EPILOGUE

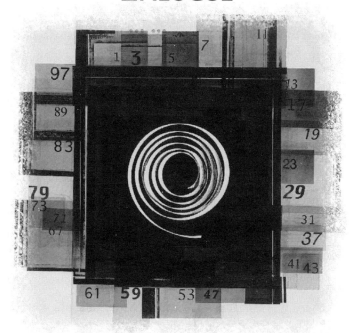

In his epic Canterbury Tales the fourteenth century poet Geoffrey Chaucer wrote that when April comes, "Thanne longen folks to goon pilgrimages."

It is April-springtime along the information highway. At this dawning of a new millennium, more and more pilgrims venture forth into cyberspace every day. As of this writing, forty-six million homes in the United States are on the information highway, and the numbers are growing daily. The Internet and other realms opened by developing communication technologies offer almost limitless new trails to explore. Internet chat rooms can connect us to companions for our life journeys just as varied and interesting as the Knight, Squire, Merchant, Wife of Bath and Chaucer's other pilgrims.

WALKING A BLESSING PATH

As they take us on a cyberspace pilgrimage, the Internet and its communication cousins usher into the holy shrine of our inner sacred space both the very best and the very worst of pilgrim-companions. That reality coupled with the increasingly frenetic daily pace of our cyberworld compels us to cultivate a spirituality of technology, if only to help us keep our footing along the way. We are becoming acutely aware of our need for a spirituality that is situated solidly within the context of our truest spiritual traditions, one that places us squarely on a blessing path.

Slowing down enough to be nourished by the holy dark, and by the wisdom of the Celtic, Native American and Jewish *berakhah* blessing paths helps us find the inner rhythm that keeps us on track even in the fast track. Allowing ourselves to be influenced by Chartes and Chimayo, *Feng Shui* and the findings of modern physics, helps us turn even the need to meet mushrooming expectations and multiplying demands into a great dance. Creating time for paused moments of noticing and pondering can help us turn seeming negatives — what we might call intrusions — into positives, into graced occasions for blessing. Whether it is the moment when we make our bed, pour a cup of morning coffee, boot up our computer or stop at the traffic signal, we can seize upon these moments as opportunities for prayer and orienting ourselves toward a blessing way.

BLESSINGS UPON BLESSINGS

Underlying this spirituality is the basic be-attitude of a positive frame of reference. This is the original attitude of our creator: "God looked upon the earth and filled it with good things" (Sirach 16: 27). Seeing the whole picture, the creator envisioned and bestowed blessings upon blessings, and everything was "very good" (Genesis 1: 31).

Such a blessing frame of reference always sees wider and deeper. What we humans see is often what we get. If we see failure and gloom, that is what we are likely to receive. On the other hand, if we see blessing possibilities even in the midst of apparent chaos, then our creative self can be moved to find something new and better. Darkness can become the passageway to light and messiness the raw material for beauty. This blessing attitude underlies Jesus' Sermon on the Mount of Beatitudes and opens us to a spirit of inner spaciousness even in the midst of constricting cynicism, a spirit of generosity and abundance even in the midst of scarcity of time and capacity.

INTERCONNECTEDNESS

The more we ponder and reflect on our journey through daily life and the treks we make between inner space, cyberspace and outer space, the more we appreciate how we do not walk alone. A critical work of the new millennium and perhaps the greatest blessing we receive from the world wide web is cultivating a deepened sense of our interconnectedness. It's an awareness of our connectedness with other humans and also with other species, with the earth itself and with the great evolutionary story that has been unfolding for 15 billion years!

In his book *The Great Work*, eco-prophet Thomas Berry writes of a new springtime, a new historical period when:

> The distorted dream of an industrial technological paradise is being replaced by the more viable dream of a mutually enhancing human presence within an ever-renewing organic-based Earth community.

Pilgrims pursuing such a dream are indeed walking on sacred ground and are blazing a holy blessing path! And as you travel this path, "may the road rise to meet you, the wind be always at your back, and the rain ever fall soft upon all the fields of your activity."

William John Fitzgerald